## ABOUT ISLAND PRESS

Island Press is the only nonprofit organization in the United States whose principal purpose is the publication of books on environmental issues and natural resource management. We provide solutions-oriented information to professionals, public officials, business and community leaders, and concerned citizens who are shaping responses to environmental problems.

In 2004, Island Press celebrates its twentieth anniversary as the leading provider of timely and practical books that take a multidisciplinary approach to critical environmental concerns. Our growing list of titles reflects our commitment to bringing the best of an expanding body of literature to the environmental community throughout North America and the world.

Support for Island Press is provided by the Agua Fund, Brainerd Foundation, Geraldine R. Dodge Foundation, Doris Duke Charitable Foundation, Educational Foundation of America, The Ford Foundation, The George Gund Foundation, The William and Flora Hewlett Foundation, Henry Luce Foundation, The John D. and Catherine T. MacArthur Foundation, The Andrew W. Mellon Foundation, The Curtis and Edith Munson Foundation, National Environmental Trust, The New-Land Foundation, Oak Foundation, The Overbrook Foundation, The David and Lucile Packard Foundation, The Pew Charitable Trusts, The Rockefeller Foundation, The Winslow Foundation, and other generous donors.

The opinions expressed in this book are those of the author(s) and do not necessarily reflect the views of these foundations.

# THE
# PORTLAND
# EDGE

# THE
# PORTLAND
# EDGE

*Challenges and Successes*
*in Growing Communities*

EDITED BY CONNIE P. OZAWA

2004

**ISLAND PRESS**
WASHINGTON · COVELO · LONDON

*Library of Congress Cataloging-in-Publication data.*


The Portland edge : challenges and successes in growing communities / edited by Connie P. Ozawa.
    p. cm.
Includes bibliographical references and index.
ISBN 1-55963-687-4 (alk. paper) — ISBN 1-55963-695-5 (pbk. : alk. paper)
1.  Regional planning—Oregon—Portland Metropolitan Area. 2.  Urban renewal—Oregon—Portland Metropolitan Area. 3.  City planning—Oregon—Portland. 4.  Environmental protection—Oregon—Portland Metropolitan Area.  I. Ozawa, Connie P.
HT394.P67P67 2004
307.1'216'0979549-dc22

                              2004012458


*British Cataloguing-in-Publication data available.*


Printed on recycled, acid-free paper ✹

Design by Teresa Bonner
Photographs of Portland today by Dr. Leslie Good


Manufactured in the United States of America
10  9  8  7  6  5  4  3  2  1

*Dedicated to our students, in whose trust we place our cities,*
*and to publicly spirited citizens everywhere.*

# CONTENTS

# TABLES, FIGURES, AND PHOTOS

## Tables

## Figures

## Photos

# PREFACE

In late spring of 2001, three Portland State University faculty, Karen Gibson, Charles Heying, and I, sat down for lunch at a restaurant near campus that offers seasonal menus of locally produced foods. In the course of our meandering conversation, we touched on what might seem an eclectic array of topics: university politics, what drew each of us to Portland and what we found once here, the broader academic and popular press discussions about livability and sustainable cities, and the fact that PSU had been selected to host the 2004 annual meeting of the Association of Collegiate Schools of Planning. Karen put forth what seemed a brilliant idea. Why not put together an edited book on Portland, with chapters written by faculty at Portland State University's School of Urban Studies and Planning?

This was a stroke of genius for several reasons. As a school of urban studies and planning with a community development undergraduate degree, a master's degree in planning, and a master's and doctoral degree in urban studies, we felt our faculty should be part of the larger national discussion on livability, sustainability, and other fashionable labels for desirable urban environments. We also were experiencing a loss of a sense of community in our own workplace as pressures of growth at our university began to impose on us. A project that created a vehicle for conversations among us about something for which we all cared deeply, community, seemed like a proactive response. Finally, hosting a national conference with planning educators seemed like a golden opportunity to present those attending with a collection of writings that would foster a deeper understanding of their experience visiting the Portland metropolitan region and the role that planning has played here.

In a truly collaborative spirit, we invited other faculty to help us scratch away at the surface of possibilities. Tom Sanchez, who was at PSU at the time, joined Charles Heying and myself on an Internet search of possible funders, guided by Tracy Prince, then director of development for the College of Urban and Public Affairs. In summer 2002, Portland State University provided a small faculty development grant to support graduate assistance in grant writing. Jennifer Porter, a master's degree planning student, compiled a list of books and articles about the buzz and the bust of the Portland urban scene. Planning graduate student Kristin Dahl provided logistical support and Carl Abbott added his publishing experience to the mix, helping to write the book proposal. And in fall of 2002, without funders or a publisher yet, the authors began meeting regularly to hear and react to proposed chapters one by one.

These "seminars" were truly one of the most enjoyable aspects of this project. While weekly or monthly seminars are a routine part of many department calendars, an opportunity to discuss our own research and interests not as a fully formed product but as an emerging idea, sometimes with little more than passion or curiosity behind it, and to feel confident that the group's response would be not only tolerant but supportive and informative, is less usual in the academy. In addition to the authors in this volume, our colleagues Charles Heying, Barry Messer, Irina Sharkova, and Richard White joined these meetings and helped enormously to expand and enliven our discussions. These sessions allowed the more recently arrived faculty to take advantage of the vast and insider knowledge of the long-term residents. Conversely, the taken-for-granted assumptions of the longer-term faculty were challenged. Most importantly, we were constructing together a shared understanding of what constitutes the fields of urban studies and planning, at least at Portland State University.

Eventually, in response to an anonymous outside reviewer's urging for a lead editor, I assumed this role. However, I prefer to think of myself as a shepherd of this project; the authors themselves, as colleagues, have been moving this project forward with their energy, mutual support, and shared commitment to sustaining a sense of community in our workplace.

As this project has progressed, our community has widened. The PSU Office of Graduate Studies and Sponsored Research provided editing support through collaboration with the PSU English Department's graduate writing program. Thanks to Bill Feyerherm and Tracy Dillon, we enjoyed the editorial assistance of graduate student Merilee D. Karr, who read our drafts with the fresh perspective of an outsider and a keen eye for good prose. We also appreciate the editorial assistance of graduate student Hilary Russell, who employed the expertise she has gained as assistant editor of the *Journal of the American Planning Association* as she reviewed the complete manuscript for consistency and continuity and provided valuable project management skills. We are most grateful to Nohad Toulan, then dean of PSU's College of Urban and Public Affairs, for stepping in with funds when needed to support our final steps toward publication.

Finally, we thank Heather Boyer and the staff at Island Press and beyond, who provided the support, push, and expertise necessary to get the manuscript to press.

# Introduction
## Challenges in Growing Communities

Urban areas across the United States and indeed the world are growing rapidly spatially and demographically. As we entered the twenty-first century, much of the talk in the United States concerned the recognition that the physical form of our cities creates costs we are unwilling to pay. Traffic congestion, loss of air quality, floods, and wildfires threatening suburban development, as in Southern California in autumn 2003, are rather unsubtle signals that continuing urban growth along past patterns will spell disaster. In the final decades of the past century a worry emerged about increasing social ills and a loss of a sense of community (Bellah et al. 1985, Putnam 2000). Homelessness, alienation of youth, and fears of random shootings in busy metropolitan areas mark the inadequacy of our social connections. Where should elected officials, planners and public administrators, and citizens look for a path out of what seems at times an inevitable downward spiral heading toward increasing law enforcement, higher walls, and greater isolation among the citizenry?

How can we organize ourselves spatially and socially to maintain and restore our sense of community? A search for ideas begins with places that have ventured off the trodden path and have arrived in the first years of the twenty-first century as places where people, at least reputedly, want to live. The Portland, Oregon, metropolitan region is one such place.

In an interview with the libertarian Reason Policy Institute, renowned urbanist Jane Jacobs was asked about the regulatory and planning approach that Oregon, and Portland in particular, have undertaken for the past 30 years. As one might imagine, the Reason Policy Institute questioner was inviting Jacobs, who has advocated for an organic, bottom-up approach to developing city form, to damn the presumed heavy hand of Oregon planners. Jacobs's response was refreshingly simple and straightforward. She said, "In Portland, a lot of good things are being done." When the interviewer asked what she liked about Portland, Jacobs replied, "People in Portland love Portland. That's the most important thing" (Reason Policy Institute 2001). And then she went on to say,

> They really like to see it [the City] improved. The waterfront is getting improved, and not with a lot of gimmicks, but with good, intelligent reuses of the old buildings. They're good at rehabilitation. As far as their parks are concerned, they've got some wonderful parks with water flows in them. It's fascinating. People enjoy it and paddle in it. They're unusual parks. The amount of space they take and what they deliver is terrific. They're pretty good on their transit, too. It's not any one splashy thing. It's the ensemble that I think is so pleasant.

Newcomers to the Portland region are often struck by a few consistent themes. Certainly the landscape is exceptional, and the location, equally accessible to the snow-capped peak of Mt. Hood and the rugged Oregon coast, offers a myriad of recreational opportunities. Nine months of the year, the land is hugged by rain-soaked clouds that (after enough years) begin to feel like a comforting blanket and seem to disappear next to the thick line of green treetops. The dry summer months offer temperate temperatures and clear blue skies. But more than just the landscape and the well-kept secret of summer keep Oregonians in Portland despite high unemployment rates and low wages. There is something else about this place.

As a recent transplant myself a decade ago, I was struck not only by the appearance of planning-related news items reported in the local papers on nearly a daily basis, but also by the high level of awareness of ordinary people, such as my dental hygienist and Little League moms, about relatively technical aspects of land use planning, such as Portland's "urban growth boundary" (UGB). But Portland's difference goes beyond the state land use system.

People seem to care about one another. Shortly after moving to the region, my then 10-year old son rode his bike to a local shop and lost the money he had stuffed into his pocket to buy a snack. Seeing him searching up and down and around the bike rack and looking rather upset, a passerby asked what the problem was. Upon hearing about my son's plight, the stranger reached into his wallet and handed him a twenty-dollar bill.

Although numerous examples come to mind, one prominent story of community activism in the region is the history of a nonprofit organization called City Repair. In 1995, some residents in the Sellwood neighborhood of Portland recognized what they perceived as an absence of public meeting spaces in their neighborhood. Banding together, they approached a landowner and got his approval to set up on his lot what they called the "Moon Day T-Hows," (Monday Tea House). The neighbors held Monday night potlucks at the T-Hows and stocked it with pillows, books, and games. The structure won the 1996 People's Choice Award from the American Institute of Architects, Portland Chapter (City Repair 2004).

The next step by these residents was a bit bolder. Noting the lack of public space resulting from the grid street pattern that characterizes much of Portland's east side, they decided to claim a local street intersection as their own public square. Although their initial efforts to gain formal permission from the city were refused, the residents persisted. They eventually constructed a tea station where free, hot tea is available 24 hours a day, reserved a place for people to obtain or give away free food, and painted a colorful design across the intersection. In January 2000, the Portland City Council passed an ordinance that allows any group of citizens to create public squares at street intersections in their own neighborhood. Since then, four additional neighborhoods have organized similar community-building efforts. Is the success of such community-based initiatives a reflection of effective activist organizing or something more elusive and pervasive in social relationships here? How significant was the apparent responsiveness of the city council in this case?

What is myth and what is reality in the Portland, Oregon, metropolitan region? Do these anecdotes resemble life in the other 100 largest U.S. cities, or is a sense of responsibility to one another unusually strong in Portland? To what extent are physical form and a sense of community related, and to what extent are conditions in the Portland region a result of intentional actions by its leaders and institutions? Is Portland a model for Smart Growth advocates and a contender for sustainability awards? Or, in contrast, is Portland simply "behind the curve" in hitting the challenges of urban sprawl, housing affordability, and environmental degradation? Will Portland continue to "look different" from other cities of its age, or will the homogenization of globalization flatten out its urban scape into a standardized metropolitan form?

As scholars, teachers, and citizens of the Portland metropolitan region, the authors of this volume have come together in a joint inquiry to examine how special the Portland region is (or isn't), in what ways, and to understand how this came to be. We are intrigued by the attention lavished upon the region by the national press for its quality of life; by the intensity of controversy among proponents, skeptics, and critics of Oregon's progressive planning system; and by the questions that still surround the design of urban form and culture. We are also struck by what is missed by out-of-town scholars in their examinations of this region, about both the institutional structures and the nature of this place and its people.

Our objective through this volume is to enhance our collective understanding of the evolution and development of the Portland metropolitan region as an example of a livable place. We focus on particular, critical elements of the urban system, choosing to address what we as residents and scholars know best and recognizing that important questions remain. Our intention is not only to speak to the current and future residents of Portland about what is special here and how such qualities can be protected, but also to contribute to a broader discussion among scholars, practitioners, politicians, and urban activists about how North American cities can accommodate growth while sustaining a sense of community for their residents. We believe that our chapters shed light selectively not only on the role of state and local government, but also on the role of citizen leaders in shaping healthy urban communities and regions.

## Organization and Structure of This Volume

The overall approach of this collection of chapters is to illuminate how institutions and people have come together to create current conditions in the Portland region. Several questions framed our research:

- What has the Portland region achieved that is special or especially valuable?
- What are the innovations in policy, planning, or plan making that we see in the Portland region?
- Where has Portland been successful or innovative in utilizing national programs or policies or adapting to national trends?

Although in some cases we may be able to suggest how this region compares with other localities, our main objective is to provide a view of this region and a point of reference for others to conduct such a comparison. Consistent with our belief that scholars *in a place* are best able to interpret the critical features of the social, physical, and political environment, we present the Portland region's case and invite others to do similar work on their own regions as they see fit.

We begin by presenting a snapshot of the demographic, economic, and civic character of the Portland region in a chapter by Heike Mayer and John Provo. They also present data for Portland and other similarly sized U.S. metropolitan areas on key dimensions of economy, equity (which considers education and homeownership patterns among various socioeconomic and ethnic groups), and environment to set a general context for the remaining chapters.

Then we progress to the institutional structures that have been put in place in the Portland region. The next three chapters describe the roles and intentions of major regional and city bodies. Ethan Seltzer's chapter explains the regional framework enabled by the 1973 state land use law and the evolution of Metro, an elected regional planning authority, over the 1990s. Metro's efforts have laid the groundwork and a frame for many of the activities described in the later substantive chapters on transportation, housing, and the environment. Karen Gibson's chapter examines how the Portland Development Commission has pursued urban redevelopment and the extent to which it has become more inclusive in its planning processes as it goes beyond large-scale, downtown development to projects that impact the neighborhoods. Gibson raises questions about the quality of citizen involvement and how it has or hasn't changed over time. Matt Witt's chapter describes Portland's unique neighborhood association program, which has been brought to scholarly attention by works such as *The Rebirth of Urban Democracy* (Berry, Portney, and Thomson 1993). Witt describes the 30-year history of the neighborhood associations, changes in the program's structure and composition over time, and some of the tensions that threaten even today to rip the system apart.

In the next group of chapters, we look at elements of the culture of this place and its people. Steve Johnson's chapter describes the level of engagement of the general population in organizations concerned about the collective good over time. Gerald Sussman and J. R. Estes describe Portland's community radio station as both an example of voluntary action and a contributing force to the creation of a sense of community.

KBOO has resisted pressures to professionalize its staff and format in the face of increasing corporate ownership of competing airwaves and, in the process, remains accessible to and reflective of the region's diverse ethnic groups and subcultures. It serves as a magnet for progressive communications. Chet Orloff's chapter describes the history of public space preservation in Portland going back to the founding years of the city and leading up to the present. This history illustrates how the hands of visionary elites and citizen advocates together worked to draw the map of Portland's parks and open spaces.

The last chapters lay out various measures of current conditions in the region and describe to varying levels how agents and structures worked together to produce these conditions. Some of these chapters address directly debates in the scholarly literature and the popular press about what is and what is not working about Oregon's land use system. Carl Abbott's chapter describes the liveliness of the central city and the deliberate efforts that occurred to sustain its prominence in the region. New challenges may be arising, however, Abbott notes, as expansion of the central city encroaches into neighborhoods that had been deliberately protected in prior decades. Deborah Howe's chapter responds to criticism about perverse effects of the urban growth boundary on housing affordability and explains the steep rise in market prices within its historical context. Nancy Chapman and Hollie Lund's chapter addresses questions of density and adds meaning to the notion of livability. Their chapter shows the influence of the combination of state, regional, and local policies on the character of growth and livability in the metro area. Sy Adler and Jennifer Dill describe deliberations around the formulation and implementation of a state transportation policy at the local and regional levels and offer an assessment of key indicators of the policy's success at this relatively early point in time. Connie Ozawa and Alan Yeakley's chapter similarly discusses the evolution of local implementation actions in the context of the state land use law and federal policy on the environment. Their chapter examines changes in one resource, riparian buffers, as a window onto the larger picture of urban ecosystem protection in the region. Although their research is ongoing, their efforts thus far provide a method for assessing and comparing the effectiveness of urban ecosystem policies. Finally, Tracy Prince argues that the city of Portland's progressive response to homeless issues has been guided largely up to this point by the influence and actions of prominent political actors. Whether the city's progressive reputation will extend to the homeless population into the future, however, may be questioned,

Prince suggests, given local ordinances that have been put in the books recently.

As we move further into the twenty-first century, there are indications of increasing stressors on the current urban political, social, and physical system. This collection of chapters helps to identify and understand what policies and processes put in place in the Portland, Oregon, region appear to be working well, and which ones suggest that the Portland region, as other U.S. metropolitan areas, may be approaching a critical "edge."

REFERENCES

Bellah, Robert N., Richard Madsen, William M. Sullivan, Ann Swidler, and Steven M. Tipton. 1985. *Habits of the Heart: Individualism and Commitment in American Life*. New York: Harper & Row.

Berry, Jeffrey, Kent E. Portney, and Ken Thomson, 1993. *The Rebirth of American Democracy*, Washington, D.C.: The Brookings Institution.

City Repair. 2004. *Moon Day T-Hows*. http://www.cityrepair.org (accessed 11 March 2004).

Putnam, Robert D. 2000. *Bowling Alone: The Collapse and Revival of American Community*. New York: Simon & Schuster.

Reason Policy Institute. 2001. *City Views: Urban Studies Legend Jane Jacobs on Gentrification, the New Urbanism, and Her Legacy*. http://reason.com/0106/fe.bo.city.shtml (accessed October 2001).

# 1 | *The Portland Edge in Context*

Heike Mayer and John Provo

Portland is known as the "Capital of Good Planning" (Abbott 2000). For many urban planners the region has been the poster child for regional planning, growth management, and other innovative urban planning policies. While the following chapters examine a variety of issue areas in which the Portland region has gained this reputation, this chapter provides a broad context for that discussion. We begin by describing the region's demographic and economic landscapes as well as the evolution of some key policies dealing with urban and regional planning. We provide some comparative statistics on metropolitan Portland and a number of similarly sized regions across the United States. We conclude by highlighting key challenges facing the region.

The Portland, Oregon–Vancouver, Washington, Primary Metropolitan Statistical Area is 30 miles north of the 45th parallel and roughly on a line with Augusta, Maine, and Fargo, North Dakota. Surrounded by high mountains at the northern end of Oregon's fertile Willamette Valley, the region's temperate climate provides mild temperatures all year with a famously wet winter and a wonderfully dry summer. Spectacular mountain views abound throughout the region and inspire a connection with a rich outdoor culture that offers boundless opportunities to kayak, camp, hike, fish, and hunt.

Portland is also known for vibrant, diverse neighborhoods that cluster around commercially active neighborhood streets like Hawthorne Boulevard, Belmont Avenue, and Northwest 23rd. The city has an excellent transportation system that is anchored by extensive regional bus, light rail, and streetcar systems. These networks support transit-oriented developments like Orenco Station in the region's western suburbs and the trendy Pearl District, formerly a warehouse district adjacent to downtown that is now home to condominiums, restaurants, and specialty shops.

Portland residents and visitors alike spend hours at Powell's City of Books, the nation's largest independent bookstore. They can drink a pint at one of the region's many microbrewery pubs or drive just outside of the city for a pinot noir tasting at a world-class winery.

## Things Look Different Here

Looking at the Portland metropolitan region through consumer marketing data and quality-of-life rankings in the popular press suggests that things really do look different here. Portlanders are more likely to spend their time and money on active outdoor recreation than observing team sporting events. They read more and they watch cable television less than folks in most places. The region ranks seventh in U.S. cities in newspaper circulation and it ranks third—after Seattle and San Francisco—in the absolute number of coffee shops (Cortright 2002). *Travel and Leisure* magazine ranked Portland high in safety, cleanliness, proximity to nature, and "getting around" in March 2003. In fact, getting around in Portland by foot is so much easier than in other U.S. cities that the American Podiatric Medical Association ranked Portland among the nation's best cities for those who love to walk. Other magazines and organizations rank Portland as the top market for wireless technology, as the leader for constructing ecoroofs, as one of the most literate cities, and as one of the least expensive cities on the West Coast to live (Portland Development Commission 2003). The cumulative impact of such accolades is apparent. In September 2003, Harris Poll ranked Portland number eight before Seattle and Denver as a place where most people want to live. Echoing this result was *Money* magazine ranking of Portland among the best places to live in the nation, second to New York City. For all that they do tell, these rankings offer only one kind of story about the Portland region. Data like these do not reveal much about the people who live in the city and how they make urban life work. In this chapter we present a thumbnail sketch of the region that goes beyond the questions in magazines.

## Demographic Landscape

The historic pace of Portland's growth has been described as temperate—more the tortoise than the hare (Abbott 2002). However, over the last three decades, the Portland region's population has grown larger and more diverse. The six-county metropolitan area counted a total population of 1,918,009 people in 2000. From 1990 to 2000, the region's population grew by 402,557 people, a 26.5% increase. The population almost doubled since the 1970s and as a metropolitan statistical area it ranks 23rd among all U.S. metropolitan areas. The Portland–Vancouver Primary Metropolitan Statistical Area (PMSA) includes six counties. Five counties are in Oregon and one county (Clark County) is in the state of Washington.

At the center of the region is Multnomah County, home to the City of Portland and accounting for 660,486 residents in the 2000 census (see Table 1.1). The surrounding counties of Columbia and Yamhill make up the rural fringe of the PMSA, while Clackamas and Washington counties include both rapidly urbanizing suburban rings around Portland and large swaths of rural areas outside of the urban growth boundary. Of the six counties, Clark County, across the Columbia River in Washington State, has seen the highest percentage change in population growth between 1990 and 2000, at 45%.

Portland population growth has been primarily attributed to the region's economic success, especially in the 1990s. According to the 1998 Oregon Employment Department's In-Migration Survey, approximately 33% of

### Table 1.1
*Population by county in the Portland–Vancouver metropolitan region*

| County | Population in 2000 | % Change 1990–2000 |
|---|---|---|
| Clackamas | 338,391 | 21.4 |
| Columbia | 43,560 | 16.0 |
| Multnomah | 660,486 | 13.1 |
| Washington | 445,342 | 42.9 |
| Yamhill | 84,992 | 29.7 |
| Clark (Washington) | 345,238 | 45.0 |
| **Total Portland–Vancouver PMSA** | **1,918,009** | **26.5** |

SOURCE: U.S. Census. 2000. *Ranking Tables for Metropolitan Areas: Population in 2000 and Population Change from 1990 to 2000.* http://www.census.gov/population/www/cen2000/phc-t3.html (accessed 21 February 2004).
NOTE: PMSA, Primary Metropolitan Statistical Area.

the survey respondents reported coming from California (Oregon Employment Department 1999). In particular, the young, single, and college educated were attracted to the region. According to a census report, the Portland PMSA ranked fifth behind Naples, Las Vegas, Charlotte, and Atlanta in attracting the young, single, and college educated between 1995 and 2000 (Franklin 2003). The report also found that this demographic group is more likely to settle in central cities than in suburbs or nonmetropolitan areas. In the Portland metropolitan region the central county, Multnomah County, experienced the greatest influx of young people (see Fig. 1.1.) The "young and restless" still flock to Portland even though the region experiences high unemployment. In contrast with the invitation issued in the 1970s by Oregon Governor Tom McCall "to visit but don't stay," Governor Kulongoski quipped that today's new residents were welcome but should bring a big savings account and a picnic basket (Wentz 2004).

In 2000, the largest ethnic minority group in the Portland metropolitan area was the Hispanic or Latino group, which accounted for 7.4% of

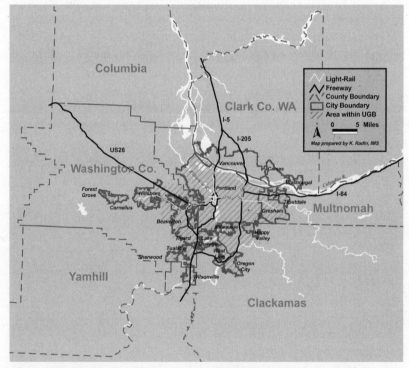

FIGURE 1.1. The Portland Metropolitan Region with the Urban Growth Boundary.
Source: Original.

the total population. The Asian/Pacific Islander population in the region accounted for 6.2%. Other ethnic groups have a rather small presence. The 2000 census reported that the region's population included 3.4% African Americans and 1.9% American Indians. These figures represent a sharp increase, with the total nonwhite and Hispanic population almost doubling from 11% in 1990 to 19.5% in 2000. This was driven by the dramatic and largely suburban phenomenon of growth in the Hispanic population, which increased its share by 4.5% between 1990 and 2000.

In general, the region's poverty rates follow national trends, with rates across the metropolitan area increasing from 1980 until a period of decrease from 1993 to 1996. Since 1997, however, poverty rates in the region have increased while national figures show decreases. The latest data on poverty from the census indicate that poverty rates in the region as a whole have risen, from 9.2% in 1997 to 9.5% in 2000. Increasing suburban poverty has contributed to this change. In Multnomah County, which includes most of the City of Portland, the poverty rate has dropped from 13.6% in 1997 to 12.7% in 2000, while Washington County's poverty rate has risen from 7.1% in 1995 to 7.4% in 2000. Poverty rates decreased in Yamhill County (11.2% in 1995, 9.2% in 2000) and in Clark County, Washington (9.3% in 1995, 9.1% in 2000).

## Economic Landscape

The Portland metropolitan economy has grown rapidly over the last decade. Underlying this growth has been a structural transformation of the region's economic drivers with the most striking change being the emergence of high technology firms. The region's economic history began with its success in trading natural resource products. Portland's proximity to the Columbia River and the Pacific Ocean was pivotal in its role as a trading gateway to the rest of the world (Abbott 1983). The region exported grain, lumber, and wood products. Consequently, the necessary infrastructure—grain elevators, wholesale operations, and warehouses—was set up in close proximity to the ports and the railroad. All this economic activity took place near Portland's downtown, and from the late nineteenth century to the mid-twentieth century the suburban counties in the region were part of the agricultural hinterland. In the latter part of the twentieth century, suburbanization and growth in the high technology industry changed the role of these suburban counties and most of them are now not only residential but also have a large share of the region's traded-sector industry clusters, networks of export-oriented firms and their specialized suppliers.

About 16% of the region's 1.2 million workers are employed in traded-sector industry clusters that include agriculture and forestry; metals, machinery, and transportation equipment; high technology; nursery stock; wood and paper products; and creative services (see Table 1.2). Even though there is only one company, Nike, that belongs to the *Fortune* 500 group, the list of export-oriented firms that call the region their home looks quite impressive: DaimlerChrysler's Freightliner manufactures trucks, Tektronix produces measurement equipment, Intel develops and manufactures high-end semiconductors, Adidas America and Nike are in the sports apparel markets, and Wieden & Kennedy produces TV commercials and advertising campaigns for companies like Nike, AOL, and Coca-Cola.

Portland's economic geography displays some distinct patterns. Most of the service-oriented firms, such as public relations companies, multimedia firms, insurance brokers, and banks, have their offices in the central city. High technology industry, in contrast, is concentrated in suburban Washington County. The nursery industry takes advantage of the availability of agricultural lands protected from development and locates at the edge of the urbanized region just outside of the urban growth boundary.

The region's traded-sector industry clusters benefit from geographic conditions and historical accidents. The nursery industry, for example, draws on the availability of fertile soil, relatively cheap agricultural land, and an urban transportation infrastructure. It also benefits from Oregon's mild climate with its wet winters and dry summers. The apparel

### Table 1.2

*Employment and average pay in select industry clusters, 2001*

| Industry Cluster | Total Employment | Average Pay |
| --- | --- | --- |
| Agriculture and forestry | 29,399 | $26,282 |
| Metals, machinery, and transportation equipment | 45,957 | $50,939 |
| High technology | 68,149 | $68,339 |
| Nursery | 4,216 | $24,062 |
| Wood and paper products | 17,195 | $42,514 |
| Creative services | 30,007 | $55,203 |

SOURCE: Oregon Employment Department. 2003. *ES-202 Data*. Portland, Oregon. Washington State Employment Security Department. 2003. *ES-202 Data*. Vancouver, Washington.

industry can trace its history back to Phil Knight, the founder of Nike, whose athletic activities began in the Oregon college town of Eugene where he ran track and field for the University of Oregon. Adidas America was later drawn to the region mainly because of the availability of specialized labor in the sports apparel market. The metals, machinery, and transportation equipment industries have their roots in the shipyards here during World War II. Employment in this industry peaked in 1944 when more than 115,000 worked for the shipyards (Abbott 1983). And the high technology industry traces its roots to 1946 when two local engineers founded Tektronix to make electronic measurement instruments (Lee 1986).

Common to all of these industry clusters is that they are more innovative and knowledge-intensive today than they were just a couple of decades ago. In that time the economy in the Portland region transitioned from a natural resource–oriented economy to one that is knowledge based. One key measure of knowledge creation is patent registration activity. By this measure the Portland region has been highly innovative over the last decades. While patent activity from 1975 to 1999 in the United States grew annually by 2%, patents in Portland were registered at an annual growth rate of 6% during the same period. The large high technology corporations such as Intel and Tektronix have been the most prolific patent holders. However, other sectors of the region's economy have adopted innovative products and production processes as well. The region's nursery industry, a national leader in the field, for example, relies on sophisticated marketing and merchandising techniques to increase sales of their products, which are different from traditional agricultural goods such as potatoes and grain.

The Portland region flourished economically in the 1990s, driven by export-oriented manufacturing. By 2000, about 12% of the region's total workforce was employed in manufacturing industries. Between 1990 and 2000, the six-county metropolitan area added 22,871 manufacturing jobs. This growth is remarkable because during the period most regions in the United States posted a loss in manufacturing employment due to the migration of these jobs overseas.

These manufacturing gains centered on the high technology industry. Echoing other high technology regions, the area branded itself with the name "Silicon Forest" in the 1980s. Tektronix sowed the seeds for the growth of this Silicon Forest in the late 1940s. The company grew quickly and became the world's leader in oscilloscope manufacturing. At its peak in the mid-1980s, Tektronix employed 15,000 people in the Portland region and 24,000 worldwide. In late 1976, Intel set up its first branch plant in Washington County. Intel chose Portland because of the availability of cheap water and electricity and a less competitive environment for attracting talented employees as well as lower costs of living compared to Silicon Valley. The region never had a world-class research university, the commonly presumed prerequisite for high technology development. However, Intel and Tektronix compensated for this lack by functioning as "surrogate universities" (Mayer 2003). With Intel's move to the region, a host of supporting firms, suppliers and subcontractors, and competitors discovered the Portland location. Over time, a complex and innovative industrial cluster evolved that today benefits from close proximity to demanding customers such as Intel. Talented employees were attracted to the region because of the opportunities the high technology industry could offer and the high quality of life.

For the most part, the aforementioned industry clusters evolved without receiving much strategic attention from economic developers. Economic development policy has been characterized by a supply-side approach. During the region's high technology boom in the 1980s and 1990s, local and state leaders used tax measures to influence economic development. During the mid-1980s, the state repealed the unitary tax and during the 1990s instituted a tax break program—the Strategic Investment Program—for capital-intensive industries such as semiconductor manufacturing. Most of the jurisdictions in the region have economic development plans but a regional consensus on where the economy should head in the future has yet to emerge. Regional discussions about economic development mainly revolve around issues related to the availability of industrial land and the ability to grow knowledge-based industries. The latter has become a discussion topic because business, higher education, and economic development leaders are realizing the role higher education institutions can play in economic development.

### Civic Landscape

Historian Kimbark MacColl (1979), chronicling Portland in the first half of the twentieth century, described an unambiguously conservative civic landscape. This was expressed in rural values, a belief in the sacred nature of private property, a deep-seated Anglo-Saxon bias, and an overriding desire for stability in the neighborhoods (see Chap. 5, Johnson). This was perhaps at odds with Portland's reputation as a wide-open port town, where sailors were warned against the risks of involuntary impressments through a series of "shanghai tunnels" along the waterfront red light district (Lansing 2003).

On the whole, however, Portland escaped most of the highs and lows of early twentieth-century capitalism. Although a region with strong unions, it never experienced the levels of labor–management conflict or ethnic strife rampant in other western cities. The upheavals of central-city urban renewal and auto-driven suburbanization that remade many U.S. regions following World War II were also slow to arrive in Portland. Carl Abbott describes this stability as advantageous for a new generation of civic leaders in the 1960s and 1970s whose relatively small, homogeneous metropolitan region could be visualized "as a single place in need of common solutions" (Abbott 2002, 7).

Playing out on the demographic, economic, and civic landscapes just described, innovations in local and regional planning have contributed to Portland's reputation as a livable place. The 1970s saw state and local policies that laid the foundation of the region's reputation as a livable and well-planned metropolitan area. Senate Bill 10 was adopted in 1969, requiring cities and counties to prepare comprehensive land use plans that meet statewide standards. Senate Bill 100 created the Land Conservation and Development Commission in 1973 to monitor local comprehensive planning and compliance with a set of statewide planning goals. These goals are still in effect and focus comprehensively on the preservation of farmland, open space, housing, public facilities and services, urban growth boundaries, and economic development. By establishing a statewide land use planning framework in the early 1970s, Oregon was at the forefront of what is termed today the smart growth movement.

Urban growth boundaries were mandated statewide in 1973–1974 and Metro, the regionally elected land use and transportation planning agency, defined the boundary for the Portland metropolitan region in 1979 (Gibson and Abbott 2002). Initially the motivation behind state land use planning was to protect the fertile farmland in the Willamette Valley (Abbott 1983, Abbott et al. 1994). As urbanization increased, however, attention has shifted toward managing the forms growth takes within the established urban growth boundaries, especially in the Portland metropolitan area.

While the 1970s saw the introduction of innovative planning policies statewide, they also saw new approaches to downtown planning. Following World War II, downtown Portland faced the same challenges as other U.S. cities: The central city area lost its attraction to shoppers, workers, and residents and it faced many other revitalization challenges. The beginnings of the downtown's revival were centered on the redevelopment of the waterfront. The Willamette River divides Portland's downtown area from the industrial district and the residential areas southeast of the center. During the 1940s a highway, Harbor Drive, had been built to bypass the central business district. But this highway cut off the waterfront from the rest of the city and citizen-initiated plans were devised to create a greenway so that residents, visitors, and workers would be able to enjoy the river. These plans culminated in the 1973 removal of Harbor Drive, which was replaced with a riverfront park named after Oregon Governor Tom McCall, one of the architects of the state's land use planning system (Abbott 1983).

Another milestone of downtown revitalization was the city's bold steps toward a more comprehensive approach to downtown planning. In 1971 a citizen advisory committee was appointed and worked on fleshing out a list of downtown goals, which then were folded into a plan

PHOTO 1. Harbor Drive in 1958, looking north from about the Hawthorne Bridge. During the 1970s, this major expressway was torn down and reclaimed for urban park use, now called Tom McCall Waterfront Park (see following photo).
Republished with permission from the Oregon Historical Society

PHOTO 2. Tom McCall Waterfront Park looking north from the Hawthorne Bridge in 2004. In the 1970s, a significant urban amenity replaced a six-lane expressway. The park runs for 22 blocks along the west bank of the Willamette River.
Note: This and all subsequent photographs contributed by Leslie Good

that was adopted in 1972. Key elements of the plan were high-intensity office and retail use at the core of downtown and a transit mall for incoming buses that would serve offices and retail. Two downtown streets were dedicated to the transit mall and are primarily restricted to use by buses. Portland historian Carl Abbott describes the plan as an "integrated solution to a long list of problems that Portlanders had treated piecemeal for fifty years" (Abbott 1983, 222).

Looking at the outcomes of these efforts, Portlanders can be proud of how their downtown developed. Downtown Portland has a healthy mix of office, retail, and residential uses and unlike so many U.S. cities is used not only from 9 to 5 but also in the evenings and on the weekends. The waterfront park, extended to the opposite shore with the recent addition of the Eastbank Esplanade, is used for numerous festivals and events. Both parks serve the daily needs of a legion of runners, bike riders, Rollerbladers, skateboard enthusiasts, and quiet strollers.

At the time when the downtown plan was adopted a new mayor was just taking office in Portland. That mayor was Neil Goldschmidt and his vision for Portland was built not only on downtown revitalization but also on a complementary effort to revitalize neighborhoods. During his tenure the Office of Neighborhood Associations (now the Office of Neighborhood Involvement) was established to fund and assist neighborhood associations across the city (see Chap. 4, Witt). Goldschmidt's goal was to make Portland's neighborhoods attractive to a wide range of people, especially young families. With this population-based strategy Goldschmidt wanted to develop a market for downtown retail, induce investments in older neighborhoods, and avoid the flight of middle-class families to the suburbs. His strategy worked and the city's neighborhoods experienced significant reinvestment while the downtown flourished.

During the 1980s the region diverted funds from a long-planned highway project to invest in a metropolitan light rail system. In 1986, Tri-Met began operating a 15-mile-long light rail line between Gresham (to the east) and downtown. Known as MAX, this light rail was extended out to Hillsboro in the western suburbs in 1998. In 2001, another line opened and connected the existing ones to Portland International Airport. In Spring 2004, Tri-Met opened a line connecting north Portland with downtown. According to Tri-Met, the region's transit authority, the region's ridership has increased steadily since the first light rail line was opened. Portland's light rail system has also had a dramatic impact on land use development along the lines. Since the decision to build light rail about $3 billion has been invested in these projects. Transit-oriented development has placed attractive high-density, mixed-use communities in close proximity to the stations.

These innovative threads drew together in the 1990s through a comprehensive regional planning effort, Region 2040. This process was led by Metro, the nation's only elected regional government, which covers the metropolitan area's three core counties of Multnomah, Washington, and Clackamas. Through a process of extensive public outreach, Metro developed a 50-year vision for how the region should manage expected growth. Metro's Growth Concept prioritized building the region up at higher densities, rather than out through expansion of the urban growth boundary. A Regional Framework Plan incorporated this growth concept, focusing development in designated urban centers, coordinated with improved transportation investments, and bound local governments to its implementation through required changes to their comprehensive plans. Region 2040 involved both substantial public outreach and the creation of ongoing advisory committees of public and private sector stakeholders that vetted matters before the Metro Council to build consensus around policy. (For a detailed examination of this process, see Chap. 2, Seltzer.)

## Portland Compared to Other Regions

To place the "Portland Edge" in context this section compares the Portland metropolitan region with five PMSAs within the continental United States that rank above and below the region in terms of population. While later chapters in the book discuss regional, city, and neighborhood planning, we present this comparative data at the metropolitan level. The most widely available sources for such comparisons, the commuting patterns on which PMSAs are based, play a role in planning at all levels of geography. Metro, the elected regional government, is a case in point. Its legislative authority is limited to the 24 cities and portions of three counties. At the same time much of Metro's data collection, forecasting, and planning efforts take into account the wider six-county geography of the Portland–Vancouver PMSA.

These comparative data are organized around emerging thought in regionalism and sustainable development. Various theoretical frameworks have suggested that environment, economy, and equity (known as the "three Es"), must interact in any model of regionalism or sustainable development (Campbell 1996, McDonough and Braungart 2002, Wheeler 2002, Yaro and Hiss 1996). Similarly, national organizations such as PolicyLink (2004) or regional efforts like the San Francisco Bay

Area Alliance (2004) and Portland's Coalition for a Livable Future (2004) are making connections across environmental, economic, and equity agendas in practice.

This framework is used for descriptive purposes rather than to advance the theory behind it. Given Portland's place in both regionalism and sustainable development literatures data were gathered around the three Es to illustrate some of the major ideas about the Portland metropolitan region and how this region performs compared to some of its peers.

As indicated in Table 1.3, the metropolitan areas in the comparison group range in population from Pittsburgh with 2.3 million to Cincinnati with 1.6 million. Within this group Portland's growth rate of 26.6% between 1990 and 2000 was among the fastest, outstripped only by Denver's 30% and followed closely by Fort Worth at 25.1%. The other West Coast cities in this group, San Francisco and San Jose, grew at a more measured pace of 8 and 12.4%, respectively.

## Economy

The national prosperity enjoyed in the 1990s produced new ideas to explain a period of rapid economic growth and industrial restructuring.

### Table 1.3
*Population in select metropolitan areas, 1990–2000*
*(ranked by population change)*

| MSA/PMSA | Population | % Population Change 1990–2000 |
|---|---|---|
| Denver, CO PMSA | 2,109,282 | 30.0 |
| **Portland, OR–Vancouver, WA PMSA** | **1,918,009** | **26.6** |
| Fort Worth–Arlington, TX PMSA | 1,702,625 | 25.1 |
| Miami, FL PMSA | 2,253,362 | 16.3 |
| San Jose, CA PMSA | 1,682,585 | 12.4 |
| Kansas City, MO–KS MSA | 1,776,062 | 12.2 |
| San Francisco, CA PMSA | 1,731,183 | 8.0 |
| Cincinnati, OH–KY–IN PMSA | 1,646,395 | 7.9 |
| Newark, NJ PMSA | 2,032,989 | 6.1 |
| Cleveland–Lorain–Elyria, OH PMSA | 2,250,871 | 2.2 |
| Pittsburgh, PA MSA | 2,358,695 | –1.5 |

SOURCE: U.S. Census. 2000. *Ranking Tables for Metropolitan Areas: Population in 2000 and Population Change from 1990 to 2000.* http://www.census.gov/population/www/cen2000/phc-t3.html (accessed 21 February 2004).
NOTE: MSA, Metropolitan Statistical Area; PMSA, Primary Metropolitan Statistical Area.

High technology industries drive an increasingly interconnected global economy where metropolitan areas or "regional economic commons" matter as much or more than nation-states (Barnes and Ledebur 1998). Further, at the center of many of these regions significant economic revitalization has occurred. In some cases both young people and aging baby boomers turned "empty-nesters" have chosen an urban lifestyle, opening the way for new investment in central cities (Gratz and Mintz 1998, Grogan and Proscio 2000). These elements are apparent in metropolitan Portland as the 1990s saw the growing presence of high technology semiconductor manufacturing and the second decade of regional planning focused on sustaining economically viable urban centers.

From 1990 to 2000, Portland increased its total employment base by 25%, or 313,970 jobs. Only sunbelt service centers Denver and Fort Worth–Arlington performed similarly or better than the Portland region. Portland's West Coast neighbors San Francisco and San Jose added only 13% and 19%, respectively. Portland, in keeping with the objectives of its regional planning system, also retains a strong central city employment base with 42% of employment in the City of Portland (see Table 1.4). Among the comparison regions it was surpassed only by San Francisco with 54% and matched by Fort Worth with 42% of jobs in the central city.

### Table 1.4

*Employment in central city and suburban areas in select metropolitan regions, 2000 (ranked by central city share)*

| MSA/PMSA | 2000 Employment Percents | |
| --- | --- | --- |
| | Central City | Suburban |
| San Francisco, CA PMSA | 54 | 46 |
| **Portland, OR–Vancouver, WA PMSA** | **42** | **58** |
| Fort Worth–Arlington, TX PMSA | 42 | 58 |
| Denver, CO PMSA | 39 | 61 |
| San Jose, CA PMSA | 37 | 63 |
| Kansas City, MO–KS MSA | 36 | 64 |
| Cincinnati, OH–KY–IN PMSA | 33 | 67 |
| Pittsburgh, PA MSA | 30 | 70 |
| Cleveland–Lorain–Elyria, OH PMSA | 26 | 74 |
| Miami, FL PMSA | 25 | 75 |
| Newark, NJ PMSA | 14 | 86 |

SOURCE: HUD User (2000). *State of the Cities Data Systems County Business Patterns Special Data Extract.*
   http://socds.huduser.org/CBPSE/CBPSE_Home.htm (accessed 26 May 2004).
NOTE: MSA, Metropolitan Statistical Area; PMSA, Primary Metropolitan Statistical Area.

Further, compared to its peers, Portland is the only region that added manufacturing jobs, generally in the high paying high technology sectors like semiconductors, during the 1990s. Each of the 10 regions we used for comparison lost manufacturing jobs during this time period (see Table 1.5). This includes high tech hot spot San Jose, for example, which lost 725 manufacturing jobs, as well as the more traditional manufacturing center of Newark, which posted the largest loss with 28,790 jobs.

Portland's reliance on the manufacturing sector is a blessing and a curse. While the region has done well in growing this sector during the 1990s, it has also become more vulnerable to economic cycles. This has become obvious in the recent recession. In early 2001, the semiconductor industry employed 36,000 people. By early 2003, the industry had shed approximately 6,000 jobs. Driven by these losses the region's average annual unemployment rate in 2002 was 7.8%, among the highest in the nation.

### Equity

A discussion of equity in Portland with respect to race or ethnicity may be challenging because of the small size of these communities in the region. Similarly a discussion of equity with respect to individual economic outcomes may be challenging given the region's largely middle-class character. However, as mentioned earlier both those features are changing. The region's nonwhite population almost doubled in the 1990s. Further, not only is the region currently experiencing some of the highest unemployment rates in the nation but it also retains significant pockets of poverty that actually persisted throughout the prosperous 1990s. Given criticism of growth management as exclusive, considering such negative outcomes in light of equitable access to economic opportunity is important. To that end we present data on rental housing costs and homeownership rates. This question of housing affordability, whose association with growth management has been debated in Portland's case (Downs 2002; Nelson et al. 2002), receives a full airing later in this volume (see Chap. 9, Howe) We also present data on the range of educational attainment within the regions suggesting readiness within labor markets for the competitive demands of the high technology development that drove the economy of the 1990s.

Fair market rents (FMRs) are a measure of rental housing costs derived by the federal Department of Housing and Urban Development through statistical and survey analysis of the distribution of rent and utility costs in individual regions. This is done in order to determine

**Table 1.5**

*Employment patterns in select metropolitan areas, 2000 and 2002 (ranked by manufacturing share)*

| MSA/PMSA | Total Full- and Part-Time Employment 2000 | Manufacturing Employment 2000 | % Share of Manufacturing Employment of Total Employment 2000 | % Average Annual Unemployment Rate for 2002 |
|---|---|---|---|---|
| San Jose, CA PMSA | 1,285,420 | 270,823 | 21 | 8.4 |
| Cleveland–Lorain–Elyria, OH PMSA | 1,405,955 | 225,849 | 16 | 6.5 |
| Cincinnati, OH–KY–IN PMSA | 1,079,465 | 144,646 | 13 | 4.8 |
| Fort Worth–Arlington, TX PMSA | 993,767 | 114,660 | 12 | 6.1 |
| **Portland, OR–Vancouver, WA PMSA** | **1,236,838** | **153,876** | **12** | **7.8** |
| Newark, NJ PMSA | 1,209,693 | 138,573 | 11 | 6.1 |
| Pittsburgh, PA MSA | 1,368,400 | 141,137 | 10 | 5.4 |
| Kansas City, MO–KS MSA | 1,198,337 | 107,821 | 9 | 5.7 |
| Miami, FL PMSA | 1,279,917 | 72,159 | 6 | 7.7 |
| Denver, CO PMSA | 1,519,288 | 95,876 | 6 | 5.9 |
| San Francisco, CA PMSA | 1,452,591 | 75,899 | 5 | 5.9 |

SOURCE: Bureau of Economic Analysis. 2002. *Regional Economic Information System.* http://www.bea.doc.gov/bea/regional/reis/default.cfm (accessed 21 February 2004).
NOTE: MSA, Metropolitan Statistical Area; PMSA, Primary Metropolitan Statistical Area.

reimbursement rates for landlords participating in the Section 8 Housing Voucher program. As Table 1.6 illustrates, Portland's FMR of $771 per month in 2003 for a two-bedroom apartment falls exactly in the middle of the comparison group. The two other West Coast metropolitan areas lead comparison regions by a substantial amount. The FMR for a two-bedroom apartment is $1,940 per month in San Francisco and $1,760 per month in San Jose.

Table 1.7 indicates that six of the comparison regions had higher rates of homeownership than Portland's 62.87%. Pittsburgh topped the list at 71.29 and San Francisco and San Jose trailed at 49.02 and 59.85%, respectively. Like most other regions in the comparison group, home-ownership rates for blacks and Hispanics lagged about 30 points behind whites in Portland. Across the comparison regions, Asians, with some exceptions, were closer to parity with whites in homeownership. In Portland's case that still means that Asians lag behind whites by 8%.

With respect to the reported percentage of the population with a bachelor's degree or higher, Portland's 32.1% is similar to many of the comparison regions (see Table 1.8). It is also substantially outstripped by three other cities with a significant profile in high tech, San Francisco at 45.1%, San Jose at 44.1%, and Denver at 37.4%. However, with respect to the percentage of those not completing high school, only

### Table 1.6
*Fair market rents in select metropolitan areas, 2003*
*(ranked by highest FMR)*

| Metropolitan Area | Two-Bedroom Apartment |
| --- | --- |
| San Francisco, CA | $1,940 |
| San Jose, CA | $1,760 |
| Newark, NJ | $949 |
| Denver, CO | $945 |
| Miami, FL | $813 |
| **Portland, OR–Vancouver, WA** | **$771** |
| Cleveland–Lorain–Elyria, OH | $748 |
| Fort Worth–Arlington, TX | $741 |
| Kansas City, MO–KS | $701 |
| Cincinnati, OH–KY–IN | $662 |
| Pittsburgh, PA | $608 |

SOURCE: National Low Income Housing Coalition. 2003. *Out of Reach.*
http://www.nlihc.org/oor2002/index.htm (accessed 21 February 2004).

**Table 1.7**

*Homeownership by race/ethnicity in select metropolitan areas, 2000 (ranked by total households)*

| MSA/PMSA | | Total Households | White Households | Black Households | Hispanic Households | Asian Households |
|---|---|---|---|---|---|---|
| Pittsburgh, PA MSA | % Owners | 71.29 | 74.57 | 40.05 | 48.41 | 39.54 |
| Cleveland–Lorain–Elyria, OH PMSA | % Owners | 68.35 | 75.06 | 43.94 | 47.15 | 51.48 |
| Kansas City, MO–KS MSA | % Owners | 67.94 | 72.35 | 47.35 | 49.92 | 50.59 |
| Denver, CO PMSA | % Owners | 66.49 | 71.41 | 44.03 | 50.77 | 57.92 |
| Cincinnati, OH–KY–IN PMSA | % Owners | 66.22 | 71.82 | 34.73 | 40.89 | 44.24 |
| Fort Worth–Arlington, TX PMSA | % Owners | 63.58 | 69.75 | 43.99 | 48.98 | 51.33 |
| **Portland, OR–Vancouver, WA PMSA** | **% Owners** | **62.87** | **65.95** | **37.12** | **32.2** | **57.68** |
| Newark, NJ PMSA | % Owners | 60.80 | 74.97 | 33.86 | 32.1 | 60.46 |
| San Jose, CA PMSA | % Owners | 59.85 | 66.56 | 37.85 | 45.53 | 57.12 |
| Miami, FL PMSA | % Owners | 57.85 | 70.02 | 49.28 | 55.34 | 58.41 |
| San Francisco, CA PMSA | % Owners | 49.02 | 52.41 | 33.58 | 34.18 | 51.88 |

SOURCE: Lewis Mumford Center. 2000. *Metropolitan Racial and Ethnic Change: Census 2000.* http://mumford1.dyndns.org/cen2000/data.html (accessed 21 February 2004).
NOTE: MSA, Metropolitan Statistical Area; PMSA, Primary Metropolitan Statistical Area.

## Table 1.8

*Educational attainment in select metropolitan areas (ranked by ratio of bachelor's to not completing high school)*

Educational Attainment, Population 25 Years or Over

| MSA/PMSA | % Bachelor's or More | % Not Completing High School | Ratio Bachelor's to Not Completing High School |
|---|---|---|---|
| San Francisco, CA PMSA | 45.1 | 13.1 | 3.44 |
| San Jose, CA PMSA | 44.1 | 12.4 | 3.56 |
| Denver, CO PMSA | 37.4 | 11.9 | 3.14 |
| Newark, NJ PMSA | 33.7 | 16.6 | 2.03 |
| Kansas City, MO–KS MSA | 32.4 | 8.5 | 3.81 |
| **Portland, OR–Vancouver, WA PMSA** | **32.1** | **9.6** | **3.34** |
| Cincinnati, OH–KY–IN PMSA | 31 | 15.3 | 2.03 |
| Pittsburgh, PA MSA | 30.6 | 9.6 | 3.19 |
| Miami, FL PMSA | 26.4 | 23.7 | 1.11 |
| Fort Worth–Arlington, TX PMSA | 26 | 15.3 | 1.70 |
| Cleveland–Lorain–Elyria, OH PMSA | 25 | 10 | 2.50 |

SOURCE: Authors' calculation from Current Population Survey. 2003. *Educational Attainment of the Population 25 years and Over by Metropolitan Area.* http://www.census.gov/population/www/socdemo/education/ppl-169.html (accessed 21 February 2004).
NOTE: PMSA, Primary Metropolitan Statistical Area; MSA, Metropolitan Statistical Area.

Kansas City at 8.5% is lower than Portland's 9.6% (Pittsburgh tied Portland). A ratio of the two scores comparing the region's distribution at both ends of the scale of educational attainment places Portland (3.34) in the middle along with Kansas City (3.81), San Jose (3.56), and San Francisco (3.44).

As represented by the ratio of high to low educational attainment, earning potential appears more equitably dispersed in Portland than in many of the comparison regions. Portland's rental housing costs are in the middle of the comparison group, and in fact are significantly cheaper than other West Coast and high tech regions. However, as in other regions the wealth-building potential represented in homeownership is distributed inequitably among racial and ethnic groups in Portland. In the end, these figures suggest that with or without Portland-style growth management policies in place, many regions face equity challenges.

## Environment

While the original impetus for Oregon's land use planning program was farmland protection, today the motive that comes to mind for many is to slow sprawling development patterns to preserve the environment and maintain a high quality of life. Both Seltzer (Chap. 2) and Abbott (Chap. 8) discuss these motives further. In measures of sprawl and air quality (see Tables 1.9 and 1.10), the Portland region clearly stands out. However, data on the release of toxic chemicals suggest that significant challenges may remain.

Table 1.9 presents the scores for the comparison regions on a sprawl index developed by Reed Ewing, Rolf Pendall, and Don Chen (2002). This index is composed of data representing four factors: residential density; the neighborhood mix of jobs, homes, and services; the strength of centers and downtowns; and accessibility to the street network. Later in this volume Chapman and Lund (see Chap. 10) discuss the pros and cons of such measures. Portland scores high, particularly for connectivity and the strength of centers, and is outscored only by San Francisco.

Table 1.10 presents the number of days that Environmental Protection Agency data indicate that ozone or smog levels exceeded healthy

### Table 1.9

*Sprawl Index Score (low scores represent areas with more sprawling development patterns)*

| MSA/PMSA | Sprawl Index Score |
| --- | --- |
| San Francisco, CA PMSA | 146.83 |
| **Portland, OR–Vancouver, WA PMSA** | **126.12** |
| Miami, FL PMSA | 125.68 |
| Denver, CO PMSA | 125.22 |
| San Jose, CA PMSA | 109.7 |
| Pittsburgh, PA MSA | 105.94 |
| Cincinnati, OH–KY–IN PMSA | 96.04 |
| Cleveland–Lorain–Elyria, OH PMSA | 91.75 |
| Kansas City, MO–KS MSA | 91.64 |
| Newark, NJ PMSA | 81.32 |
| Fort Worth–Arlington, TX PMSA | 77.23 |

SOURCE: Ewing, Reed, Rolf Pendall, Don Chen. 2002. *Measuring Sprawl and Its Impact.* http://www.smartgrowthamerica.com/sprawlindex/MeasuringSprawl.PDF (accessed 21 February 2004).
NOTE: MSA, Metropolitan Statistical Area; PMSA, Primary Metropolitan Statistical Area.

**Table 1.10**

*Unhealthy ozone (smog) levels, 2002 (ranked by number of days)*

| MSA/PMSA | Number of Days | | | | | |
|---|---|---|---|---|---|---|
| | 1998 | 1999 | 2000 | 2001 | 2002 | Average |
| San Francisco, CA PMSA | 0 | 0 | 0 | 0 | 0 | 0 |
| Portland, OR and Vancouver, | | | | | | |
| WA PMSA | 3 | 0 | 0 | 0 | 1 | 0.8 |
| Miami, FL PMSA | 8 | 5 | 0 | 1 | 0 | 2.8 |
| San Jose, CA PMSA | 8 | 3 | 1 | 3 | 6 | 4.2 |
| Denver, CO PMSA | 9 | 3 | 2 | 2 | 7 | 7.6 |
| Kansas City, MO–KS MSA | 14 | 3 | 10 | 4 | 7 | 7.6 |
| Cincinnati, OH–KY–IN | | | | | | |
| PMSA | 13 | 11 | 4 | 6 | 26 | 12 |
| Newark, NJ PMSA | 22 | 21 | 6 | 13 | 27 | 17.8 |
| Cleveland–Lorain–Elyria, | | | | | | |
| OH PMSA | 13 | 11 | 4 | 17 | 29 | 18.2 |
| Fort Worth–Arlington, | | | | | | |
| TX PMSA | 17 | 19 | 16 | 17 | 23 | 18.4 |
| Pittsburgh, PA MSA | 39 | 23 | 4 | 19 | 28 | 22.6 |

SOURCE: Surface Transportation Policy Project. 2003. *Clearing the Air.*
   http://www.transact.org/report.asp?id=227 (accessed 21 February 2004).
NOTE: MSA, Metropolitan Statistical Area; PMSA, Primary Metropolitan Statistical Area.

levels within a PMSA. The Portland region experienced only one such day in 2002 and averaged less than one day of unhealthy ozone over the last five years. This was surpassed only by one of the comparison regions, coastal San Francisco, which experienced no unhealthy ozone days in the last five years.

Table 1.11 reports data from the Environmental Protection Agency's Toxic Release Inventory. This database includes gross figures on releases of air, ground, and water contaminants, self-reported by the largest manufacturing facilities. With more than 7 million pounds of toxic releases, Portland is in the center of the comparison group. It is worth noting that more than half of the releases in the Portland region were from just three facilities, one steel works within the City of Portland and two rural pulp mills. This facet of Portland's industrial heritage contrasts sharply with other western regions in the group. For example, San Jose reported just over 459,000 pounds, and only 89,000 pounds were reported in San Francisco, the lowest total among the comparison regions.

**Table 1.11**

*Toxic releases, 2001*

| MSA/PMSA | Total Releases (lbs.) |
| --- | --- |
| Pittsburgh, PA MSA | 26,590,532 |
| Cincinnati, OH–KY–IN PMSA | 20,335,202 |
| Cleveland–Lorain–Elyria, OH PMSA | 16,479,732 |
| Kansas City, MO–KS MSA | 9,355,857 |
| **Portland, OR–Vancouver, WA PMSA** | **7,495,478** |
| Newark, NJ PMSA | 4,618,164 |
| Denver, CO PMSA | 1,799,200 |
| Fort Worth–Arlington, TX PMSA | 1,571,804 |
| Miami, FL PMSA | 1,311,088 |
| San Jose, CA PMSA | 459,247 |
| San Francisco, CA PMSA | 89,252 |

SOURCE: Compiled by authors from Right to Know Network. 2004. *TRI Search.*
http://www.rtknet.org/tri/ (accessed 21 February 2004).
NOTE: MSA, Metropolitan Statistical Area; PMSA, Primary Metropolitan Statistical Area.

## Summary

In sum, during the 1990s, the Portland region experienced population and employment growth beyond most comparably sized metropolitan areas. Unique facets of that growth include the retention of a strong central city employment base and growth in manufacturing employment, both of which were almost unheard of among the comparison regions. While fair market rents and overall homeownership rates were near the middle of the comparison group, they compare favorably with other West Coast cities. Negatively, the distribution of the wealth-building opportunity of home-ownership was distributed inequitably among racial and ethnic groups just as in other comparably sized regions. At the same time, the distribution of educational attainment suggests that earning potential, reflected in a high ratio between college graduates and high school dropouts, is distributed more evenly among individuals than in many of the regions in the comparison group. Additionally, keeping sprawl in check and maintaining high air quality, even through a period of rapid growth and expansion in the 1990s, represents a significant environmental asset, while toxic release data suggest that serious challenges to the environment remain.

## Regional Challenges

With a population that is growing both in raw numbers and in the diversity of its ethnic and racial composition, the Portland region's future will certainly be a more complicated economic and civic project than it was in the past. Many of the challenges faced by metropolitan Portland are affecting cities and regions all across the United States. However, other challenges are unique to the region as it attempts to sustain and build upon the innovative planning policies that make up the "Portland Edge."

While hardly a new issue, the overarching challenge faced by metropolitan Portland is the continued management of urban growth. The region is projected to add 525,000 persons by the year 2022. The regional and local governments are required to make decisions within the framework of the statewide land use planning system, the 2040 Growth Concept, and the Regional Framework Plan about how to accommodate this growth (see Chap. 2, Seltzer). These decisions may have implications for the three Es mentioned earlier: economy, equity, and environment—cornerstones of the Portland region's highly valued quality of life. Are governance and fiscal systems across the region prepared to make these choices? What will be the results?

Urban growth will influence not only the consumption of land but also the institutional structure and governance capacities of the region. In 2002 the Metro Council approved the largest expansion of the urban growth boundary (UGB) to date. In the Damascus area of Clackamas County, for example, stakeholders are preparing for a 13,000-acre portion of that expansion with an extensive discussion related to responsibility for infrastructure and service provision.

Business leaders and economic development policymakers have adopted a particular discourse around the UGB expansion. Their primary concern is the availability of large tracts of land that could accommodate capital-intensive firms, provide employment, and strengthen the public revenue outlook. Metro is undertaking a study of industrial lands in the region to develop criteria for designating "regionally significant" industrial lands (see Chap. 2, Seltzer). Blending industrial sanctuary zoning and land banking on a regional scale, such lands would be preserved for specific categories of future industrial development.

Development pressures on land within the boundary also conflict with some environmental measures, such as setbacks required as riparian buffers to meet federal Endangered Species Act requirements. This conflict leads some developers to question the economic cost of these regulations. Ozawa and Yeakley (see Chap. 12) provide a broader description of this issue.

Development pressures also raise equity challenges. Some neighborhoods in Portland are experiencing gentrification. In these areas, housing costs increase due to rising property values that in some cases are associated with city-financed urban renewal projects. Active urban renewal programs generated the revenue that underwrote not only such neighborhood redevelopment, but also regionally significant projects like downtown Portland's Pioneer Courthouse Square and Intel's Ronler Acres plant located in Washington County. While the City of Portland in particular has made efforts to include more citizens in the urban renewal process and to discuss the gentrification issue openly, the impact of this in the face of a growing revenue imperative for local governments in Oregon is uncertain (see Chap. 3, Gibson).

Like most states, the bursting of the high tech bubble has led to fiscal problems in Oregon. With no sales tax the state budget relies largely on income tax and thus was particularly vulnerable as incomes dropped in the downturn. The revenue shortfalls have interfered with the delivery of basic services such as education, which became a state responsibility following a series of voter-approved initiatives early in the 1990s that capped property taxes. Jurisdictions within the region cut school days to balance their budgets and made national news headlines. At the same time, state higher education budgets declined, crimping efforts to make the state's universities into high technology development engines.

From this discussion, under the overarching challenge of continuing to manage the region's growth, two further challenges stand out. First, while the recent economic downturn obscures the region's stellar economic performance in the 1990s, how prepared are the region, its people, and its institutions for the next turn in the business cycle? Second, the Region 2040 planning process created a complex web of stakeholders and consensus-building mechanisms. How will the increasingly diverse new residents moving to the region react to the policy decisions flowing from Region 2040 that occurred before they arrived? Will the confines of regional governance challenges narrow the scope of the region's planning activities? Or will the newcomers continue to buy into the "Portland Edge?"

REFERENCES

Abbott, Carl. 1983. *Portland: Planning, Politics, and Growth in a Twentieth-Century City.* Lincoln: University of Nebraska Press.

Abbott, Carl. 2000. The Capital of Good Planning: Metropolitan Portland since 1970. In *The American Planning Tradition: Culture and Policy.* pp. 241–262. Edited by Robert Fishman. Baltimore: Johns Hopkins.

Abbott, Carl. 2002. *Greater Portland: Urban Life and Landscape in the Pacific Northwest.* Philadelphia: University of Pennsylvania Press.

Abbott, Carl, Deborah Howe, and Sy Adler. 1994. *Planning the Oregon Way: A Twenty Year Evaluation.* Corvallis: Oregon State University Press.

Barnes, William, and Larry Ledebur. 1998. *The New Regional Economies: The U.S. Common Market and the Global Economy.* Thousand Oaks: Sage Publications.

Bay Area Alliance. 2004. *Bay Area Alliance for Sustainable Communities.* http://www.bayareaalliance.org/overview.html (accessed 5 February 2004).

Campbell, Scott. 1996. Green cities, growing cities, just cities? Urban planning and the contradictions of sustainable development. *Journal of the American Planning Association* 62 (3): 296–312.

Coalition for a Livable Future. 2004. *About CLF.* http://www.clfuture.org/aboutclf.html (accessed 5 February 2004).

Cortright, Joe. 2002. The economic importance of being different: Regional variations in tastes, increasing returns, and the dynamics of development. *Economic Development Quarterly* 16 (1): 1–16.

Downs, Anthony. 2002. Have housing prices risen faster in Portland than elsewhere? *Housing Policy Debate* 13 (1): 7–33.

Ewing, Reed, Rolf Pendall, and Don Chen. 2002. *Measuring Sprawl and Its Impact.* http://www.smartgrowthamerica.com/sprawlindex/MeasuringSprawl.pdf (accessed 21 February 2004).

Franklin, Rachel. 2003. *U.S. Census Bureau. Migration of Young, Single, and College Educated: 1995 to 2000.* http://www.census.gov/prod/2003pubs/censr-12.pdf (accessed 9 February 2004).

Gibson, Karen, and Carl Abbott. 2002. City profile: Portland, Oregon. *Cities* 19 (6): 425–436.

Gratz, Roberta, and Norman Mintz. 1998. *Cities Back from the Edge: New Life for Downtown.* New York: John Wiley.

Grogan, Paul, and Tony Proscio. 2000. *Comeback Cities: A Blueprint for Urban Neighborhoods.* Boulder: Westview Press.

Lansing, Jewel. 2003. *Portland: People, Politics, and Power: 1851–2001.* Corvallis: Oregon State University Press.

Lee, Marshall M. 1986. *Winning with People: The First 40 Years of Tektronix.* Portland: Tektronix, Inc.

MacColl, E. Kimbark. 1979. *The Growth of a City: Power and Politics in Portland, Oregon, 1915–1950.* Portland: The Georgian Press.

Mayer, Heike. 2003. Taking root in the Silicon Forest: The role of high technology firms as surrogate universities in Portland, Oregon. Ph.D. diss., Portland State University.

McDonough, William, and Michael Braungart. 2002. *Remaking the Way We Make Things: Cradle to Cradle.* New York: North Point Press.

Nelson, Arthur, Rolf Pendall, Casey Dawkins, and Gerrit Knapp. 2002. *The Link between Growth Management and Affordability: The Academic Evidence.* Washington, DC: The Brookings Institution.

Oregon Employment Department. 1999. *1999 Oregon In-Migration Study.* Salem: Oregon Employment Department.

PolicyLink. 2004. *About PolicyLink.* http://www.policylink.org/about.html (accessed 5 February 2004).

Portland Development Commission. (2003). *Facts and Praises.* http://www.pdc.us/ bus_serv/praises/default.asp. (accessed 24 September 2003).

Wentz, Patty. 2004. *As Young Singles Flock to Portland, Oregon Enters a Long, Hard Winter.* http://www.secretplan.org/npn/Zephyr/Winter%20Zephyr.pdf (accessed 12 February 2004).

Wheeler, Stephen. 2002. The new regionalism: Characteristics of an emerging movement. *Journal of the American Planning Association* 68 (3): 267–278.

Yaro, Robert, and Tony Hiss. 1996. *A Region at Risk: The Third Regional Plan for the New York–New Jersey–Connecticut Metropolitan Area.* New York: Regional Plan Association.

# 2 | It's Not an Experiment: Regional Planning at Metro, 1990 to the Present

Ethan Seltzer

Regional planning is notable for the way that it has, from time to time, captured the imagination of planners and scholars, but generally failed to establish a compelling movement across the United States. One of the most notable exceptions to this history has been the regional planning undertaken by Metro, the regional government in the Portland metropolitan area, over the last 24 years.

Metro is a relatively young institution, still actively finding its way and making adjustments in form and function. Metro was established by a vote of the people in the late 1970s. The development of the Metro Charter (Metro 2003a), Regional Urban Growth Goals and Objectives (Metro 1991), Region 2040 Growth Concept (Metro 1997, Metro 2000b), Regional Framework Plan (Metro 1997), Regional Land Information System (Knaap et al. 2003), Regional Greenspaces Program (Metro 1997, Metro 2001), and the Future Vision (Metro 1995), all adopted or implemented within a period spanning the years 1991 to 1997, stands out as a watershed for regional planning in the Portland metropolitan area.

This chapter describes these pivotal regional planning efforts of the early 1990s, beginning with the Regional Urban Growth Goals and Objectives and ending with the Regional Framework Plan. I then consider a key recent regional planning "event," the 2002 expansion of the urban growth boundary (UGB). The chapter concludes with an assessment of lessons learned and prospects for the future. Observations regarding the role that region-specific factors have played in Metro's regional planning will be offered as a way for presenting lessons learned here to outside observers interested in pursuing similar planning projects in their own region.

## Metro

Metro's origins can be traced to a grant-funded initiative in the mid-1970s to study and propose regional governance options for metropolitan areas (Abbott and Abbott 1991, Abbott 2001). That project resulted in a report to the legislature and the referral of a proposal to the voters to create Metro in the Portland region through the merger of the old, and out-of-favor, council of governments with a limited-purpose regional services district. The voters approved the measure in 1978, and in 1979 the first Metro Council was elected.

Metro was originally set up using a "separation of powers" model. The Council consisted of twelve members elected from districts. The Council then chose its presiding officer from among its members. An executive officer was elected at-large in the region, charged with managing the administrative affairs of the new government. Metro's powers were described in statute and included both existing functions from its predecessors as well as the ability to engage in new regional activities, including assuming responsibility for the regional transit agency, should it so desire.

In 1990, the voters approved a constitutional amendment to allow home rule charters for metropolitan governments and to enable existing metropolitan governments to appoint charter committees. The measure passed statewide, Metro appointed a charter committee, and in 1992 the voters within Metro's boundaries approved a home rule charter for the agency. Significantly, that charter

1. reduced the number of councilors from twelve to seven,
2. added an elected auditor,
3. established a standing system of policy advisory committees,
4. spelled out provisions for engaging in new areas of regional concern, and
5. most significantly, declared urban growth management to be Metro's primary responsibility.

In 2000, the Metro Council referred a charter amendment to the voters to end the separation of powers structure by replacing the elected executive officer with an appointed manager, decreasing the number

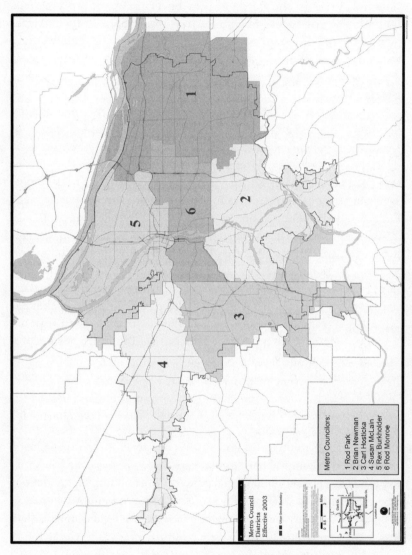

FIGURE 2.1. Metro Council Districts. Source: Metro.

of councilors from seven to six, and adding a presiding officer elected at-large. Figure 2.1 shows the six Metro councilor district boundaries.

Today, Metro has primary responsibility for regional land use, growth management, and transportation planning on the Oregon side of the Columbia River in the Portland–Vancouver metropolitan area (see Chap. 11, Adler and Dill). In addition, it is responsible for the management of the region's solid waste disposal system; regional convention, visitor, and performance spaces; management and further development of a regional greenspaces system; and ongoing maintenance of a regional data and GIS.

By state statute, Metro plays a unique role in land use planning. By law, only cities and counties have the responsibility and authority to develop comprehensive land use plans. Comprehensive land use plans, under the Oregon statewide land use planning program, are the primary legal documents guiding all local planning and development decisions. By law in Oregon, zoning codes must implement comprehensive plans (Oregon Department of Land Conservation and Development 2001).

Though Metro has not been given the authority to engage in comprehensive land use planning, it has been given the authority to develop regional functional plans. A functional plan addresses one or a narrow set of issues associated with an issue of regional significance. Furthermore, Metro has also been granted the power to require changes in local comprehensive plans to make them consistent with regional functional plans (Metro 2003a). This is an astounding power for a regional agency in this country, more so because of the fact that comprehensive plans are such central legal and policy documents for Oregon communities.

Significantly, the state has assigned to Metro the responsibility for establishing and managing a UGB for the 24 cities and parts of three counties within its jurisdiction. In this instance, Metro furnishes a component of a comprehensive plan, here the UGB, to each of the jurisdictions. They are required to make their plans and implement actions consistent with the UGB, and by virtue of doing so are not required to show any other basis for asserting that their plan is consistent with state law on this point.

For the first decade of Metro's existence, the region was mired in a deep and prolonged recession, with little call for either new plans or expansion of the UGB. Most of Metro's regional growth management planning activity revolved around coordinating locally developed comprehensive plans with each other. However, the prospect (specter to some) of functional plans emanating from Metro loomed as a source of tension in the regional–local relationship.

In fact, for most of its first decade, Metro's major planning activities focused on its role as the metropolitan planning organization for federal transportation planning and resource allocation purposes, and on the siting of landfills and management of the solid waste and recycling collection system.

## RUGGO and the Region 2040 Concept

The conventional wisdom is that if you aren't growing, then nothing is happening. However, during the early 1980s in Portland, a time when the region's economy was in a deep and prolonged recession, a lot was happening. The metropolitan region lost both population and jobs in what turned out to be a major restructuring of the area's economy. Though the region was, by most accounts, declining, construction in the downtown core continued, a light rail system opened, and comprehensive land use plans that were prepared consistent with Oregon's statewide planning goals were adopted locally and approved by the state.

In the late 1980s, as the region's economy began to rebound, a "new old" concern emerged to galvanize a landmark regional growth management effort. In 1987 Metro was asked by the state to assess the functioning of the UGB as part of an ongoing "periodic review" process in the Oregon land use planning program. UGBs were intended to provide an "efficient transition between rural and urban land use," and above all to be based on a demonstrated need for urban land over about a 20-year period. As land needs changed, urban growth boundaries were expected to change as well.

By late 1988 three issues began to dominate land use and policy discussions about the Metro UGB:

- Inside the UGB the region was experiencing many of the same issues associated with sprawl development elsewhere. Increasing traffic congestion, vehicle miles traveled per capita, and disappearing open space were becoming neighborhood, jurisdictional, and regional concerns.
- Outside, in rural areas, speculation was occurring everywhere, even on lands reserved for exclusive farm use. As the economy picked up, adjacent rural residential zones began to be occupied by high-end residential development. This posed a paradox to the region and the state: if the adjacent rural residential lands were built up with very expensive

single-family structures, then the use of those areas for future urban use, at urban densities, would be highly unlikely and future changes in the UGB would be forced to occur on the "vacant" resource land, the very land Oregon set out to protect in 1973.

• At the boundary itself there was no policy, no guidance for farmers, investors, elected officials, and local service providers as to where expansion might most likely take place.

Consequently, a simple review of the boundary, as it was adopted in 1980, would leave too many questions unanswered. For that reason, in early 1989, the Metro Council adopted a workplan for periodic review of the UGB that called for the creation of regional urban growth goals and objectives (RUGGOs) as the underpinning for an overall regional urban growth management plan.

This important step was not without controversy. For its first nine years of existence, Metro's commitment to land use planning amounted to a weak coordination function as local comprehensive plans were adopted, and by 1987 had dwindled to one half-time position charged with overseeing the boundary. Taking on a planning process like this raised the stakes on Metro's commitment to its land use role and was accompanied by a growing regional growth management staff.

In addition, it raised the prospect of Metro exercising its functional planning powers, something it had never done in its first nine years. Local governments within Metro's jurisdiction knew of the functional planning authority and made it clear that exercising that power would be regarded as a serious usurpation of local control. On the other hand, environmentalists, concerned by what they viewed as lax local concern with land use planning objectives, wanted Metro to step in and take action to counter local decision making viewed as fueling sprawl.

Metro created the Urban Growth Management Policy Advisory Committee to oversee and propose goals and objectives for adoption by the Council. The Committee was chaired by Metro councilor Jim Gardner and consisted of representatives from local government, the development community, environmental organizations, state and regional agencies, and citizens. It began its work in mid-1989, and in late 1991, the RUGGOs were adopted (Metro 1991, 1997).

The goals and objectives accomplished two important tasks. First, as the result of a year-long negotiation, they spelled out for the first time how regional planning would be done, when Metro would exercise its considerable powers, and what the roles would be for other jurisdictions and interests in the regional planning process. Second, RUGGO served as the "sketchbook" for the region, providing a common framework for the growth management challenges of the day.

Parallel to the initiation of the periodic review effort, the staff in charge of Metro's data and information services started to create what is now the internationally recognized Regional Land Information System (RLIS). RLIS is a geographic information system (GIS) that links a wide range of public records to a land parcel base map. Metro began developing RLIS in 1988; it was designed to be an urban planner's GIS, incorporating data essential for regional urban planning and growth management (Knaap et al. 2003).

Designing RLIS was a collaborative effort involving regional, county, and city planners. The objective was to identify the data and functional requirements of a GIS supporting community and regional planning. Its regionwide usage for planning and environmental management was to provide consistent land information across jurisdictional boundaries for GIS users in government and business, enabling data exchange and sharing of maintenance responsibilities.

In addition to developing a parcel-level base to support modeling and analysis, RLIS provided regional planners with a number of "firsts" essential for supporting existing and emerging regional planning efforts. It provided the first parcel-level base map for the region, showing the impact of the UGB in bold relief, regionwide, for the first time. It provided the first composite comprehensive plan and land use maps for the metropolitan region.

The system provided the first data on rural and southwest Washington land cover and land use plans on the same maps showing the territory inside Metro's boundaries on the southern or Oregon side of the Columbia River. It enabled the development of a complete set of "McHargian" overlays needed to support environmental planning efforts linked to actual landscape characteristics. Finally, it provided the basis for creating new tools for citizen involvement, including real-time experiments showing the impacts of user-defined land use policy choices. Significantly, RLIS directly supported the complex land supply accounting needs required by state and regional expectations for the management of the UGB.

All three of these efforts—RUGGO, the Metro Charter, and RLIS— were developed through participatory processes that involved jurisdictions, citizens, business, and civic interests. Whereas Metro faced a large amount of skepticism, if not fear and opposition for expanding its regional planning role in the 1980s, by the early 1990s a significant amount of trust had been built with key regional partners. In fact, it was suburban jurisdictions themselves that called for the next phase of regional planning, recognizing that the region's "sketchbook" needed further elaboration to serve as a vision. The Region 2040 Planning Project was developed specifically to add structure to the region's conception of its physical form. Through the Region 2040 planning process the region would

1. specify the degree of expansion, if any, required of the UGB and the locations for any future expansions;
2. identify the major components for the regional transportation system, especially transit components and the creation of a regional pedestrian system;
3. identify a hierarchy and system of places, ranging from downtown Portland to existing town centers to regional centers and neighborhoods; and
4. incorporate a system of greenspaces in the urban region, both for purposes of accommodating outdoor recreation and for maintaining the viability of wildlife habitat.

The Region 2040 process was financially supported by Metro; Washington, Multnomah, and Clackamas Counties; Tri-Met (the regional transit agency); and Portland General Electric. Representatives from each of these organizations constituted a management team, which met regularly, sometimes weekly, to advise Metro on project strategy and content.

In addition, the Metropolitan Policy Advisory Committee, created as part of the Metro Charter, provided Metro with an advisory committee of local government officials, state agency heads, and citizen interests. The Metropolitan Technical Advisory Committee provided Metro with the advice of local planning directors for both Region 2040 and other ongoing planning efforts. Finally, the Regional Citizens Involvement Coordinating Committee at Metro provided Region 2040 staff with advice regarding citizen outreach and involvement.

The first step in the Region 2040 project was to characterize base conditions (beginning with the history of settlement in the region) and community values and expectations, and to create what became known as the "do nothing" or "base" case—the probable future if nothing was done and existing development patterns and dynamics went unchecked (Metro 2000b). The information on base conditions and community values was then used to propose three potential alternative urban form strategies for the region from which a preferred alternative could be constructed.

Alternative A called for less UGB expansion than the base case along with changes in the land use–transportation relationships along major corridors. Alternative B called for no expansion of the UGB, a large expansion of the transit system, and major rezoning. Alternative C called for minor changes in the UGB, a large expansion of the transit system, and the creation of satellite cities outside or separate from the current UGB.

Each of the alternatives and the base case were evaluated using a set of criteria developed through a public process (see Chap. 5, Johnson). Extensive modeling of the transportation system, air quality, and land use allocations accompanied each scenario. Throughout this process, numerous public hearings and workshops were held, the project was publicized on cable TV and through the news media, over 25,000 newsletters were mailed to area households, and hundreds of presentations were made to local governments and civic organizations. Over 500,000 copies of a tabloid outlining the alternatives and the trade-offs involved in selecting different growth management strategies for the region were mailed to every household, resulting in over 17,000 citizen comments and suggestions.

Throughout the public involvement activities, Metro asked citizens to respond to four central growth management techniques: reducing average residential lot sizes, reducing parking, encouraging new growth to locate proximate to transit stations, and encouraging new growth to locate in existing city centers. Six other management techniques, ranging from the establishment of greenbelts to encouraging growth in neighboring cities, were also tested.

From the public involvement activities conducted over about a two-year period, Metro learned that participating citizens generally supported

- holding the current UGB in place;
- utilizing the growth management "building blocks" tested throughout the process, especially establishing greenbelts and encouraging development in existing neighborhoods and close to transit;
- reducing traffic and encouraging the use of alternative modes for travel;
- retaining open space both inside and outside the UGB;
- a combination of increasing density inside the UGB and encouraging some growth in neighboring cities; and
- ongoing public education and dialogue regarding the trade-offs inherent in growth management.

Citizens questioned why growth had to occur and whether planning to accommodate growth would only encourage it to happen. They were skeptical of using neighboring cities to accommodate growth, since they believed that it would be unlikely that enough jobs would be created in those locations to keep people employed close to home.

The preferred alternative resulted from a blend of public comment and aspects of each of the scenarios. What ultimately became the adopted 2040 regional growth concept called for very little UGB expansion over the next 50 years, amounting to about 7% of the existing area (see Fig. 2.2). These future expansions were targeted at parts of the region needing additional urban growth but avoided the use of lands protected for farm and forest use.

In contrast, the base case and Alternative A called for massive increases in the acreage devoted to urban use and expected very little in the way of redevelopment on existing urban land. Unlike Alternative B, the adopted growth concept for 2040 calls for a minor amount of urban expansion, though it reflects an overall desire on the part of the public to limit urban expansion to the extent possible.

The transportation system concept called for additions to the light rail system backed up by higher expectations for pedestrian trips within and at each end of trips between important regional centers. Each center will likely serve different functions since this region cannot sustain a large number of places that offer the same things. Note that light rail is intended not so much as a replacement for the automobile but as a device that allows people to inhabit the region as pedestrians (see Chap. 11, Adler and Dill).

A system of greenspaces was identified to separate communities from each other and to continue to protect open space resources within the urban area. Finally, specific expectations were stated for the relationship between the urban area inside Metro's UGB and small rural communities outside the UGB.

Table 2.1 summarizes a number of the measurable differences between the alternatives and the preferred alternative as would be expected in the year 2040.

The preferred alternative and what became the final adopted Region 2040 Growth Concept received extensive public review using the same techniques just outlined. A video outlining the preferred alternative and its impact on the region was made available to the public for no charge through Blockbuster Video outlets, a chain of video rental stores.

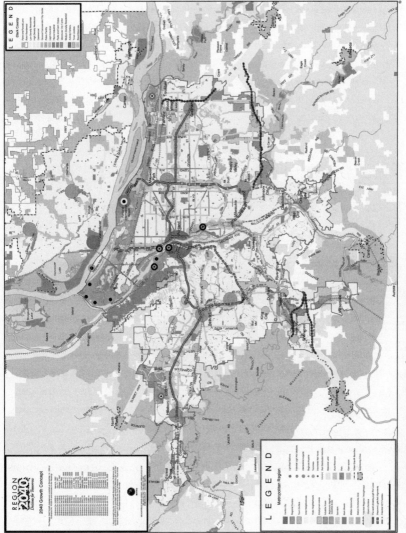

Figure 2.2. Region 2040 Growth Concept. Source: Metro.

**Table 2.1**

*Comparison of 2040 alternative scenarios*

| Attributes | 1990 | Base Case | Alt. A | Alt. B | Alt. C | Preferred Alt. |
|---|---|---|---|---|---|---|
| Single-family/multi-family (%) | 70/30 | 70/30 | 74/26 | 60/40 | 69/31 | 65/35 |
| % Growth in 1990 UGB | 100 | 83 | 71 | 100 | 63 | 87 |
| % Growth via redevelopment | – | 0 | 6 | 18 | 8 | 19 |
| Acres farmland converted | – | 63,900 | 17,200 | 0 | 11,400 | 3545 |
| VMT/capita | 12.4 | 13.04 | 12.48 | 10.86 | 11.92 | 11.76 |
| Mode split (auto/trans/ped/bike) | 92/3/5 | 92/3/5 | 91/4/5 | 88/6/6 | 89/5/6 | 88/6/6 |
| Congested road miles | 151 | 506 | 682 | 643 | 404 | 454 |
| Transit riders (1,000s) | 137 | 338 | 372 | 528 | 437 | 570 |

SOURCE: Metro.
NOTE: UGB, urban growth boundary; VMT, vehicle miles traveled.

Architect Peter Calthorpe, retained earlier in the process, developed a series of "regional design images," "before-and-after" elevations and site plans for locations throughout the region helpful for making the potential effects of the plan more tangible to a broader audience. In December 1994, after two-and-a-half years, the Metro Council adopted the Metro 2040 Growth Concept at the urging of local governments, citizens, and business interests (Metro 2000b).

## Implementation

Since its inception, Metro has been engaged in transportation planning aimed at developing a multimodal transportation system able to meet the wide range of needs for accessibility and mobility in the metropolitan area (see Fig. 2.3). Region 2040 provided new guidance for the incorporation of land use objectives into transportation system models, policymaking, and planning. Further, Region 2040 provided Metro and the state with explicit guidance regarding the management of the UGB, something that had prompted the creation of RUGGO and Region 2040 in the first place.

Parks and greenspaces, a signature structural element of the Regional 2040 Growth Concept, also made a major advance in the wake of the regional planning effort (see Chap. 7, Orloff). Beginning in the late 1980s, advocates for parks and natural areas worked with Metro staff to make the provision of greenspace an issue of regional concern. In 1992, the first Metropolitan Greenspaces Master Plan was adopted by the Metro Council. It outlined a vision for an interconnected system of regional parks and greenspaces able to meet needs for both habitat and recreation (see Fig. 2.4). The plan identified important sites as well as key links in a regional trails system, and implementation roles for citizens, local government, nonprofits, and businesses.

Then, concurrent with the development of the Region 2040 Growth Concept, parks and greenspaces advocates worked closely with Metro councilors to bring forward a regionwide bond measure to raise $135.6 million to acquire key properties identified in the master plan. The greenspaces planning and campaign were spearheaded by legendary greenspaces activist Mike Houck and a coalition of about 100 local advocacy groups known as Friends and Advocates of Urban Natural Areas (FAUNA). FAUNA provided the grassroots muscle in every corner of the region to support the levy, and the voters strongly supported its passage.

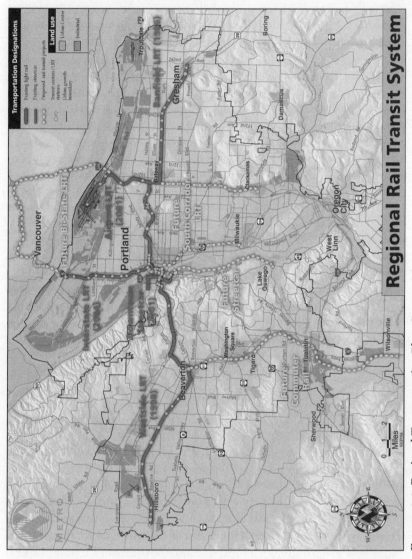

FIGURE 2.3. Regional Transportation Plan. Source: Metro.

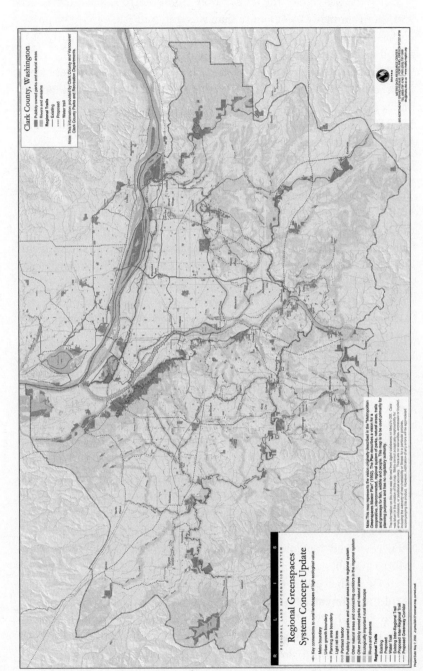

FIGURE 2.4. Greenspaces Master Plan. Source: Metro.

Since the passage of the levy in May 1995, Metro has acquired over 7,915 acres, roughly 2,000 more than was originally thought to be possible (Metro 2001). These sites and corridors are now permanently protected as part of the regional greenspaces system, itself an important structural element envisioned by Region 2040. Metro is now considering a second levy both to add to the inventory and to begin development of sites and corridors for public use. The Metropolitan Greenspaces Master Plan continues to provide guidance and a prioritized list of future acquisitions.

Finally, in December 1997, as directed by the 1992 Metro Charter, the Metro Council adopted the Regional Framework Plan (Metro 1997). The Regional Framework Plan was expected to be the document that unified all of Metro's regional planning activities. It would be based on the RUGGO and the Region 2040 Growth Concept but would specifically address 10 key regional planning concerns, including management and amendment of the UGB, the transportation system, greenspaces, urban design and settlement patterns, and coordination with Clark County, Washington.

The objective was a coordinated, integrated plan for accomplishing the Region 2040 concept, the preferred long-term vision for metropolitan growth and development. In addition to broad statements of policy and goals, the plan would also include specific expectations for both Metro and local government action. In essence, the Regional Framework Plan would be a collection of regional functional plans, implemented through a combination of local actions and Metro initiatives.

Today, the Regional Framework Plan continues to be amended and enhanced as implementation proceeds. Recent efforts have focused on clarifying expectations for the use of industrial land, advancing goals for affordable housing, and the achievement of goals for natural resources and watershed management (see Chap. 12, Ozawa and Yeakley). All of the local comprehensive plans in Metro's jurisdiction have been reviewed for compliance with the Regional Framework Plan (Metro 2003b).

In December 2002, the Metro Council took the unprecedented step of adding almost 18,000 acres to the UGB, increasing its area by approximately 7% (Metro 2002). Though small additions had been made through the years, this was the largest single legislative addition to the boundary in its history. The amendment was the result of state legislation requiring the maintenance of a 20-year supply of land for residential purposes.

After an extensive process of meetings, surveys, workshops, conferences, and other outreach activities, Mike Burton, Metro's executive officer, recommended that the Council expand the boundary in August 2002. His recommendation provided for the needed residential land but noted that there was an unmet need for additional industrial sites. After adjusting his recommendation throughout the fall, he presented a proposal to the Council that still left some 1,500 acres of unmet industrial land needs.

However, in submitting his recommendation, he noted that the region was simply adding small acreages without adequately looking far enough into the future to anticipate what the cumulative impacts might be. He raised the concern that inadequate long range planning was leading the region toward what seemed to be the unavoidable urbanization of prime farmland.

When the Council acted on the executive officer's recommendation in December 2002, it directly addressed the issue of industrial land by initiating efforts to identify additional lands for industrial expansion, creating new elements in the Regional Framework Plan pertaining to the acceptable uses and partitioning of industrial parcels, and the identification of a small number of what would become "regionally significant industrial areas" (RSIAs).

RSIAs were to be protected for uses able to provide "family wage" jobs. Local jurisdictions would be prohibited from allowing uses that did not meet this criterion, and from allowing parcelization that would decrease the region's supply of relatively large industrial sites. In return, regional investment in transportation infrastructure would be coordinated with the RSIAs.

Though the region had identified certain centers as key sites for promoting downtown-like function, this represented the first time that Metro's regional planning had specifically singled out a relatively narrow class of land uses and locations as being of regional significance.

This action of the Metro Council has taken place against a backdrop provided by a deep economic recession that has savaged employment in the manufacturing-rich Portland region. The desire to do something quick, effective, and simple to "cure" the economy has historically led to amendments of urban growth boundaries and reexamination of the state's commitment to land use planning generally (see Fig. 2.5).

Metro expects to make its final amendments to the UGB by the end of 2004 and to include the identification of RSIAs in that action.

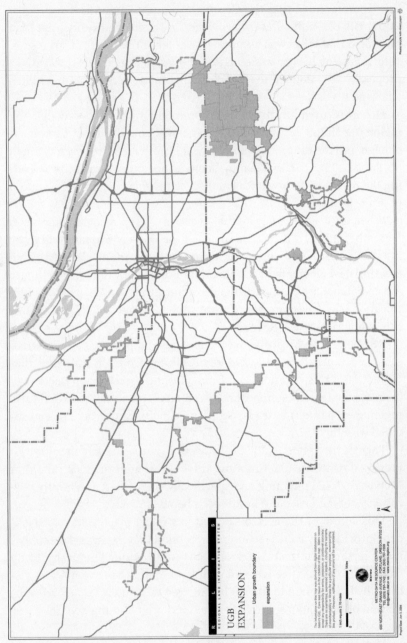

FIGURE 2.5. 2002 UGB Amendment. Source: Metro.

Controversy is growing as local economic development interests have begun to resist an expanded Metro interest in economic development. At the same time, the Metro presiding officer David Bragdon has publicly chastised those same interests for plotting against the broader wishes of the public.

This may prove to be a pivotal moment for Metro and its regional planning effort. There is probably nothing more "local" in its orientation than economic development. Local jurisdictions and business groups overwhelmingly hire economic developers, and their rewards are all tied to performance within very local geographies. Metro represents a strong countercurrent to that very local orientation, bringing the notion of a metropolitan economy forcefully to the table.

The conflicts in style, philosophy, and objectives are profound. The resolution of this issue may put the issue of land supply to rest for awhile. On the other hand, the amount of controversy and ill will being generated around the development of RSIAs and the rules for their use could lead to a more uncertain future for Metro's regional planning efforts, if not for Metro itself.

## Observations and Lessons Learned

There are typically three motivations for localities to join together to engage in regional planning. The first is that a more "senior" level of government requires it. For example, the requirement that metropolitan planning organizations create regional transportation plans has been essential in motivating the planning associated with efforts to build and expand transportation systems.

Second, regional planning efforts can occur because of self-interest. Sometimes it simply makes too much sense to ignore. Most often, these initiatives are associated with creating service efficiencies that directly and demonstrably reduce costs. Regional solid waste system management, emergency dispatch and "911" services, and water source development clearly fall into this category.

Third, regional planning efforts can arise, though infrequently, in an organic manner, emerging from a set of local cultural norms that make regional cooperation and collaboration a more highly valued path. Efforts associated with major natural features, such as the Columbia River Gorge (Abbott et al. 1997), the Adirondacks, or the recent "Yellowstone to Yukon" effort (Yellowstone to Yukon undated), often emerge not because of a mandate from above or a clear demonstration of cost saving but because the landscape and the people who live there demand it.

The regional planning described here was promoted by several factors. The biggest set of reasons was internal to the region and organic in nature. The Portland metropolitan area encountered the same urban development challenges as other places, despite a solid legacy of comprehensive planning. This was in direct conflict with the image of the place revered by residents and attractive to in-migrants, the source for about 70% of the region's population growth.

A portion of the planning here resulted from a state mandate—the development of urban growth boundaries—but the desire for a regional growth management strategy, and even the Metro Charter itself, went well beyond the dictates of state law. A quick scan of the categories covered by the Regional Framework Plan reveals a number of things, like parks and urban design, that aren't even addressed by state planning law.

The opportunity to take a regional response came at a time when individuals and communities found themselves in slightly more comfortable circumstances as the economy rebounded. Things seemed to be moving in the right direction, but the uncritical "growth at any cost" spirit of the recession years was just being replaced by a new concern for quality of life as growth began to accelerate.

Finally, Metro's regional planning was also backed up locally by emerging national interest in the challenges of sprawl and the failures of traditional suburban development patterns. The New Urbanists began to emerge during this period, and public and media fascination with places like Seaside, Florida, supported an environment for questioning old ways of doing things (Leccese and McCormick 2000).

What lessons, then, can be gleaned from the Portland experience? Clearly, contextual factors have been profound in shaping the nature and timing of this experience. Nonetheless, there are nine salient and transferable lessons, discussed in the following sections, that can be gleaned from this region's planning activities.

### Planning Matters

Through planning, patterns that rule urban landscapes can be changed. As Lew Hopkins, Gerrit Knaap, and their colleagues have shown, plans matter (Knaap et al. 1999). Prior to the creation of the UGB, the total number of new households that could be accommodated by the urban land supply was about 160,000. After adoption of the UGB, that same supply yielded about 310,000 potential new units. Further, the development of a more compact, efficient settlement pattern in combination with careful transportation planning has yielded rates of transit ridership increasing substantially faster than rates of either overall population growth or vehicle miles traveled per capita. In fact, the most recent figures from the Federal Highway Administration suggest that this region is actually registering a slight decline in vehicle miles traveled per capita, the opposite of the experience observed in other comparable U.S. metropolitan areas (Metro 2003b).

## Participation Matters

Citizen involvement in planning is not a particularly dramatic notion these days. There are several reasons for seeking widespread participation in local planning efforts. Participation offers cover and legitimacy to decision makers and planners. However, it also contributes two essential elements that contribute to successful plans. First, widespread participation increases the range of ideas at the table. More eyes on the problem means more insight into its real nature and possible solutions (Hwang 1996). Second, involving a wide range of folks makes ownership of the results, the plan, widespread, particularly over the years and decades that it takes to act on plans.

Planning is an important part of the kind of community building needed to sustain values and visions over the long haul. Participation made Metro's Region 2040 planning process possible. In the Portland way, a "Noah's Ark" of a committee was constituted to guide the process of developing the RUGGOs, with membership consisting of elected officials from throughout the region, environmentalists, home builders, business interests, and citizens.

At the end of the two-year RUGGO process, it was suburban elected officials who observed that although they and Metro had developed a great description of the pieces of a well-functioning region, there was no vision, no overall description of where we were heading. Hence, it was the participants themselves that called for the creation of the Region 2040 Growth Concept, not Metro. Metro's signature growth management planning effort would never have happened without the participation of a wide range of interests.

## Leadership Matters

Unquestionably, Oregon and the Portland region have benefited from terrific leaders that have made critical contributions at different points in time. Former governor Tom McCall and key legislative leaders from both parties made the Oregon statewide land use planning program a reality. The former governor and mayor of Portland, Neil Goldschmidt, has been widely credited with leading the revival of Portland's downtown, neighborhoods, and civic culture (see Chap. 8, Abbott). Today the region continues to benefit from key leaders in critical positions: people able to accurately name the problem, see the connections between interests, and inspire people to be better than they are.

However, the role for leadership has changed substantially in the last 25 years. Leaders no longer control information like they used to. Neighborhood activists run ArcView on their home computers. Information is now everywhere. Furthermore, in this region, interests are divided finely enough that there are no longer single "lead" issues that dominate the public policy agenda, pull interests together, and focus their efforts.

### Good Things Take Time

The region is a work in progress. It's not done and it never will be. Things weren't always like they are today. Lewis Mumford visited the Portland region in the 1930s at the behest of a group of leaders investigating the ways that electrification could be integrated into the Pacific Northwest. Mumford (1939) had this to say about Portland and Seattle:

> Neither Portland nor Seattle show, from the standpoint of planning, more than metropolitan ambitions that have over-reached themselves. The melancholy plan to increase Portland's population from 300,000 to three million succeeded in disordering and unfocussing its growth: but it did little to give it the benefit of modern city planning practice; meanwhile, the apparent financial prospects of these port cities undermined the base of the sounder development that could well have been taking place in other parts of the region, on strictly modern lines.

His solution: Build new towns in a landscape that literally took his breath away. Some 60 years later, downtown Portland is a national model, but downtown was being rebuilt in the depths of the recession of the 1980s because of initiatives put into motion 20 and 30 years before. Creating a great place is the legacy of a lifetime, not a matter of months, a single term of office, or the cutting of a single ribbon. Stewardship takes place over generations, not all at once.

### You Can't Regulate Quality of Life into Existence

Planners have lots of tools for limiting damage. However, community quality of life is a collective achievement. The great parks of this region didn't result from exactions, but from bond measures and other collective action. Modeling work done for the Region 2040 Growth Concept found that even with the ideal arrangement of buildings with relation to the transportation system, transportation system goals would not be met without changes in trip-making behavior.

That is, absent a culture of inhabitation to go along with the physical development of the landscape, plan objectives would not be realized and community values wouldn't be served. Achieving quality of life goals is a partnership between what is required and the choices made by individuals. Regulation alone is not sufficient. Putting choice into context remains a central challenge for planners.

### Growth Management Has Costs as Well as Benefits

Planners have known for some time that sprawl is not free. Recent studies revisiting the "costs of sprawl" question in Oregon and elsewhere have reconfirmed that sprawl and its inefficiencies carry a cost. However, we've also learned that the alternatives to sprawl aren't free either. Every choice entails a cost, and growth management can make the nature of the challenge of creating equitable regions even more explicit.

Although numerous studies have been developed to determine the cost imposed by the UGB, none has been able to demonstrate that the UGB alone is the reason, even a significant reason, for rising housing costs in this region (Downs 2002, Metro 2000a, Nelson et al. 2002, Phillips and Goodstein 2000) (see Chap. 9, Howe). Nonetheless, choosing a UGB both incurs a cost of some magnitude and, perhaps most important, implies that traditional methods for supplying affordable housing—devaluing central cities and older suburbs while minimizing land costs elsewhere—won't be available here. The challenge, like that throughout the country, remains identifying ways to house the least affluent households in the region in locations close to services and jobs (see Chap. 3, Gibson). Growth management doesn't relieve planners and decision makers of the responsibility for facing up to that challenge, just as sprawl doesn't relieve other regions of the same challenge.

### Growth Management Is Not Enough

Growth management is primarily a game of rates: forecasting rates of growth, assigning growth to locations, attempting to match rates of growth with the provision of infrastructure and services. Growth management has been portrayed in the past as a means for accommodating new growth as if it never happened. That is, the impact of new growth would presumably be minimized as its requirements were recognized and addressed in advance through growth management efforts.

Though it is important to know how big things might get and by when, and to ensure that communities can grow into themselves gracefully when the time comes, we've learned that you can't manage away the effects of growth. More people means more activity, more competition for fishing holes, and more folks in the checkout line no matter how good the growth management effort has been. Growth, like decline, results in change.

There are several questions worth exploring through planning, but these are not typical growth management questions. First, how can new growth assist communities with maturing? Most often, discussions of growth are about adding something new. Rather than focusing on newness, how can growth assist places with becoming more mature, with better making the fit between local aspiration, environmental quality, and sustainability? Second, no matter how many people show up, and no matter when they get there, what ought to still be true about the community?

Planning cannot prevent change. Change is a given. However, planning can advance values. What are the qualities that ought to still be evident, still be true about the place in the future? Planning can make great strides in that direction as evidenced in Portland's downtown, its neighborhoods, and the vitality of the working landscape surrounding the rapidly expanding "Silicon Forest."

### Community Building, Both Locally and Regionally, Is an Ongoing Responsibility

At the turn of the twentieth century, Portland's booster message was simple. Portland just wanted to be big, the "Queen City" of the Pacific coast. Today, a quest for bigness is not a sufficient booster message. Attention has turned to being better, and improving the quality of a place automatically brings into focus questions of cost, collective responsibility, and political will. Our experience is that regional planning is fundamentally a community-building task. Furthermore, if people aren't empowered locally, if they don't feel effective in arenas close to home, they won't be able to relate to a regional plan.

Consequently, an ongoing effort needs to be made to build both strong local communities and collective recognition of a shared metropolitan future. One without the other won't ring true and won't go far. Ultimately competitiveness at a metropolitan scale is not just about doing things well that other places can do, but doing things well that are unique to your own metropolitan area.

In Portland we live in a landscape with oceans, mountains, deserts, wilderness, and incredible fresh food all within the same day's drive. We can drink the water from the tap and still see the mountains on the horizon. If Portland can continue to make and remake itself as the best place it can be, then the strength of our collective ideas and action will continue to be of interest to the world. No one will visit this region simply to see a better version of some other place.

## This Is Not an Experiment

Often the Portland experience is described as an experiment. It's not. This region did not set out to become a national model. Instead, it sought to serve the values that have consistently characterized this community: a real desire to make up our own minds and solve our own problems, and significant concern for the environment.

As Carl Abbott has noted, this is an intentional place, and what has happened is the result of an ingrained desire to serve it well (Abbott 2001). As former governor Tom McCall, "father" of the Oregon planning program, once said, "Heroes are not giant statues framed against a red sky. They are people who say: 'This is my community and it's my responsibility to make it better.'"

When it comes to the growth and change of any particular metropolitan area, there are no controls in the classic experimental sense. You can't go back and "run the experiment" again with a different set of parameters. Consequently, what has been taking place at the regional level in the Portland metropolitan area is not an experiment, just as what is happening in other communities, intentional or not, is no experiment either. Every choice made or avoided is part of what a place will become. More than most, the Portland region has chosen to make its future by choice, not by accident.

REFERENCES

Abbott, Carl. 2001. *Greater Portland: Urban Life and Landscape in the Pacific Northwest.* Philadelphia: University of Pennsylvania Press.

Abbott, Carl, and Margery P. Abbott. 1991. *Historical Development of the Metropolitan Service District.* Portland: Metro.

Abbott, Carl, Sy Adler, and Margery P. Abbott. 1997. *Planning a New West: The Columbia River Gorge National Scenic Area.* Corvallis: Oregon State University Press.

Downs, Anthony. 2002. Have Housing Prices Risen Faster in Portland than Elsewhere? *Housing Policy Debate* 13 (1): 7–31.

Hwang, Sang W. 1996. The implications of the nonlinear paradigm for integrated environmental design and planning. *Journal of Planning Literature* 11 (2): 167–180.

Knaap, Gerrit, Lewis D. Hopkins, and Chengri Ding. 1999. *Do Plans Matter? Effects of Light Rail Plans on Land Values in Station Areas.* Working Paper WP99GK1. Cambridge: Lincoln Institute of Land Policy.

Knaap, Gerrit, Richard Bolen, and Ethan Seltzer. 2003. *Metro's Regional Land Information System: The Virtual Key to Portland's Growth Management Success.* Working Paper WP03GK1. Cambridge: Lincoln Institute of Land Policy.

Leccese, Michael, and Kathleen McCormick. 2000. *Charter of the New Urbanism.* New York: McGraw-Hill.

Metro. 1991. *Regional Urban Growth Goals and Objectives.* Portland: Metro.

Metro. 1995. *Report of the Future Vision Commission.* http://www.metro-region.org/ article.cfm?ArticleID=433 (accessed 19 February 2004).

Metro. 1997. *Regional Framework Plan.* http://www.metro-region.org/ article.cfm?ArticleID=432 (accessed 19 February 2004).

Metro. 2000a. *Regional Affordable Housing Strategy.* http://www.metro-region.org/ article.cfm?ArticleID=417 (accessed 19 February 2004).

Metro. 2000b. *The Nature of 2040: The region's 50-year strategy for managing growth.* http://www.metro-region.org/article.cfm?ArticleID=422 (accessed 22 February 2004).

Metro. 2001. *Land Acquisition Report to Citizens.* http://www.metro-region.org/ article.cfm?ArticleID=469 (accessed 19 February 2004).

Metro. 2002. *2002 UGB Decision and Map.* http://www.metro-region.org/ article.cfm?ArticleID=2504 (accessed 19 February 2004).

Metro. 2003a. *Charter.* http://www.metro-region.org/article.cfm?ArticleID=3724 (accessed 19 February 2004).

Metro. 2003b. *The Portland Region: How Are We Doing?* http://www.metro-region. org/article.cfm?ArticleID=3795 (accessed 19 February 2004).

Mumford, Lewis. 1939. *Regional Planning in the Pacific Northwest: A Memorandum.* Portland: Northwest Regional Council.

Nelson, Arthur C., Rolf Pendall, Casey J. Dawkins, and Gerrit J. Knaap. 2002. *The Link between Growth Management and Housing Affordability: The Academic Evidence Center on Urban and Metropolitan Policy.* Washington, DC: The Brookings Institution.

Oregon Department of Land Conservation and Development. 2001. *Oregon Statewide Land Use Planning Goals and Guidelines.* http://www.lcd.state.or.us/ goalhtml/goals.html (accessed 19 February 2004).

Phillips, Justin, and Eban Goodstein. 2000. Growth Management and Housing Prices: The Case of Portland, Oregon. *Contemporary Economic Policy* 18 (3): 334–344.

Yellowstone to Yukon Conservation Initiative. Undated. *Yellowstone to Yukon Vision.* http://www.y2y.net/overview/default.asp (Accessed 20 February 2004).

# 3 | Urban Redevelopment in Portland: Making the City Livable for Everyone?

Karen J. Gibson

The test for the city isn't whether we can make it livable. I think we've learned how to do that. The question is whether we can make it livable for everyone.[1]
—ERIK STEN QUOTED IN LEESON 2002.

In 1958, Portland voters approved the formation of a quasi-independent development agency, the Portland Development Commission (PDC). From the start it developed an autocratic organizational culture that resembled a law firm more than a public bureaucracy. Mayor Terry Schrunk appointed business-man Ira Keller chair of the citizen commission that governed its activities. His first urban renewal project, South Auditorium, is a classic case of "slum clearance" that dismantled an ethnic enclave of Jewish and Italian residents.[2] Keller, a successful businessman from Chicago, was single-minded and confident. His leadership style set the tone and culture of the agency. Decisions were made in closed-door deals, and public commission meetings were scripted. The PDC ignored other planning agencies. According to historian Carl Abbott, Fred Rosenbaum, chairman of the Hous-ing Authority of Portland (HAP), said his agency "didn't get the time of day" from the PDC throughout the 1960s. In fact, even though it provided the funds for PDC's first renewal projects, HAP failed to get land to develop public housing projects. Nor did the Portland Planning Commission have influence over deci-sion making at the development agency, despite its role as coor-dinator of development and renewal projects. Mayor Schrunk had given the city's business establishment free rein over urban redevelopment and expected the agency to produce results under Keller's leadership (Abbott 1983, 172).

Fast-forward 40 years. Mayor Vera Katz appointed Felicia Trader as executive director of the PDC in 1997. She expected Trader to deliver a far different product: a change in the culture of the PDC, which, over the years, had developed a reputation for arrogance. Despite the PDC's successful record of using urban renewal to remake downtown Portland, it was still operating on its own, unaccountable to anyone but the mayor, developers, and big business.[3] Elected officials and neighborhood activists put pressure on the mayor to make the PDC more accountable to the public and more attentive to neighborhoods. Trader, Portland's transportation director for 10 years, understood the importance of the participatory planning process. The creation of two new urban renewal areas (URAs) in 1998 and 2000 gave the PDC its first chance to involve the public since the 1970s.

This chapter examines the public involvement processes in the Lents Town Center and Interstate Corridor URAs to analyze the extent to which the PDC has changed its organizational culture. Is it still arrogant and closed or has it become open and available to public input on its decision-making processes? How has increased public involvement affected urban renewal outcomes? The Lents and Interstate cases are particularly interesting because both URAs comprise neighborhoods that have had negative experiences with city government, resulting in a lingering distrust (see Chap. 4, Witt).

The Lents Town Center URA is located in outer Southeast Portland (see Fig. 3.1). In the early twentieth century, Lents was a small, thriving town on the eastern outskirts of Portland. In 1913 it was annexed by the city. Annexation and two other events hurt Lents and caused some residents to feel bitter toward Portland's city government. Much resentment was stirred up when the City, because of state environmental requirements, forced the residents to pay for connection to a sewer system in the 1970s. But Lents and its surrounding neighborhoods had represented the largest area within city bounds without a sewer system in the United States. Then in 1983, the Interstate 205 highway split Lents in two, destroying its town center.

The Interstate Corridor URA is the largest in Portland, comprising 3,700 acres in 10 neighborhoods (see Fig. 3.1). A highway also sliced these neighborhoods in two, separating whites on the west side and blacks on the east side. African Americans had experienced the urban renewal bulldozer a few times before. In the late 1950s they were moved out of the Broadway area for the Memorial Coliseum and the Lloyd Center Mall, and in the late 1970s they were moved out of the Eliot neighborhood for Legacy Emanuel Hospital. These events left a bitter taste in the mouth of residents. More recently, these areas have experienced gentrification, resulting in the displacement of low-income residents.

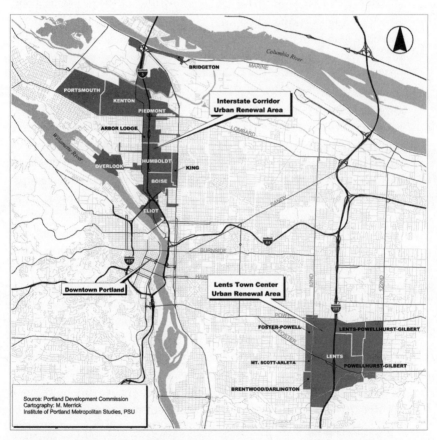

FIGURE 3.1. Urban Renewal Areas, 2003. Source: M. Merrick; adapted from Portland Development Commission.

The city, motivated by the region's 50-year plan, the 2040 Growth Concept (see Chap. 2, Seltzer), and the quest for more light rail, instigated the PDC's venture into parts of town that had not reaped the benefits of urban redevelopment. The PDC's successful urban renewal projects are well known among admirers of the city's strong downtown. As in many other cities in the United States, urban renewal has helped revitalize Portland's central business district by providing public squares such as Pioneer Courthouse Square, Lovejoy Park, and Urban Center Plaza, and greenspaces such as Pettygrove Park, Tom McCall Waterfront Park, and the Park Blocks. It has revitalized industrial districts with mixed-use, mixed-income developments, such as the Pearl District, River District, River Place, and Brewery Blocks. It has kept crowds living, working, shopping, and entertaining in the downtown and been a boon to the city's coffers and the local economy (see Chap. 8, Abbott).

However, as is often the case with urban renewal, the benefits of redevelopment have not been widely distributed. The need for city governments to pursue private capital investment to increase tax revenues creates a bias toward developers, bankers, and large businesses (Judd and Swanstrom 1994). In many cities this plays out through struggles between neglected neighborhoods and downtown, and city hall becomes an object of resentment for neighborhood groups. Often it takes the form of battles over gentrification, displacement, and the loss of low-income housing (Fainstein et al. 1986). In Portland, it is too early to tell how average residents from Lents and Interstate will benefit from urban renewal, but an examination of the PDC's public involvement process hints at a wider distribution of benefits than usual.

According to planning scholar Susan S. Fainstein, the "crux of the policy debate" about inner-city real estate development concerns two issues explored here: (1) the exclusion of the public from decisions about property and (2) the influence of public and private development activity on social equity (Fainstein 2001, 107). Has the PDC been able to change its organizational culture to genuinely become more open and inclusive in planning for its development projects? Have citizens, local business owners, and community-based organizations effectively been given a voice in the decision making that affects their neighborhoods? Will public involvement result in expanded access to resources for those groups previously excluded from the benefits of redevelopment? These are questions that concern communities all across the nation.

## Background on the Portland Development Commission

Felicia Trader came in to redirect the PDC. It had a reputation of being arrogant and she wanted to change that. (Arthuree interview 2003)

The PDC, like most urban renewal agencies, is legally structured so that it can move faster than the typical public bureaucracy. Portland created its own quasi-independent agency to administer its renewal program; its structure is "unique nationally" because urban renewal, housing, economic development, and redevelopment are all under its purview. It retains an independent reporting structure, accountable only to the mayor and a governing board the mayor appoints, leaving the city council without direct oversight. Although the council and planning commission must approve urban renewal districts, decisions about the allocation of tax increment financing resources for projects within the district are made by the five-member governing board, which is typically composed of professionals from real estate and private business.[4]

The logic underlying this organizational form in cities across the nation is that the nature of deal making and real estate development requires the ability to move quickly. The acquisition of property also requires a certain level of secrecy unusual for the public sector. As Fainstein (2001) notes:

[Urban development corporations] retain many of the governmental powers of their participating agencies while not being subject to the normal requirements on the public sector, such as holding open public meetings, filing extensive reports of their activities, and providing avenues for community participation. . . . [They] operate much like private firms, employing the entrepreneurial styles and professional image-building techniques more customary in the corporate than governmental world. (107)

The PDC is much more formal than the Bureau of Housing and Community Development (BHCD), the agency responsible for implementing the city's affordable housing programs. Tonya Parker, former BHCD director, contrasted the two cultures as "the Birkenstocks" versus "the suits" (Parker interview 2003). In summary, while Portland has excelled in its ability to implement land use, transportation, and redevelopment planning to keep downtown vibrant, it uses a traditional redevelopment agency model that has both hurt and ignored neighborhoods in the past. This resulted in political pressure on the PDC to change, especially once it began to eye projects in residential neighborhoods again.[5] The Lents Town Center and Interstate Corridor urban renewal planning processes provide interesting case studies to explore whether it has indeed changed.

## Urban Renewal in Lents

### Origins of the Lents Town Center Urban Renewal Area

The history of planning in Outer Southeast Portland is very recent. In 1992, a plan for the Brentwood–Darlington neighborhood (formerly known as Errol Heights) was adopted. In early 1996 the city council adopted the Outer Southeast Community Plan, which was developed as part of Portland's comprehensive planning process at the district level. This plan provides the specific policy framework for the Lents Town Center Urban Renewal Area (LTCURA). At around the same time, BHCD and the PDC were doing economic development planning with area merchants. However, the driving force behind the creation of a URA was the 2040 Growth Concept (see Chap. 2, Seltzer). Adopted in 1995, this plan identified the interchange of highway Interstate 205 and SE Foster Road as a "town center" because of its strategic location as a "regional multimodal" transportation node (Portland Development Commission, 1998, 23). The 2040 plan also identified one of the few remaining undeveloped industrial parcels in the region, a 100-acre property in Lents owned by the Freeway Land Company, as a Mixed Use Employment Center in its 2040 Growth Concept. It has the potential to accommodate over 2,000 jobs. According to PDC development director Abe Farkas, because "market forces are not strong enough" for the town center to develop on its own, the city decided to use tax increment financing, through urban renewal, to spur physical development (Farkas interview 2003). This required the PDC to again engage in a large community planning process.

### Public Involvement and the Plan in Lents

Public involvement to develop the urban renewal plan consisted of a series of meetings between the PDC and area stakeholders over an eight-month period from January to August 1998. The PDC's project manager, David Nemo, began discussion of urban renewal with the

Foster and 82nd Avenue Business Associations. The Lents Neighborhood Association played a role in the initial planning, along with four other neighborhood associations. A few nonprofit organizations, representing the interests of low-income households and other residents, also participated early on, but more than half of the 17 original members on the Urban Renewal Advisory Committee (URAC) had some sort of business interest. This group hammered out the goals and objectives of the plan to improve the physical capital and counter the negative image of the area (one neighborhood was labeled "Felony Flats"). The Lents URAC was experimental, but its structure and format were institutionalized by the PDC and are currently used in all subsequently formed URAs.

The vision that "forms the cornerstone" of the Lents urban renewal plan consists of four elements: jobs, wealth, livability, and community (Portland Development Commission, 1998). Key to the vision of community is a "strong neighborhood residential environment surrounding a revitalized central town center business district that integrates the neighborhood into its purpose and function." The revitalized center reflects the desire of residents to revive the former business district, as well as the 2040 Growth Concept's goal of directing population density around regional town centers. Industrial employers are sought to move into the large industrial parcel and create living wage jobs. The housing element mentions housing for a "range of incomes and housing needs, recognizing the value of the existing affordable housing stock." The majority of committee members perceive that there is already an ample supply of affordable housing because many poor whites and immigrants live in the area; therefore no more is wanted, regardless of the city's commitment to increase affordable housing (see Table 3.1).

## Urban Renewal in Interstate

### Origins of the Interstate Corridor Urban Renewal Area

In contrast to Lents, planning in the neighborhoods that make up the Interstate Urban Renewal Area goes back to the 1960s with the Albina Neighborhood Improvement Plan and Model Cities. In the early 1990s the Portland Planning Bureau worked with citizens to develop the Albina Community Plan, a comprehensive plan for the nine neighborhoods of Inner Northeast and North Portland. Again, however, it was the regional 2040 Growth Concept that played a vital role in the creation of this urban renewal district, for in the plan Interstate Avenue was designated a regional transportation corridor. Before the Interstate 5 freeway was

**Table 3.1**

*Characteristics of urban renewal plans*

| Characteristic | Lents Town Center | Interstate Corridor |
|---|---|---|
| Start–expiration dates | 1998–2015 | 2000–2020 |
| Size | 2,472 acres | 3,710 acres |
| Number of neighborhoods | 5 | 10 |
| Maximum indebtedness | $75 million | $335 million |
| Related plans | Portland Comprehensive Plan<br>Outer Southeast Community Plan<br>Lents Neighborhood Plan | Portland Comprehensive Plan<br>Albina Community Plan |
| Relationship to 2040 Growth Concept | Transportation Node at I-205 & Foster Rd. | Regional Transportation Corridor |
| Primary goals | 1. Plan is community based<br>2. Increase neighborhood livability<br>3. Provide new and rehabbed housing<br>4. Increase vitality of commercial areas<br>5. Create family-wage jobs<br>6. Protect and enhance natural environment<br>7. Minimize impact of Johnson Creek Flooding<br>8. Improve transportation within area and between area and region<br>9. Develop parks, open space, and public facilities<br>10. Promote development that creates strong identity for downtown Lents and neighborhoods | 1. Plan and implementation have inclusive public involvement processes<br>2. Prevent displacement of current residents<br>3. Strengthen businesses; expand employment and wealth creation<br>4. Optimize benefits of light rail and potential commercial/residential investment; enhance transit access for residents and workers<br>5. Focus redevelopment around light rail stations; foster mixed-use development as outlined in 2040 Growth Concept<br>6. Promote historic preservation, honor cultural heritage, promote public art and public parks<br>7. Maintain and improve existing open space assets<br>8. Maintain existing and create new public facilities |

built, this avenue was the major north–south transportation artery; because it can potentially relieve traffic congestion on Interstate 5, transportation planners seized the opportunity to build light rail along its path. Although voters defeated a bond proposal for a north–south light rail line in 1996, Oregon's congressional representatives secured a $300 million commitment from the federal government for its construction. The catch was that Portland had to match the $300 million with $30 million. The PDC provided that match with tax-increment financing through urban renewal.

The politics of bringing urban renewal to north and northeast Portland were difficult, especially given the history of major land redevelopment initiatives in the area.[6] Gentrification and displacement complicated the situation even further. Between 1990 and 1996 housing prices rose so rapidly that north and northeast neighborhoods saw prices double and in some places triple (Gibson and Abbott 2002). Suddenly, an area that in the 1980s had held more than 2,000 vacant and abandoned properties became a hot market due to its central location and Victorian housing stock. The city's housing and planning agencies, along with the nonprofit housing sector, had helped to revitalize the area during the early 1990s, but the regional economic revival had the greatest effect on housing demand (see Chap. 9, Howe). Although some residents appreciated the increase in their property values and revitalization of commercial strips, others were forced out of both rental and owner markets. This limited the residential choices of low-income residents of the only African American community in the state. The idea of creating another URA reminded some of the powerful impact that condemnation and clearance had on their viable neighborhoods. Harold Williams, president of the African American Chamber of Commerce, threatened to sue the city if residents and businesses were not included in the planning this time.

## *Public Involvement and the Plan in the Interstate Corridor*

The first step in this process was to ask community groups to nominate representatives for membership on an advisory board. In contrast to Lents, the Albina community (see Chap. 5, Johnson) had a significant "community-building infrastructure" with numerous nonprofits, businesses, neighborhood associations, and institutions that had willing participants (Southgate interview 2003).[7] In fact, Mayor Katz appointed 54 people from the nominees to the advisory board. The Interstate Corridor Urban Renewal Advisory Committee (ICURAC) met monthly from September 1999 to May 2000 to develop the plan. They determined the 3,700-acre boundary that includes 10 neighborhoods, commercial areas, industrial zones, and Columbia Villa, the largest public housing development in the state of Oregon (see Fig. 3.1). After the required public hearings, the city council adopted the plan devised through the community process nearly verbatim. In addition to the monthly meetings, in which public comment was taken, the outreach effort involved presentations to 40 stakeholder groups, two large public forums, a monthly bulletin with a mailing list of more than 600, and a door-to-door community survey of spending priorities from 1,300 residents. The survey identified jobs and affordable housing as the top two priorities. Following the initial year of plan development, a second year of planning ran from September 2000 through May 2001 in which subcommittees devised strategies for housing, economic development and jobs, transportation, revitalization, urban design and historic preservation, parks and open space, and community facilities and infrastructure.

The ICURAC developed a set of "general principles" that "apply to all decisions affecting the urban renewal area," and a set of specific principles and goals pertinent to each topical area. (Portland Development Commission, 2000, 3–11). The two overarching principles developed by the committee were that (1) community outreach will be comprehensive and long term and will build community capacity, and (2) projects will primarily benefit existing residents and businesses in the URA. Significantly, the plan ruled out the use of eminent domain for condemnation of land and property unless specifically requested by a member of the advisory board (see Table 3.1).

## Assessment of Process and Outcomes

The staff members and boards of these organizations believe that they do their best to represent the interests of the public. They view the protesting community groups as narrowly favoring their own interests and unable to conceptualize or sacrifice for programs that would benefit the whole city. The community groups, on the other hand, justifiably feel that they bear the costs of improvements while others realize the gain, that wealthy citizens are rarely asked to give up their privileges for the common good and that their intimate knowledge of their neighborhoods is disregarded. (Fainstein 2001, 226)

According to Development Director, Abe Farkas, the recommendations of advisory committees are "attended to," but they do not "determine" the plans; the PDC commission retains that authority (Farkas interview 2003). If the ultimate power is situated with the PDC and its five commissioners, is the process anything more than mere tokenism so that city and regional planning agencies can achieve their goals? Or has the PDC created a genuinely inclusive process and thus become more accountable? An evaluation of the public involvement processes and the early outcomes leads to the conclusion that the PDC has become more accountable *than it was before.* There is evidence to support PDC's claim that it "embraced the ethic of citizen participation" during the Lents and Interstate planning processes (Southgate interview 2003). The question remains, however, whether this movement forward represents a change that meets a standard of true public involvement adequate for representation of traditionally marginalized citizens. If measured by Arnstein's classic typology, the "ladder of citizen participation" (see Fig. 3.2) do these processes truly redistribute power to Lents and Interstate citizens, or do they merely manipulate people to gain their support? (Arnstein 1969). Three criteria used to assess the processes are (1) what is the composition of the committee, (2) what is the quality of the participation, and (3) what are the outcomes?

### Composition of the Lents URAC

According to Baruti Arthuree, former deputy director of the PDC, their public involvement in Lents "stretched the envelope" (Arthuree interview

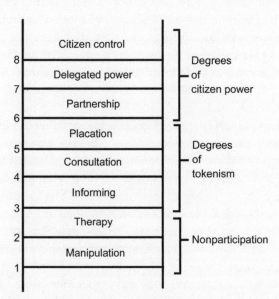

FIGURE 3.2. Arnstein's Ladder of Citizen Participation. Source: *AIP Journal,* Vol. 35, No. 4, July 1969, p 217. Reprinted with permission of the American Planning Association.

2003). This pilot test has been problematic due to conflicts between committee members and the strong distrust of the city by many of the commercial stakeholders. Joanne Davis, a Lents homeowner, complained that "from the beginning the PDC let the business community have a strong say," and therefore it thinks it has "more rights" than residents (Davis interview 2003). After complaints that the initial committee overwhelmingly represented business interests, membership was expanded to include more residents and community groups. Still, the relationship between business and residents has been conflicted. Davis suggested that although the PDC project manager, David Nemo, was a "lovely person who worked hard and did a lot of good," the committee included too many of the "wrong people" who posed "road blocks." Especially when planning the redevelopment of an industrial site, the business people "took over" to the point of excluding city agencies and those "not on the inside" (Davis interview 2003). Nemo asserted that committee members pose barriers to PDC's plans because they generally do not "buy into the vision of density and transit oriented development" (Nemo interview 2003).

The lack of low-income representation on the committee is problematic for Nick Sauvie, executive director of Rose Community Development Corporation (Rose CDC). His organization is the only entity "representing the interests of more than 10,000 renters" in the urban renewal district (Sauvie interview 2003). Besides his organization, there are few established community organizations that have the capacity to be involved over the life of the planning process. The area is home to many low-income white and ethnic immigrant populations less involved in public affairs (a large Russian and Slavic population and growing numbers of Asians and Latinos).

Four years into the planning process, commercial interests on the committee remained dominant. Rose CDC and a commercial developer, Morrison Company, were planning a mixed-use development project for the Lents Town Center site. Rose CDC had secured $2.7 million of federal tax credits to develop the housing units. When the commercial developer could not find clients in the weak economic environment and pulled out of the project, the Lents Town Center Urban Renewal Advisory Committee (LTCURAC) was unwilling to approve the housing development as a stand-alone project on the site, even if it meant losing the tax credits. The vote against Rose's proposal was 17 to 3. Since Rose CDC had already paid the predevelopment costs, this posed a real risk to the organization's solvency (Sauvie interview 2003). Neither the city nor the PDC wanted to lose the tax credits, so after a long delay the PDC overruled the URAC's recommendation and approved the project. It is ironic that the PDC had to overrule the committee to build more affordable housing in a neighborhood with many low-income and working class residents.

### Composition of the Interstate Corridor URAC

The appointment of 54 people to the ICURAC gave the appearance that most constituencies were adequately represented. In fact, one might argue that if there was a problem, it is that too many people were included. Mark Kirchmeier, a committee member from North Portland, suggested that the committee was "twice as big" as it should be, making the planning process "unwieldy" (Kirchmeier interview 2003). In his opinion, the "pendulum had swung" away from "heavy-handed redevelopment" to an excessive focus on the process of participation, to the detriment of projects.

Although representation of a variety of citizen stakeholders is apparent in Interstate, representation from some key city agencies is scarce. Jennie Portis, who runs a nonprofit workforce agency, says the absence of the city agency that disburses federal workforce funds, Worksystems, Inc., makes it difficult to make progress on the issue of job development (Portis interview 2003). This reflects a larger issue generally that surfaced in interviews with nonprofit and city agency staff: although citizen participation has increased, the PDC "does not necessarily promote inter-agency relations" (Wadden interview 2003). Thus some of the players that are essential for a comprehensive implementation strategy remain absent from the planning process. When Mayor Katz appointed Felicia Trader to run the agency, she knew that Trader was an insider who appreciated the idea of community involvement. Trader advocated the notion in Interstate that this urban renewal was not of the traditional kind; it was actually a big community development process. But Trader retired from her post early in 2001. Katz then hired Donald Mazziotti as executive director. Educated in law and planning, he was experienced in public administration as well as private real estate development. Chief planner for Portland's Bureau of Planning from 1974 to 1978, his appointment represents a return to the leadership style of Keller and a turn away from the community orientation of Trader. Kip Wadden, staff member at Parks and Recreation, regrets his orientation toward developers and away from his management counterparts in other city agencies. Frustrated in her attempt to plan with the URACs for parks, she says Mazziotti "has a separate empire" and "does not want to collaborate"; she feels that if the citizens want a park and the PDC does not want to fund it, she cannot succeed (Wadden interview 2003).

## Quality of Participation

The truly interesting thing is that there was this idea that there was going to be a chicken in every pot—people were led to believe that many things were available. (Galbraith interview 2003)

The two key factors inhibiting the quality of participation are (1) the unequal distribution of technical expertise between PDC staff and the committee members and (2) poor communication. Marshall and Ozawa (2004) assert that because "presence does not ensure participation," all involved should be "brought to a comparable level of substance and process competency." This has not occurred in either urban renewal advisory committee.

### Lents

It is generally acknowledged that there is less experience with urban planning processes among the citizens in Outer Southeast than in Northeast Portland. Educational attainment in this area is lower than average for the city. The local high school, Marshall, has the highest dropout rate in the state, about 40%. Joanne Davis said "the community as a whole is very unknowledgeable" (Davis interview 2003). Nick Sauvie argues that since "residents are not knowledgeable on how to do development," he would like to see the PDC staff take "leadership to create a plan and increase understanding and implement it" (Sauvie interview 2003). In other words, PDC should take more seriously the need for residents to become more educated (increase understanding) so that they can participate in a more competent fashion. It is likely that low-income residents shy away from participation because they do not share the same level of substantive knowledge as the "suits" from downtown. They also have much less experience with the public involvement process and are intimidated by its formality. At most meetings they are far outnumbered: there are usually more professionals from city agencies and representatives of local business interests than there are residents.

URAC members often perceive lack of information and unclear priorities as a lack of sincerity. Communication is quite a problem in Lents, and it is connected to the issue of trust. In early 2002, the PDC replaced David Nemo with John Southgate as project manager in Lents. The manager of a local workforce center said that committee members representing business interests have such "incredible mistrust" for the PDC that they have slowed the process, frustrating other residents and representatives of community development organizations. Although "it was pretty hard" to work with some members, the PDC "did a great job taking their concerns seriously" (Soderberg interview 2003). Communication improved when the PDC brought in facilitators to run meetings. But budget pressures in 2001 eliminated the facilitators. Nick Sauvie has "lots of respect" for Southgate's ability to communicate information, but still the PDC staff is "deciding [the] plan [for Lents] because the committee is not knowledgeable" (Sauvie interview 2003). Given the paucity of knowledge and lack of trust, the PDC should increase investment in the process and offer more than superficial information to participants. Gretchen Kafoury, former city commissioner in charge of housing and community development, suggests that where there is true commitment there is no shortage of staff (Kafoury interview 2003). The issue of trust arose in the Interstate Corridor as well.

### Interstate

The following excerpt from the testimony of Larry Mills ICURAC member to the city council illustrates how the lack of consistent information and clear communication raised questions about the PDC's sincerity:

Good communication will be essential for the success of this plan. As we all know, PDC has a somewhat tainted past. The future can be positive or negative depending on how PDC administers and implements the plan. Every attempt should be made to promote open dialogue with the community. During the planning of this proposal there were a number of times it seemed that we, as members of the committee, were shooting at a moving target. Issues such as the city's portion of the light rail funding, boundaries and the right of eminent domain lacked any definite direction. This influences the credibility of the process. There were times that many issues changed from meeting to meeting. That brings us back to the trust issue again. In the future clear and concise priorities should be established. That way everyone is starting from the same place. (Mills 2000)

Several participants involved in planning for Interstate expressed high regard for the effort put forth by John Southgate, the project manager, as well as the efforts of other PDC staff. Yet they felt misled by the city and the PDC: "The community is upset that promises including jobs, housing, and business growth and development have not materialized" (Portis interview 2003). Southgate is aware that the public was allowed to believe that more money would be available in the early years; he says he did not know that the city's $30 million light rail obligation would come due so fast. The "fiscal people" decided to repay the debt in a shorter time frame than he had anticipated, and if he could have changed anything, it would have been to stress that tax increment financing would represent a "huge economic engine in the long haul" (Southgate interview 2003). This causes one to wonder about the flow of information within the PDC and to the public. Why didn't Southgate know about the status of funding early on, so that he could keep the public accurately informed? Why were there so many moving targets?

Another example of how PDC keeps information "close to its chest" concerns the budget. The cochair of the Interstate advisory committee, Walter Valenta, said that he had to be "very persistent" just to "get an understanding of the budget" (Valenta interview 2003). Although the PDC shares budget information, it is usually presented in a very superficial format, with little explanation of budget items. It is difficult to tell where administrative costs are and how money carries over from year to year when left unspent. It is presented during the same meeting in which committee members are expected to vote, allowing little time for review or consideration.

A striking illustration of the top-down flow of information was the Interstate Corridor Urban Renewal Area Base Data and Trends Report, prepared by the PDC to launch the second year of strategic planning on housing, economic development, etc. The PDC produced the report with little or no consultation with committee members. It was accepted with some surprise and disappointment because participants felt that they had knowledge about the community that was not included. Had they been consulted, they would have included additional kinds of information in the report, such as more detailed employment information. This is an example of what Arnstein calls "bureaucratic technical assistance" (Arnstein 1969, 222). It is typical of a citizen involvement process that is designed to "placate" the public but not really grant them meaningful participation. At the bare minimum this report should have been a collaborative effort between the PDC and participants; in a true partnership the PDC would provide the committee its own funds for independent technical assistance.

### Outcomes in the Lents Urban Renewal Area

There are few completed projects in Lents, despite the fact that the urban renewal plan was adopted five years ago. The largest investment was made for development of the Marshall Technical Center. This is a workforce-training center that the PDC had constructed in partnership with a few manufacturing firms such as Gunderson and Stream International. However, because tax increment funds are restricted to physical development and closely related costs, there is no operating support for training. Initially it was supported by a federal grant, but its operation has been unstable, switching administration from the Southeast One Stop Employment Center to Portland Community College. When the economy declined in 2001, manufacturing firms no longer demanded workers. According to BHCDs economic development director, Howard Cutler, when the economy began to pick up, Gunderson began looking for welders outside of the state (Cutler 2003). This is an example of what occurs when there is no collaboration between the employment and training agency, which is Worksystems, Inc., and the economic development agency, which is the PDC. It is also a good example of one limitation of tax increment financing as the chief tool for economic development. As the saying goes, "When the only tool is a hammer, then all problems are nails." Because of this limitation it is imperative that the PDC actively partner with other city agencies so that programs can operate in the buildings it develops.

Other projects that have been completed or are in progress include major rehabilitation of the Boys and Girls Club, park and lighting improvements, storefront improvements, street paving, and tree planting. Some seniors' homes are being rehabilitated, and Rose CDC completed its 24-unit housing development at the Lents Town Center. This area is still the centerpiece of the revitalization effort and the PDC is still trying to acquire seven properties so that it can attract a "home run" development to the site (Southgate interview 2003). Very little has been accomplished regarding the highest priority goals: jobs, commercial development, and housing. This has frustrated participants and kept other residents and stakeholders from joining the effort.

A new addition to the original urban renewal plan for Lents is a station for the proposed north–south light rail extension envisioned in the 2040 Growth Concept. It appears that regional planners who favor light rail have latched onto the idea of using urban renewal tax increment financing to support the large capital investment it requires. While local residents want living-wage manufacturing jobs and the Marshall Tech Center does not have the funds to train welders, money is available for light rail.

## Outcomes in the Interstate Corridor Urban Renewal Area

Throughout the planning for this urban renewal district there were times when it seemed that expectations were outside the scope of an urban renewal process. Many ideas seemed a little like "pie in the sky."

I think that it is misleading to allow citizens and organizations to think that financial resources are there, when they probably aren't. Establishing criteria for resources should be a top priority. Accountability for allocation of funds should be a top priority. (Mills 2000)

The Interstate Urban Renewal Plan, adopted a little more than three years ago, has borne relatively more fruit. The light rail line began operations in mid-2004. Three of the intersections selected to concentrate intensive transit-oriented developments have projects in the works. The PDC has purchased a building on Killingsworth and Interstate Avenues and released a request for proposal for a mixed-use commercial/housing development. New Seasons Market, an upscale, locally-owned grocer, will open a new store at a major intersection, and the older traditional store is undergoing major renovation. The demand for storefront improvements has increased along Interstate Avenue, and a Tri-Met program helped retain businesses that experienced revenue losses during the construction period. Many parks are undergoing improvements.

Looking at the biggest priorities in Interstate—housing and jobs—very little has been accomplished. To be fair, over 70 programs were frozen for more than a year beginning in 2002 because of a lawsuit against the city, brought by the owner of a hotel chain (Shilo Hotels) over property tax. Because the funding was frozen, many staff were shifted away from renewal projects and onto "resource development" (Arthuree interview 2003). As of June 2003, the housing and economic development subcommittees on Interstate had not met for over a year, while the parks, transportation, and livability committees kept meeting regularly. Very little explanation was offered, except for the fact that there was little money flowing. Although the housing and economic development project coordinators are administering housing and storefront projects for the renewal area, the fact that meetings are a low priority illustrates what many call the PDC's bias toward projects over planning. According to Colin Sears, the coordinator for economic development, because there is no money and there are no projects, it is not necessary to meet. Meanwhile he says that the Oregon Convention Center URA (his other area of responsibility) is quite busy (Sears interview 2003). But if the PDC is not planning, then the capacity of existing residents and stakeholders to participate in development is not being built. Jobs are the second highest priority in Interstate, yet the PDC can do little to help with human capital development. According to Baruti Arthuree "pulling workforce out [of the PDC] was not a smart thing" (Arthuree interview 2003).

The biggest development deal in Interstate, after the train, involves the revitalization of Columbia Villa, a public housing development in Portland. The Interstate Urban Renewal Area is providing $6.4 million to HAP to support the revitalization of Oregon's largest public housing development. Although HAP was included in the URA to enhance its HOPE VI grant application to the Department of Housing and Urban Development, and not for tax increment financing (TIF) revenue, it eventually came to the ICURAC with hat in hand. The City of Portland had committed $20 million to help HAP develop roughly 800 units of mixed-use, mixed-income housing, called New Columbia, scheduled to open in late 2005. The city tapped the Interstate Corridor urban renewal TIF revenue to meet its commitment. But the planning for allocation of funds to HAP occurred only partially within view of the advisory committee, according to Walter Valenta, one of the committee cochairs who helped negotiate the deal. Remarking on the advisory committee process he said,

> Citizen involvement is a profession. I am fine with it, but there is phoniness. In places they are good—and then they revert to the back room stuff. I have had tremendous access with HAP deal brokering, but I am a white guy. We haven't had anything yet to test the goals of urban renewal. I am still willing to give PDC the benefit of the doubt. (Valenta interview 2003)

## Discussion

> We put a lot of blood, sweat, and tears into the guiding principles [of the renewal plan]—are they to stand for something? (Member of ICURAC during discussion of annual budget, 2003)

Based upon the three criteria (committee composition, quality of participation, and outcomes), the PDC has become more open and accessible to the public than before. While URAC members in both Lents and Interstate commented that Southgate, Nemo, and other PDC staff should be commended for their efforts, there was still a feeling that they were being "managed." This is a far cry from how the involvement process was envisioned by Interstate committee members and embodied as the first guiding principle of the plan:

> This process will build capacity within the community by providing specific, consistent, and culturally appropriate opportunities for all community residents, businesses, and organizations to access and impact urban renewal decision making and by providing educational resources necessary to an informed decision. (PDC 2000, 4)

According to Elizabeth Rocha, one of the pitfalls of a mediated empowerment process (guided by professional planners) is that it does not build "community capacity," even though the process and outcomes can be somewhat empowering (Rocha 1997, 37). Building community capacity is a core principle of community development; it is a process whereby members become more educated and informed and therefore have more meaningful participation.

What rung on Arnstein's ladder of participation do these processes reach? (See Figure 3.2 on p. 71) The ladder has eight rungs that range from low to high in terms of the amount of citizen power over the end product. The first two rungs (manipulation and therapy) are nonpartici-pation; the second two rungs (informing and consultation) are mere tokenism; the fifth rung (placation) is a higher form of tokenism; and the last three rungs (partnership, delegated power, and citizen control) give citizens power (Arnstein 1969, 217). Based upon the evidence found (imbalance in citizen representation, citizen knowledge, and misleading and incomplete communication) the Lents and Interstate processes only reach the rung of placation. Arnstein argues that placation exists when "the ground rules allow have-nots to advise, but retain for power-holders the continued right to decide" (Arnstein 1969, 217). The URACs are advi-sory bodies—the PDC retains final decision-making authority. Although there may be the illusion of partnership on occasions, it often occurs when the PDC or the city find it necessary to appease the committee so that it can get what it wants. For example, although the Interstate adviso-ry committee leaders negotiated with the PDC around funding for New Columbia, and Arnstein does consider negotiations a partnership, this is not a routine experience. In fact, as Walter Valenta pointed out, he is a "white guy" and a realtor, and therefore his level of access is greater than other members'. It was because the city had to meet its obligation to sup-port New Columbia that it had to engage in negotiation. But it was done in a closed-door, behind the scenes deal, and not at the regular public advisory committee meeting. This is why the ICURAC member asked whether the effort put into the guiding principles was in vain; most were unable to access that decision-making process.

## Conclusion

It seems evident that because the PDC needs tax increment financing to help achieve the city's plans for its future development as mandated by the 2040 Growth Concept, it has had to appease the citizens in URAs. But the PDC has not fundamentally changed its organizational culture.

Former Portland journalist and director of BHCD Tonya Parker characterized the PDC's evolution: "its underlying goals are the same—what has changed is how it has been said, how it has been presented" (Parker interview 2003). The PDC retains the technical expertise and funds to engage in big redevelopment projects that privilege established market actors. Decision making remains in their hands and little is trickling down to the residents in Lents or Interstate. Because physical renewal primarily benefits those already well connected to markets (financial, commercial, housing, or labor markets), the current pattern of poverty, gentrification, and displacement will continue. Low-income populations in the Lents and Interstate URAs will not experience the livability that Commissioner Sten suggests unless they are included as partners in the decision-making process. These findings have relevance for cities across the nation where fiscal pressures cause local governments to focus on physical development rather than human development. Citizens and planners have an important role to play in holding quasi-independent public agencies accountable.

ACKNOWLEDGMENTS

I wish to express my appreciation to all those who were willing to share their thoughts in interviews, and to acknowledge the superb research assistance of Ms. Lisa Abuaf, a graduate student of Urban and Regional Planning at Portland State University.

NOTES

1. Erik Sten made this comment about Interstate Urban Renewal due to the impact of gentrification and displacement. He is the city commissioner in charge of the Bureau of Housing and Community Development (BHCD). BHCD administers the federal Community Development Block Grant program for Multnomah County, and the PDC executes some of its low-income housing programs.

2. After World War II, Portland, like many other cities across the nation, began to lose population and retail sales to the growing suburbs. The Housing Acts of 1949 and 1954 made federal urban renewal funds available for revitalization of urban built environments. Urban renewal was primarily an economic development tool that focused on clearing slums and reusing potentially valuable land near the central city for institutional and commercial purposes. Low-income residents were displaced as much more housing was destroyed than ever built. Thousands of businesses were displaced as well.

3. The PDC currently has 10 active urban renewal districts, covering 12,086 acres, nearing the limit of 15% of the city's eligible land. The maximum indebtedness for all areas, over an average of a 20-year life span, is $1.7 billion. This does

not include debt service or refinancing costs (PDC Proposed Budget FY 2003–04, Urban Renewal Q & A, S-7).

4. In addition to federal urban renewal funds, these projects were financed with local bond money through the use of tax increment financing (TIF). In 1960, following California's lead, Oregon became the second state in the nation to pass a constitutional amendment authorizing the use of TIF. This financing tool allows local governments to sell bonds and pay them off with the future increases in tax revenues; the bond monies provide the capital for physical redevelopment of neighborhoods.

5. City commissioners Gretchen Kafoury, Jim Francesconi, and Erik Sten began pressuring Mayor Katz to make the PDC's activities more transparent around 1996. Pressure on the PDC to become more transparent dates back to the late 1960s, and in the late 1970s this culminated in a change to the state law enabling urban renewal, which required the PDC to have a more open public involvement process. For more about the history of urban renewal see Carl Abbott's *Portland: Planning, Politics, and Growth in a Twentieth-Century City* and Craig Wollner, John Provo, and Julie Schablitsky, *A Brief History of Urban Renewal in Portland, Oregon.*

6. Three redevelopment projects had displaced the African American community: the construction of the Memorial Coliseum, Interstate 5, and Emanuel Hospital.

7. The Albina Community is the name for inner Northeast neighborhoods whose residents occupy an area that used to be a town separate from Portland, called Albina. The term is often used to refer to the African American population in Northeast Portland because this is where they became concentrated after World War II and the Vanport Flood.

## REFERENCES

Abbott, Carl. 1983. *Portland: Planning, Politics and Growth in a Twentieth-Century City.* Lincoln: University of Nebraska Press.

Arnstein, Sherry. 1969. A ladder of citizen participation. *Journal of the American Institute of Planners* 35 (4): 216–224.

Cutler, Howard. 2003. Director of Economic Development, Bureau of Housing and Community Development. Personal communication. 17 November.

Fainstein, Susan S. 2001. *The City Builders: Property Development in New York and London, 1980–2000*, 2nd ed., rev. Lawrence, KS: University Press of Kansas.

Fainstein, Susan S. and Norman I. Fainstein, Richard Child Hill, Dennis R. Judd, Michael Peter Smith. 1986. *Restructuring the City: The Political Economy of Urban Redevelopment*, rev. ed. New York: Longman.

Gibson, Karen J. and Carl Abbott. 2002. City Profile: Portland, Oregon. *Cities* 19(6): 425–436.

Judd, Dennis R. and Todd Swanstrom. 1994. *City Politics: Private Power and Public Policy.* New York: HarperCollins.

Leeson, Fred. 2002. Council backs Interstate area renewal goals. *The Oregonian.* 8 July. Page B-2.

Marshall, Gary, and Connie P. Ozawa. 2004. Mediation at the local level: Implications for democratic governance. In Peter Bogason, Sandra Kensen and Hugh Miller, eds. *Tampering with Tradition: The Unrealized Authority of Democratic Agency.* Lanham: Lexington Books.

Mills, Larry. 2000. Interstate Corridor Urban Renewal Advisory Committee member. Written testimony to City Council, 16 August.

Portland Development Commission. 1998. Lents Town Center Urban Renewal Plan. Amended 2000.

Portland Development Commission. 2000. Interstate Corridor Urban Renewal Plan. Amended 2001.

Portland Development Commission. 2003. Proposed Budget FY 2003–04, Urban Renewal Q & A, S-7

Rocha, Elizabeth M. 1997. A ladder of empowerment. *Journal of Planning Education and Research* 37: 17–44.

Wollner, Craig, John Provo, and Julie Schablitsky. 2001. *A Brief History of Urban Renewal in Portland, Oregon.* http://www.pdc.us/pdf/about/urban_renewal_ history.pdf (20 November 2003).

INTERVIEWS

Arthuree, Baruti. 2003. Interview with author. 14 April. Former Deputy director of the Portland Development Commission.

Davis, Joanne. 2003. Interview with author. 21 April. Lents Urban Renewal Advisory Committee member.

Farkas, Abe. 2003. Interview with author. 10 March. Development director, Portland Development Commission.

Galbraith, Cathy. 2003. Interview with author. 29 October. Director, Bosco-Milligan Foundation, Interstate Corridor Urban Renewal Advisory Committee member.

Kafoury, Gretchen. 2003. Interview with author. 14 March. Former Portland city commissioner.

Kirchmeier, Mark. 2003. Interview with author. 21 April. Interstate Corridor Urban Renewal Advisory Committee member.

Nemo, David. 2003. Interview with author. 19 November. Lents project manager, Portland Development Commission.

Parker, Tonya. 2003. Interview with author. 16 May. Former director, Bureau of Housing and Community Development.

Portis, Jennie. 2003. Interview with author. 18 April. Executive director, Northeast Workforce Center and Interstate Corridor Urban Renewal Advisory Committee member.

Sauvie, Nick. 2003. Interview with author. 19 May. Executive director, Rose Community Development Corporation.

Sears, Colin. 2003. Personal communication with author. Senior Project Coordinator, Portland Development Commission.

Soderberg, Heidi. 2003. Interview with author. 8 May. Director, Southeast Works and Lents Urban Renewal Advisory Committee member.

Southgate, John. 2003. Interviews with author. 14 March, 12 November. Project manager, Portland Development Commission.

Valenta, Walter. 2003. Interview with author. 4 November. Cochair, Interstate Corridor Urban Renewal Advisory Committee.

Wadden, Kathleen. 2003. Interview with author. 4 April. Portland Parks and Recreation.

**4** | *Dialectics of Control:*
*The Origins and Evolution of*
*Conflict in Portland's Neighborhood*
*Association Program*

Matthew Witt

In 1985, Tufts political scientists Jeffrey Berry, Kent Portney, and Ken Thomson began a major study of neighborhood associations (NAs) in the United States, eventually entitled, *The Rebirth of Urban Democracy* (Berry et al. 1993). Besides its scholarly significance, this research held special meaning for Portland, Oregon. As one of only a handful of metropolitan areas nationwide selected for the study, Portland made the grade because its then 11-year-old NA program featured an unprecedented level of commitment to citizen involvement by comparison with other major cities nationwide. Among the cities studied, the Tufts research team ranked Portland second only to St. Paul for its overall program design and democratic appeal. The total study included an in-depth analysis of five "core" cities of comparable size (also including Dayton, Birmingham, and San Antonio), as well as analysis of 10 matched cities, two per core city studied. The Tufts study has been the most significant effort to analyze citizen participation in local governance ever undertaken.[1]

Very recently, Robert Putnam, noted scholar of civic involvement in America, writing with colleagues Lewis Feldstein and Don Cohen, has remarked upon the unusual level of civic involvement Portland has maintained compared with comparable cities across the nation (Putnam et al. 2003). In this analysis, Portland's NA program is merely one feature of an ethos of participation drawing from several sources of inspiration—from progressive land use legislation to an aura of can-do populism and a fervent desire to maintain Oregon's vaunted livability. These attributes imbue Portland's civic culture with what these authors refer to as a "civic dialectic," deriving its form as follows: "More grassroots activism has (often through conflict) led to more responsive public institutions, and more responsive institutions have in turn evoked more activism" (Putnam et al. 2003, 262) (see Chap. 5, Johnson).

Accolades similar to these, as well as those resulting from the in-depth analysis of the Tufts study, have contributed to Portland's mystique for being one of America's most livable cities, decade after decade. In keeping with the intentions of this volume, the current chapter is an attempt to peer behind Portland's hard-earned façade, to give an up-close account of Portland's civic ethos as lived by the people who have been central to its cultivation. Though intact, Portland's NA institution today is a distinctively different creature from the one that emerged in 1973.

This chapter explores how Portland's NA institution evolved through five epochs, spanning the era between 1973 and 2004, always shaped by a complicated blend of organizational dynamics and metropolitan politics. I hope to provide the critical reader a deepened appreciation for both the fragility and the resilience of Portland's ethos of neighborhood-based citizen involvement.

## Nuts and Bolts

Thirty years after its inception, Portland's NA system is, though altered, still in operation. Through "district coalitions" (DCs), NAs have access to staffing, funds for newsletter mailing, and other logistical support services by which they are able to undertake a wide range of livability campaigns on behalf of their residents. These coalitions are governed by boards of directors—made up of delegates from member NAs—which serve as citizen participation "contractors" of sorts, in that they receive funding from local tax dollars contingent upon submitting annual work plans downtown, to the Office of Neighborhood Involvement (ONI).[2] These work plans are reviewed by ONI and checked for correspondence with a set of "guidelines" as well as baseline citizen support priorities the city has established. Upon approval, DC work plans form the basis for yearly contracts that their boards of directors then hold with ONI. As contractors, DC boards of directors (DCBs) are required to provide quarterly fiscal and operational accounting reports.

Besides receiving base funding from general fund tax dollars—a necessary condition for inclusion as a core city in the Tufts study—Portland's model has drawn both popular and academic notice because it promises a level of autonomy, in contrast to centralized, top-down (e.g., downtown) control. As contractors, Portland's DCBs have, for the most part, independent authority over staff hiring and firing, and, to a large extent, agenda setting.

## Lingering Questions

The key function of DCBs is to provide organizational capacity to their member NAs.[3] This means, nominally, that a DC serves primarily as an administrative support structure. But in fact, Portland's DCBs regularly establish policy priorities on issues such as public safety and traffic management that cut across individual NA boundaries. Moreover, city administrators often attend DCB meetings in lieu of individual NAs to gain some sense of broad-based community concerns. This is where norms for discourse among member NAs are set, and where DC staff are most dominant in establishing the tone of relations between member NAs and in helping to adjudicate differences between DCs and downtown perspectives. It is also here that interest group processes are most apparent and in some cases, most problematic. In sum, the DCB level of activity is integral to the overall working of Portland's NA system, yet this level has received almost no scholarly scrutiny.[4]

The organizational and political dynamics that have shaped Portland's NA culture have at times flared into destructive conflict. Thus, in July 1992, the Office of Neighborhood Associations (ONA, as ONI was then called) did not renew its contract with the North Portland Citizens Committee, the DCB of record for the North Portland community. This severance followed more than a year of hobbled negotiations between disaffected NA delegates to the DCB who had been fighting amongst themselves—intermittently for several years—over various operational and management issues. In spring 1997, ONI discontinued its contract with the East Portland District Coalition after a similar round of internal conflict tore that coalition apart. In each case, ONI eventually cobbled together a hybrid arrangement with NA participants whereby the City would assume administrative responsibility, including staff hiring and review, but would leave policymaking authority up to an advisory board consisting of NA delegates.[5] Although other DCBs in Portland had incurred periods of internal strife, none had, until the North Portland Citizen's Committee, chosen to give up the "sovereign" status vis-à-vis downtown purview that the Tufts team had found so laudatory.[6] In both cases—East and North Portland—neither district has sought to resume independent contract administration; those who endured the infighting in either case continue to ardently oppose any return to the status quo ante.

This situation poses challenges to claims proffered by the Tufts study regarding citizen autonomy from downtown control over NA activity. The Tufts researchers argued that, all things held equal, "more is better" when it comes to an NA's control over its own destiny. This conclusion was derived in part from basic deductive reasoning. Since local politics are powerfully influenced by the imperative to maximize growth and development, NAs can potentially serve as an important bulwark against an inherently unbalanced political agenda. But to do so, neighborhoods must be as free as possible from pressures to accept conditions set by more powerful interest groups—namely, large business interests aligned with local politicians and development agencies (see Chap. 3, Gibson). To the Tufts researchers' way of thinking, Portland's DC model guaranteed citizens a strong degree of control within the overall scheme of NA involvement in Portland.

How significant is Portland's experience with DCB conflict and dissolution within the context of its overall NA program? Were the episodes in East and North Portland essentially anomalous events within an otherwise successful and momentous history of metropolitan-scaled citizen involvement? Are these episodes merely inconsequential blips on Portland's otherwise perfect EKG of "civic dialectic"? Or is the dialectic driving Portland's experience more problematic than the Tufts or Putnam team would have us believe?

## Modeling Conflict

Portland's commitment to citizen participation has been lasting and significant, but it has also been conflicted about its program identity and definition. Since the program's inception, it has remained unresolved how much citizens shall be granted predominant authority to shape and influence decisions and actions that impact their lives and communities. Berry et al. (1993) claimed that, in Portland, as with the other cities they studied, citizens have a real and ongoing capacity not only to influence but also to shape policy outcomes in accordance with their stated preferences through participation in their respective NAs.

The problem with these conclusions is that they predate key shifts in Portland's program. These shifts have included:

*The dissolution of the bureau advisory committee (BAC) program.* Berry et al. (1993) emphasized this component of Portland's NA model as evidence for Portland's ongoing and successful commitment to citizen participation. This program had been initiated under Mayor Neil Goldschmidt in 1974 to open up the City's budgetary process to citizen scrutiny and involvement. After eventually encompassing nearly every city bureau by 1991, the BAC program steadily declined following flagging support by ONA (which had staffed its steering committee, the Bureau Advisory Coordinating Committee) and the city council. By 1994, the Bureau Advisory Coordinating Committee was discontinued, along with most of the BACs.

*The breakup of two DCs that followed intense levels of conflict and infighting.* Although beginning prior to Tufts' research efforts, these episodes did not peak, for the most part, until after Berry et al. had published their findings. This conflict included infighting among NA delegates to DC boards in North and East Portland—two of Portland's seven DCs. The fights on these boards shared several traits, including socioeconomic dimensions, and were triggered by weaknesses and vulnerabilities that are endemic to citizen involvement programs everywhere, but which also have parameters that are unique to Portland's program. The acrimony spawned by these disputes calls into question key survey findings of the Tufts study, which claim that Portland's NAs provide hospitable venues for civic discourse.

*A decisive shift in ONI's historic focus on NAs toward an assimilation of other interest groups, including, notably, neighborhood business associations.* This shift followed recommendations from a task force convened by (then) ONA and its commissioner-in-charge in 1995. The task force was convened at the height of infighting in East Portland. Several participants in and observers of this process criticized the task force for balking at key issues and for failing to clearly define objectives. For these critics, the task force signaled the continuation of a drift in Portland's NA program that had been building for some time.

As Putnam et al. (2003) stress, citizen involvement in Portland has been marked by intense episodes of contention and "raucous activism." Not fully accounted for by these scholars, though, is that matters of conflict are intimately linked to issues of control; and the question of where control should reside in Portland's NA program has always been contested. Moreover, the outcome of this contest has varied not only over time but also by place; neighborhood districts have varied significantly in terms of their ability and inclination to sustain a challenge to downtown control.

Thus the parameters of a "civic dialectic," or its conceptual cousin, "routinized policy making" (Berry et al. 1993), have been in nearly constant flux since the inception of Portland's NA ethos. To understand shifts occurring throughout the program's history, the question of control first must be theorized adequately. In accordance with the concerns already stated, a fundamental premise proposed here is that Portland's NA program has undergone significant change over the course of its history. Related to this premise is the following set of theoretic propositions:

1. Change within Portland's NA program can be understood as a *dialectical process* within which several forces are at play. These forces operate within and across four principal domains that form discrete venues lying between Portland's downtown and its neighborhoods. These venues include the political center (city council), a periphery (ONI, along with development agencies), a subperiphery (DCs), and a target (NAs).

2. Although there are competing forces within each domain, a lasting feature of Portland's NA program has been (and shall continue to be) a primary tension that derives from an enduring pull toward the center on one side of this continuum (or downtown control of the program), and toward the target on the other side (neighborhood control over the program). This tension stems from competing and antithetical imperatives at each end of the NA program. Forging consensus is the predominant imperative for NAs and DCBs; as such, *emergent process* issues drive their agendas. The center (city council) and periphery (ONI and various development and service bureaus) face the imperative of arriving at conclusions and implementing policies; as such, the sorting and ranking of *service imperatives* drives downtown agendas. The former struggle to reach agreement, the latter seek to standardize and routinize decision making: the grassroots versus the bureaucracy.

3. Shifts or key events in the NA program's history can be understood as efforts to restore balance to this tension over control and definition of the program.

4. A fundamental ambiguity in the program exists over how roles and responsibilities are to be equitably and prudently assigned.

5. This ambiguity has served to both vitalize and threaten the program. It vitalizes the program by enlisting NA participants who are granted a certain prerogative in defining terms for engagement, thereby enabling a degree of innovation and flexibility in how the program is carried out. But this ambiguity threatens the program when terms for engagement are viewed as inequitable or imprudent in some way, or to the point of eliciting strong and sometimes misguided challenge. Challenge may originate from any of the four principal venues already identified here.

6. To limit the potential damage stemming from outward conflict, the stakeholders within the NA program have adapted to a "control/counter control" dynamic whereby outward displays of consensus punctuate ongoing control struggles. These contests revolve, principally, between the periphery (ONI) and subperiphery (DCBs). This is where the enduring tension between center and target has been smoldering over the course of the program's history.

## The Five Epochs

The next sections of this chapter summarize the five epochs through which Portland's NA program has evolved since 1974. These summaries are presented from the viewpoint of ONA/ONI's various directors since they have served as a central locus of change and adaptation.

### Capacity Building: The Program's First 10 Years, 1974–1984

ONA's first director, Mary Pederson, faced significant obstacles in launching Portland's NA program. First, she had to operate within a climate of two-pronged distrust. Furthermore, the challenges she faced called for solutions that, at first glance, appeared contraindicated.

On the one hand, Pederson had to dispel the suspicions of existing neighborhood groups that ONA was a front for downtown control. On the other hand, she had to demonstrate to the city council that her program had sufficient backing in the community to warrant the council's ongoing support. The first case would suggest working closely with indigenous groups in order to foster necessary trust and buy in for the program. The second case would require mobilizing new NA groups in a way that signaled to council members that the program addressed a latent demand. Yet, in mobilizing new NAs, especially in circumstances of close proximity to existing groups, ONA's efforts would appear to diminish the authority of indigenous community leadership: ONA would face criticism that it was out to "divide and conquer."

Within this context, Pederson worked diligently to see that neighborhood concerns were made sufficiently visible that the city council, as well as downtown bureaus, would have to take notice. Her administration therefore worked from a "capacity building" logic. Pederson drew support and assistance in these efforts from several sources, most notably the sympathetic efforts of Mayor Neil Goldschmidt and his staff, with whom she shared a close working relationship. Both Pederson and Goldschmidt were individuals passionate about public service and very able tacticians. Although they viewed the role of NA activity quite differently—and, in fundamental ways, antagonistically—there was a strong congruence between their efforts to see that the program succeeded.

Upon leaving her post, Mary Pederson expressed concerns to her boss, Charles Jordan, then city commissioner-in-charge of ONA, about the direction the agency needed to take to consolidate the gains it had made during its first five years. Central among these were the needs to build the capacity of district staff as well as the leadership skills of NA participants. Also noted were the needs to establish a regular (annual or biennial) process for goal setting, as well as the codification into city ordinance of the budget advisory process. Patti Jacobsen, who had worked closely at ONA with Pederson since 1974, undertook these recommendations in earnest.

Jacobsen's administrative style was well suited to this task. Her soft-touch management skills would often be compared to Mary Pederson's brisk, intellectual, and frequently confrontational approach. As much as possible, Jacobsen administered from a "relational" basis. Jacobsen inherited the lingering suspicion of downtown from neighborhood activists with whom Pederson had had to contend. But unlike Pederson, Jacobsen faced the necessity of grooming activists into a more administrative role. Since the various parts of the City differed in their capacity and inclination to assume more formal contract relations with ONA, there was no "standard" approach available for inculcating a sense of contractor accountability and responsibility. Coupled with this was an often indignant attitude taken by NA and DC leadership who viewed ONA contract dollars as entitlement funding. This outlook has remained thematic and problematic until the present day, and is, in a sense, encoded into the program. But Jacobsen's approach to this dynamic was unique. Capacity building under Jacobsen involved a degree of "hand holding" that subsequent directors would, for a variety of reasons, be loathe to undertake.[7]

### Institution Building: 1984–1989

ONA's third director, Sarah Newhall, entered the post roughly concurrent with Bud Clark's mayoral victory against incumbent Frank Ivancie, ending an era against which Mayor Goldschmidt had first mobilized in the early 1970s. Ivancie had been the last scion of what Portland's 1970s activist vanguard viewed as the city's "old boy's club." Bud Clark's decisive victory signaled that liberal populist sentiment had not withered in Portland in spite of the conservative backlash, ascendant in many other U.S. cities, and emblematic of the Reagan presidency—a backlash that would play a central role in dismantling citizen involvement programs around the country (Berry et al. 1993).

Newhall's administration pursued several initiatives that, though in some ways carried forth the programmatic adjustments undertaken by Jacobsen, ended up markedly shifting ONA's focus.[8] Most notable among these was a set of "ONA Guidelines" that specified in detail, for the first time in the program's history, the roles and responsibilities of ONA's various stakeholder groups. These shifts were in part triggered by events beyond Newhall's control, including a heated neighborhood dispute at the Central Northeast Neighbors DC over the siting of a Fred Meyer Superstore, catalyzing a crisis of identity for the ONA; an NA boundary dispute within the Northeast DC; brimming conflict surrounding the North Portland DCB; and the reaction against annexation in East Portland. Besides these, Newhall was forced, early in 1981, to head off a budget battle that—as with the Ivancie effort in 1983— threatened to halve the ONA program by doing away with the DC offices.

Newhall's responses to these challenges signaled a clear shift of direction and outlook from the Jacobsen era, notably with regard to formalizing ONA/DCB relations. Whereas Jacobsen had hoped to achieve some of the same goals through building relationships within the system, Newhall initiated a regulatory response to external (political) and internal (organizational) issues then threatening the NA program.

Besides standardizing relationships within the program, Newhall supported ONA staff efforts to strengthen the role and stature of the BACs. Patti Jacobsen's administration inaugurated the BAC structure, but her efforts to push for BAC influence were not a decisive feature of her administrative strategy. At the time that she supervised ONA, the BAC program was still relatively small. But by 1986, shoring up the BAC process fit well with Newhall's institution-building aspirations. Linked together, the BAC program and the routinization of ONA/DCB relations won for ONA a manifest institutional profile in city politics.

Fatefully, the formal stature the DC boards acquired as a result of the ONA guidelines did not give rise to the more democratic practice Newhall and her supporters had hoped for; rather; interest group processes, as anticipated by critics of Newhall's guidelines agenda, often compelled alliances between DC office staff and key DCB activists. This was triggered in part as a result of the premium ONA placed upon contract compliance as it endeavored to actualize the guidelines. ONA's ongoing lament then became its inability to fulfill its stated aspirations of strengthening the program through a rule-driven approach. The tension wrought by this dynamic would come to a head for ONA's next director and would drive ONA reform efforts for the next several years.

### Retrenchment: 1989–1993

The 1988 budget skirmish between ONA and the Office of Finance and Administration (OF&A) was followed by a significant alteration in ONA's programmatic obligations. Beginning in July 1988, ONA took on responsibility for staffing three citizen commissions that had previously been served by the City's Bureau of Human Resources (BHR), including the Portland/Metropolitan Commission on Aging, the Metropolitan Human Relations Commission, and the Youth Commission.

Following a plan first formally proposed in 1988 by then city commissioner Earl Blumenauer, the city council resolved to place these commissions under ONA's purview, stressing the concordance between ONA's citizen-focused mission and the citizen makeup and advocacy orientation of the three human resources commissions. Rachel Jacky, previously director of the now dissolved BHR, was installed as ONA director in March 1989, under Mayor Bud Clark. Jacky served under Clark until ONA, in January 1991, was shifted to the portfolio of newly elected commissioner Gretchen Kafoury, under whom Jacky would serve until leaving ONA in November 1993.[9]

Jacky's tenure was one of the most difficult periods in ONA's history. Jacky had to deal with suspicion from within the ranks of NA activists for her association with the BHR. Although having received approval by the ONA BAC, many NA leaders were suspicious of the transfer of the advocacy commissions, fearing it signaled a drift in ONA's mission away from its historic role of NA support and toward human services delivery.

Resistance to a service delivery function for ONA had been long-standing, dating to the origins of the program. These concerns were exacerbated during the 1980s budget woes. There was also increasing pressure from the city council to enact the provisions of an intergovernmental agreement with Multnomah County that called for a swap of service delivery obligations.[10] Resentment over this transfer simmered and reemerged, and suspicion about Jacky's affiliation with the process would linger throughout her time at ONA.

Budget cutting in 1991 following the passage of Oregon's property tax limitation initiative, Measure 5, strained to the limit ONA's relations with the DCBs and fostered renewed resentment over ONA's obligations to deal with BHR functions. Beginning first in spring 1990, rancor over DCB contract negotiations between the West–Northwest DC and ONA triggered another round of DCB discontent, which peaked during FY 91–92 budget negotiations the following year, in May 1991. The contract dispute garnered support for West–Northwest from around the City against Jacky and ONA's commissioner-in-charge, Gretchen Kafoury.

Finally, simmering North Portland community politics came to a boil between fall 1991 and February 1992, leading eventually to a lawsuit against Jacky, Kafoury, and several North Portland DC members. Ironically, one of Jacky's major accomplishments was to help cobble together a hybrid service delivery arrangement in North Portland that, though by several accounts was quite successful, would be anathema to Tufts's valorization of Portland's DCB model.

### Recapturing, Recasting: 1993–1998

Two issues dominated the agenda of ONA's next director, Diane Linn: East Portland neighborhood politics, and another round of ONA soul searching, the 1995 ONA Task Force on Neighborhood Involvement (TFNI). The latter would also deliver subsequent ONA guidelines revisions and new rule making.

Linn entered ONA at a moment when East Portland NA politics had reached a new plateau of intensity. Thus, before she even had time to take a compass reading, she found herself mired in mid–Multnomah County politics. The Task Force therefore served, in part, as an exit strategy out of the East Portland morass in which Linn was embroiled throughout her tenure. Although ONA woes with East Portland would play an important part in establishing an agenda for Linn vis-à-vis the Task Force undertaking, other forces would also propel that phase of ONA introspection.

On the surface, the TFNI seems analogous to Newhall's rule-making efforts between 1985 and 1987. Both efforts were triggered by crises confronting Portland's NA institution. In Linn's case, NA skirmishing in East Portland, particularly over NA boundary disputes, had for the previous two years absorbed tremendous ONA time and effort. Formal grievance piled upon grievance, and threats of lawsuit by East Portland activists against ONA either as a target or caught in the crossfire, sustained intense pressure on Linn. Continuing drift in the program and ongoing DCB disgruntlement and intransigence stemming from the unresolved bouts with former ONA director Rachel Jacky and

Commissioner Kafoury, along with the uneasy acceptance by long-time NA activists of the North Portland "model," continued to fray NA/DCB/ONA relations. Also, antagonism between the Portland Police Bureau and DCBs over control of the City's community policing program had grown steadily since that program's inception in 1990. In addition, clear signals of new alignments between downtown policymakers and development interests, beginning around 1991 and continuing throughout the decade, signaled NA and DCB activists that their role in the land use development review process was increasingly uncertain.[11]

Newhall had tried to consolidate the NA program by specifying roles and allocating necessary coercive powers, by which activists could gain some needed control over their agenda-setting activities. She had wanted and sought to define a regulatory framework for the NA edifice; moreover, she made this part of her agenda quite apparent. Linn's approach, under significant guidance from Commissioner Charlie Hales (then ONA's commissioner-in-charge) took a different tack.[12] Whereas Newhall kept the stakeholder interests deliberately narrow as she set out to establish a mandate for reforming Portland's NA program, Linn—following Hales's direction—sought to enlarge the ONA "tent" to incorporate new stakeholder groups. Newhall based her "gambit" upon constituting a rule-based regime built upon the logic of DCB administration. Linn likewise staged a gambit, but with different parameters. Enlarging ONA's purview—by codifying new stakeholder interests and redefining the terms of engagement by which the program operated—enabled Linn to recapture Portland's citizen participation institution. The imperatives Newhall faced compelled her to build an institution; the pressures bearing upon Linn compelled her to reshape it.

### Present Tense: Soul Searching, Round Five

In one analysis, the innovations undertaken by ONA in the mid-1980s under Newhall's administration constituted the first round of what would become a cyclical pattern of soul searching for Portland's NA institution, which would cycle back intermittently over the next two decades. Beginning in 1992–93, following raucous jostling between Rachel Jacky and a coalition of DCB activists, then again in 1995–96 with the Task Force on Neighborhood Involvement, NA stakeholder groups would grow accustomed to a recursive exercise in identity formation and reformation.

Portland's latest round of soul searching occurred over the summer of 2003. Dubbed the "Public Involvement Standards Task Force" by then

ONI commissioner Jim Francesconi, this process took its cue from rising disgruntlement among NA and DCB stalwarts that the NA involvement process has become increasingly bureau-defined. Whereas some bureaus have operated in an open and accessible fashion, including regularly updating and informing NAs through online and other media, several bureaus have seemed to NAs ever more secretive and intransigent, triggering the long-standing suspicion of activists that they have been relegated to rubber-stamping decisions made by downtown bureaucratic elites. The thrust of this effort is to craft a set of standards each bureau would follow in dealing with NA requests. But City staff have felt put on the spot. A "standards" approach signals to them potential lawsuits for malfeasance, with staff vulnerable to scapegoating in the process.

The notion of "cycles" evokes an image of regularity, as in the return of a set of conditions that replays itself following some sort of wave frequency pattern. Thus in this latest round of soul searching, activists are asserting perennial claims of "not enough," "too late," and "inauthentic" public involvement processes. At one level, this cycling of concerns indicates the health and vitality of Portland's NA institution, a body politic that is vigorous and alive to improvement and possibilities. As Commissioner Gretchen Kafoury once declared, in the face of vigorous DCB discontent, "I'd rather have citizens criticize than say nothing at all."

There also appears to be an awareness of the need to signal the importance of interest groups whose involvement in Portland's NA institution has been mostly nominal: youth, ethnic immigrants (from Central America and Southeast Asia), and Portland's African American community. Each of these groups shares one common and poignant set of impacts on their lives: Portland's ever rising housing costs, both driven by and reinforcing gentrification, and the increasing displacement of working class groups from central city neighborhoods.

It may be a mistake to view these forces as merely the recycling of NA disenfrachisement and reenfranchisment, as merely another spin of Portland's dialectic of control between citizens and City. Portland is not the city it was when its maverick mayor, Neil Goldschmidt, realized what a potent influence an NA institution could serve in restoring Portland's hegemony within a metropolitan region facing imminent decline in the 1970s. At that time, Goldschmidt was able to craft a simple message that would govern his political tactics for seven years: "Downtown and neighborhoods need one another." The city Goldschmidt faced then was geographically much smaller than it is today, not yet having acquired East Portland. Nor had it begun to absorb the burgeoning non-English-speaking immigrant population, which is now such a vibrant part of the city, beginning with Southeast Asian immigrants following the Vietnam War, then Russian and Hispanic immigration throughout the 1990s.

By the early 1990s, Portland had achieved more than it dared dream possible in 1973. For the most part, its central city neighborhoods had bounced back dramatically (see Chap. 8, Abbott). Housing values were steady and rising, shored up in large part by immigration of California settlers driven northward by the allure of Portland's still deflated housing market relative to the slump in California real estate, which followed the state's loss of defense-based revenue in the early 1990s (see Chap. 9, Howe). This process would also drive, and be driven by, an invigorated retail industry catering increasingly to the lifestyle preferences of postindustrial America: upscale restaurants and retail establishments rooted and flourished in Portland's oldest commercial districts, all but abandoned in the early 1970s.

Portland's city council, once wary of Goldschmidt's vision, and openly suspicious of NAs, would by the early 1990s fully assimilate what might facetiously be called Portland's doctrine of Manifest Density. In so doing, the city council found itself on the receiving end of an increasingly restive NA contingent, whose disgruntlement would derive only partially from the age-old democratic discontent with process. A major theme of the battle between downtown and NAs in the 1990s was captured in the NA chorus of "Enough already!": enough traffic, enough parking problems, and enough growth pressures invited by an overzealous density doctrine (see Chap. 10, Chapman and Lund).

It is within this context that Portland's most recent round of soul searching needs to be considered. NA institution building and rebuilding was, in the 1970s and 1980s, largely driven by the administrative entrepreneurialism of ONA's various directors. Starting with Pederson, then Jacobsen and Newhall, city council had in large part depended upon its ONA directors to sort out the various administrative and process concerns that defined the NA enterprise. Beginning with Rachel Jacky, the council began to confront the NA institution more directly. It was also noteworthy that the Standards Task Force was announced by a coalition of three council members. Never before has any ONA soul searching drawn such a broad city council profile.

Some observers close to this process have commented that this latest round of reflexive engagement signals an increasing drift from the moorings that Portland's NA ethos once depended upon. These critics point to several sources of concern. Some trace what they view as the decline of an independent NA voice to the Newhall regime, which, in this view, emphasized procedure in a fashion that invited top-down control of NA activity. For these critics, the Standards Task Force is merely a bureaucratic impulse to control neighborhood-based initiative and activism. In this analysis, the Task Force initiative is another manifestation of a creeping bureaucratization of the NA ethos. This viewpoint pegs the beginning of Portland's NA demise to the reform initiatives of Sarah Newhall, and to a tendency since that time to view NAs as sources of bureaucratic legitimacy, not as agents in their own right focused on challenging downtown-driven agendas.

Other critics point out the failure of Portland leadership to define and seize a rhetorical high ground that could help sort and order the hyperpluralism of interest group skirmishing in a city that is now more than ever a mosaic of balkanizing interests, lifestyles, income brackets, and ethnic identities.

## Auguring Not Well: Tax Revolt and Metropolitan Balkanization

Oregonians are not likely to draw parallels between their world and Southern California. But since 1999, Los Angeles has embarked on developing a neighborhood involvement structure that aspires, in many respects, to achieve the stature Portland's system has attained for outsiders looking in. And though Oregonians are likely to insist that comparisons end at that point, there is little doubt that the tax revolts that roiled Southern California in the 1970s were harbingers of the same fiscal tremors that would rock Oregon in the 1990s.

Los Angeles's courtship with NAs (there called Neighborhood Councils) cannot be fully explained without taking account of the "fiscalization" of land usage that would result from California's property tax limitation legislation of the 1970s. This chapter is not the place to depict this history in any detail. But the enduring criticism of Los Angeles's management of NA building has been that public involvement boosterism originated in large part as a downtown initiative intended to head off the threat posed by the San Fernando Valley, whose secessionist aspirations drew heavily from antitaxation, anti–big city doctrine, and attendant race-based undertones (Diaz 2002, Hogen-Esch 1998). Los Angeles's antagonism toward this push can only partially be explained as an impulse for political hegemony within the region. Thirty years of hobbled property tax revenue has made the City of Los Angeles heavily dependent upon maintaining its geographic base against a surge of secessionist sentiment. According to this perspective, Los Angeles's neighborhood organizing efforts were intended to signal good faith intentions to be responsive to its citizenry. But since its inception this process has been dogged by claims that a top-down, heavily politicized leadership style signals mostly rhetorical interest in neighborhood mobilization, intended more to subvert secessionist claims of governmental nonresponsiveness than to build an authentically democratic, neighborhood-based public involvement system.

Did Oregon's property tax revolts of the 1990s stiffen downtown Portland's resolve to retain control of urban growth politics? Most likely. And would this serve to foster the creeping bureaucratization of the NA edifice under the banner of this or that soul-searching effort? Complaints about nonresponsiveness do not in themselves prove anything. As Commissioner Kafoury observed, complaints mean people care. Moreover, complaints assume a faith that things could be better, that improvement is possible. From this perspective, Portland most likely retains the dynamism necessary to propel a "civic dialectic," the *deus ex machina* that Putnam and his colleagues believe explains Portland's civic magic. Still, nothing fails like success. The simplicity of the Goldschmidt doctrine that "neighborhoods and downtown need one another" is nowhere evident in current discourse about what Portland should do next.

Observing Portland's then infant NA institution in 1976, Pacific University professor Russ Dondero (1976) commented, "CP [citizen participation] is a part of Portland's political 'equilibrium'—it is beyond dismantling." Several years later, Portland historian Carl Abbott (1983) would observe:

> If past experience in the public metropolis is a predictor of the future, [Portland] residents can expect planning efforts to arise from both local governments and private groups. The future will belong to leaders who can bring together grassroots activists and members of the civic elite in new coalitions for the improvement of Portland's metropolitan environment and the lives of its citizens. (277)

History has yet to determine if Portland's leadership will find ways to incorporate an ever more complex citizenry into the routines of local decision making as this city embarks on the challenges of being a "success."

NOTES

1. Though many case studies of neighborhood-based planning activity have been undertaken over the last 30 years, the Tufts study was the first to undertake a study of nationwide scope. The extent of its sampling procedure and extensive survey efforts were also groundbreaking. In total, the study was eight years in production.

2. Formerly the Office of Neighborhood Associations.

3. Member NAs are geographically contiguous. Portland's system conforms to a set of wedge-shaped districts emanating, for the most part, from the downtown core.

4. The emerging conflict in North and East Portland was the catalyst for a dissertation (Witt 2000), which found that organizational dynamics were central forces driving Portland's changing relationship to NA involvement.

5. Portland's city council consists of four commissioners and the mayor. All members are elected to at-large seats. The mayor has the authority to assign bureau portfolios as she sees fit, and may reshuffle these assignments at her pleasure. Portland lacks a city manager's office, as such; city council members serve as "demi" city managers for the bureaus within their portfolios.

6. Both the Central Northeast Neighbors (CNN) and the West Northwest Review Board have experienced fairly intensive internal turmoil. In the case of CNN, the board briefly disbanded in 1987 but then soon after reformed. Though never actually disbanding, the West Northwest Review Board sought mediation in 1995 following a year of division and antagonism on its board.

7. This would take various forms. A key feature of Jacobsen's approach would involve engendering a sense of *esprit de corps* among DC office coordinators. This served two functions. It signaled office staff that ONA would support them when necessary—in several key instances in the face of district board member disputes and staff scapegoating. Courting staff also laid the groundwork for slowly building the trust of key DC leadership. These efforts would face obstacles, however, as funding inequities across DCs would strain relations among district office coordinators.

8. Newhall came to ONA following her work at the Center for Urban Education (CUE), which provided outreach and assistance to immigrant populations. Throughout the early and mid-1980s, Portland had undergone waves of migration from southeast Asian and eastern European countries, and the CUE served a kind of settlement house function for these dislocated groups.

9. Jacky had started at the BHR in mid-1985, following her work as program director at the Center for Urban Education (CUE). Like Sarah Newhall, Jacky had also grown as an activist working on refugee resettlement issues in Portland prior to taking the ONA director's post.

10. Under Resolution A, the City of Portland would phase out its human service obligations and the County would phase out road and sewer development services.

11. These were eventually codified by Mayor Vera Katz's "Blueprint 2000" and aggressively endorsed and implemented by Commissioner Charlie Hales.

12. Hales had been elected, with Mayor Vera Katz, in 1992. Hales had been a lobbyist for the Portland Metropolitan Home Builders Association. He had also served as President of the Hayhurst NA in Southwest Portland. Hales requested and received from Katz a portfolio including ONA and the Bureau of Planning.

REFERENCES

Abbott, Carl. 1983. *Portland: Planning, Politics, and Growth in a Twentieth-Century City*. Lincoln: University of Nebraska Press.

Berry, Jeffery, Kent E. Portney, and Ken Thomson. 1993. *The Rebirth of Urban Democracy*. Washington, DC: The Brookings Institution.

Diaz, David. 2002. *Neighborhood Council and Minority Communities in Los Angeles: Will the History of Racism in Planning Negate the Promise of the Program?* Los Angeles: Center for Southern California Studies, College of Social and Behavioral Sciences.

Dondero, Russ. 1976. Memorandum to Neil Goldschmidt, August 7. In private document collection of Carl Abbott, Portland State University.

Hogen-Esch, Thomas J. 1998. *Race, Class, and the Formation of Enclave Consciousness: A Comparative Analysis of Urban Secession Movements in Los Angeles, New York, Boston, and Seattle*. Los Angeles: Center for Southern California Studies, College of Social and Behavioral Sciences.

Putnam, Robert, Lewis Feldstein, and Don Cohen. 2003. *Better Together: Restoring the American Community*. New York: Simon & Schuster.

Witt, Matthew. 2000. Dialectics of control: The origins and evolution of conflict in Portland's neighborhood association program. Unpublished Ph.D. diss., Portland State University.

# 5 | The Myth and Reality of Portland's Engaged Citizenry and Process-Oriented Governance

Steven Reed Johnson

It is widely accepted that Portland is a city of engaged citizens and that government agencies routinely involve citizens in public policy debates and public works, even at times at great cost and considerable frustration.

In *Better Together*, Putnam and Feldstein (2003) dedicate an entire chapter to Portland, where there has been, in their words, "a positive epidemic of civic engagement." Putnam argues that in the early 1970s metropolitan Portland looked virtually identical to other American metropolitan areas (including Seattle) in civic terms. Two decades later Portland suburbs, by Putnam's measure, were roughly two to three times more civic than comparable suburbs elsewhere, and Portland proper had become roughly three to four times more civic than comparable U.S. cities. For example, 21% of Portlanders attended at least one public meeting on town or school affairs in 1974, compared to 22% for comparable cities. By the early 1990s, the figure for the rest of the country had dropped to 11%, whereas in Portland it had risen from 30 to 35%.

The exceptionalism of Portland's civic life is one significant reason for the city's reputation as a well-planned city with a lively downtown and a strong creative community. Newspaper reporters and magazine writers have praised Portland as a "progressive" place where all the neighborhoods are handsome, new development is respectful of its context, and all the planners are above average.

However, trouble is brewing in Puddletown. An examination of civic trends since the 1950s in Portland suggests the upward surge of civic participation Putnam documented has begun to slow. While some indicators, as Putnam documents, reflect Portland's strong civic life, public discourse has become more contentious, and the City of Portland itself has undercut support for citizen involvement programs.

There's a sense that many civic issues are polarized, with wide uncivil divisions among citizens, and between citizens and local government. Among the divisions are urban versus rural, central city versus suburbs, west versus east Multnomah County (clearly split on the recent vote for an additional tax to save schools). There are new urban enclaves that make electoral consensus over critical issues difficult, such as reverse commuters who live in downtown and work in Silicon Forest west of Portland; they support culture and Starbucks but not necessarily schools and social services. There are many ways to divide Portlanders, but so few effective ways to bridge these differences that Portland is on the brink of losing its civic exceptionalism.

Portland's rise in civic stature is extraordinary by any standard. It is even more astounding if you picture Portland in the 1950s, a strikingly dull and derivative city, only a restaurant or two above a logging town. Civic Portland circa 1950s is summed up by a photograph of Portland's Redevelopment Board, a predecessor to the Portland Development Commission, Portland's urban renewal agency: all men, sitting around a rectangular table, in suits and ties, ashtrays lined up like today's water bottles (see Chap. 3, Gibson). It was a Pleasantville kind of place, if you were male, white, Christian, and patriotic. Urban renewal, a tool the city has used to spectacular effect in the last three decades, was itself suspect in those days. A city commissioner at the time noted that it was "the very essence of communism" (Humphrey 1955).

In the 1950s over 60% of all the civic organizations in Portland were clubs: women's clubs, ethnic social clubs, fraternities, and sororities. There was a virtual army of women roaming the civic byways in those days: 600 women's clubs, with at least 18,000 (about one out of ten women in Portland) members involved in civic activities. The repertoire of civic actions in the 1950s of civic organizations was relatively limited. In a news sample from 1960 (still soundly the 1950s in terms of civic life) the most often reported activities were the election of officers, accounting for 25%, and education forums, 33%. The two activities accounted for 58% of all the reported news by civic groups. Other traditional civic actions, including fund-raising, benefits, and honors and awards, made up an additional 29% of the news. The remainder of activities (13%) included a handful of advocacy actions, neighborhood actions, participation in hearings, and conducting studies or developing plans—all actions that became much more important to civic players during and after the civic reconstruction period (1967–1975). Even as late as 1969, the *Oregon Journal* summarized the activities of women's clubs in terms of the goodwill they generated by raising "funds from bake sales, rummage sales or book sales with proceeds earmarked for hospitals, schools, nursing homes, or any of a thousand other places where there's a need." The editors also noted, that "along with self-improvement the professionally oriented woman is concerned about her community. Climbing the business ladder is vertical, but alert and aware women are constantly challenged to reach out horizontally to help others" (Salute to Women 1969).

The city was run by white men. Citizen involvement was achieved by rounding up the usual elites, professionals, and elected officials. Abbott summarizes the process of neighborhood planning between 1957 and 1967: " . . . as straightforward as its content. City Planning Commission reports make no reference to neighborhood groups or citizen involvement. They were prepared by city employees for their colleagues in city hall. . . . During Terry Schrunk's first three terms as mayor (1957–1972) planners worked from the top down, applying professional values and expertise to small-scale problems and informing local residents of the resulting proposals" (Abbott 1983). An examination of city authorized citizen involvement through commissions, boards, and advisory committees, reveals no participation by minorities. In fact a 1967 City Club (City Club 1967) report on race in Portland identified only one civic body, other than the emerging Model Cities Program, that had black representation. This was the Metropolitan Relations Commission, which the City Club committee accused of being a public relations arm of the mayor's office. Women likewise were dramatically underrepresented in civic politics. Of the 711 members of City of Portland civic bodies (all commissions, citizen advisory committees, and professional licensing boards) in 1960, 591 were men (71%). Women were also channeled into specific civic niches. Of the total of 120 women on civic boards in 1960, about half (58 of 120) served on five commissions: The Arts Commission, Metropolitan Youth Commission, Zoo Commission, Pittock Mansion Commission, and Japanese Garden Commission, all valued civic institutions, but hardly comparable to more powerful commissions such as the Planning Commission, Portland Development

Commission, or Housing Commission on all of which there were only 10 women out of a total roster of 53.

Civic life in Portland went through a dramatic change in the later part of the 1960s and early 1970s. The city endured civic unrest, in its own mild form commensurate with its mild climate and homogeneous population. As in the rest of the country during this time, antiwar protesters took to the street, and in Portland's diminutive "ghetto" in northeast Portland a couple of nights of unrest in the late 1960s, hardly comparable to the riots of back east cities, unsettled the establishment. A strike at Portland State College (now University) was put down with a show of force that pitted the civic establishment against the brokers of academic freedom. A curfew was established in certain city parks, and drug busts were increased to limit the insurgence of freedom-loving young people, a part of the newly constituted "counter culture."

As in other communities, overt actions on the streets in the form of protests and demonstrations declined during the 1970s. The alumni of social movements in the 1960s refocused their attention from demonstrations to institutionalizing social movement ideals in the civic infrastructure of Portland. (For an example of the institutionalization of social movement ideas, see Chap. 6, Sussman and Estes.) Table 5.1, a comparison of the civic organization population in Portland between 1960 and 1972, reveals the dynamics of the civic revolution.

By 1972 traditional civic organizations still made up 30% of the total population of civic groups in Portland, combined with labor (15% of the total population), and business associations (17%), the mainstay of traditional civic life accounted for 62% of the total population of civic groups. The most dramatic shift in the population of civic groups is the

### Table 5.1
*Total number of civic organizations in 1960 and 1972*

|  | 1960 | 1972 | Total Loss or Gain |
|---|---|---|---|
| Advocacy | 31 | 184 | 153 |
| Arts and culture | 19 | 58 | 39 |
| Business | 174 | 195 | 21 |
| Labor | 164 | 172 | 8 |
| Social services | 124 | 199 | 75 |
| Traditional civic | 370 | 341 | −29 |
| TOTAL | 882 | 1149 | 267 |

SOURCE: Original

rise of advocacy groups, from 31 in 1960 to 184 in 1972, a fourfold increase. However, looking only at the total population of civic groups does not reveal the fundamental change under way in civic life in Portland. The best way to understand the more complex cycle of the civic organizations is to not just examine total numbers, but to analyze each sector in terms of births, deaths, and survivors. Figure 5.1 reveals the percentages of types of groups made up of surviving organizations and new ones. In 1972, the advocacy and arts and culture sectors were made up mostly of new organizations. The birthrate of advocacy was twice that of traditional civic organizations. The other sectors were made up of almost equal numbers of new groups and survivors. The population dynamics of civic organizations in Portland also reflects the civic tension that shows up in a more careful examination of civic events during this period. In simple terms, both traditional and the new civic worlds coexisted, sometimes in stubborn or belligerent opposition, and in other ways as though existing in parallel universes.

The alumni of the social movements, which in some ways worked together in an idealistic ether and in other ways on separate identity and issue tracks (feminism, environment, minority rights), attempted at times to storm the gates of the existing civic institutions. For the most part they were turned away. It would take years for women and minorities to break regulatory boundaries, let alone more subtle social and psychological ones, to even enter civic spaces such as the City Club of Portland, or the exclusive social clubs such as the Arlington Club.

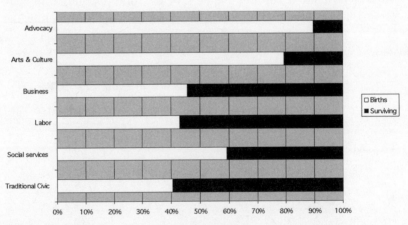

FIGURE 5.1. Organizations Born and Surviving in Portland, 1960–1972.
Source: Original.

It is interesting to note that, although the population of traditional civic organizations held their own in 1972 in terms of total numbers, a content analysis of news about civic organizations at the same time reveals how attention shifted away from traditional civic organizations. In 1960 advocacy organizations only accounted for 4% of the news while traditional civic groups accounted for 48% of the news. In 1972 it was reversed, with advocacy accounting for 50% of the news, and traditional civic organizations only accounting for 7%. It is important to note, however, that the drop in news about traditional civic organizations was accompanied by a drop in the population of traditional civic groups. In contrast, the number of advocacy groups increased fourfold, while the news about advocacy organizations increased over 12-fold.

The reconstruction of civic life in Portland was further propelled by new federal, state, and local programs like Model Cities, that mandated public participation (see Table 5.2). In 1964, the Office of Economic Opportunity (OEO) was created by Congress to lead the charge for President Johnson's War on Poverty. How cities around the country interpreted the new mandates for federal funding, which included facilitating maximum participation of the affected residents, dramatically affected the physical outcome of the urban renewal efforts and the local civic infrastructure.

The Albina neighborhood in northeast Portland, which contained the city's largest concentration of African Americans, was a Model Cities target area. In the early 1960s the Albina Neighborhood Council and the Community Council (previously, the Community Welfare Council) conducted an inventory and survey of agencies in northeast Portland in order to develop a proposal from Albina to secure OEO funding. In October 1964, a neighborhood service center for Albina was proposed, and an Albina Community Action Plan was drawn up. The action plan was submitted to the Portland Metropolitan Steering Committee, Portland's newly formed coordinating body for OEO actions. In February 1965, the Albina group, calling itself the Albina Citizens War on Poverty Committee (ACWPC), was recognized as the official representative for OEO programs in Albina.

The formation of the ACWPC, under the guidance of the community council, followed an interagency track to develop the Albina plan to combat poverty. The members of the original group were for the most part agency representatives, not lay citizens. It was expected that each participating agency would submit its own ideas and needs, which would be consolidated into one overall application to the federal OEO

## Table 5.2
*Changing rules governing citizen's right to participate in public policy deliberations*

| | |
|---|---|
| 1946 | Administrative Procedure Act: requires review of governmental actions by affected parties |
| 1954 | Federal Urban Renewal Act: calls for local advisory groups to be established |
| 1964 | Federal Economic Opportunity Act: requires antipoverty boards to be created with maximum participation of residents of affected area |
| 1966 | Quie amendment: requires specific make-up of antipoverty boards be at least one-third poor |
| 1966 | Model Cities programs: continue federal requirement that citizens be involved in federal programs |
| 1966 | Freedom of Information Act |
| 1969 | National Environmental Policy Act: requires citizen involvement in environmental impact assessments |
| 1972 | Clean Water Act: includes extensive citizen involvement procedures |
| 1972 | Oregon public meetings law: outlines rights of citizens to be notified of and be present at wide range of public meetings |
| 1972 | Coastal Zone Management Act: includes extensive procedures for citizen involvement |
| 1972 | *Sierra Club v. Morton:* eliminates the so-called direct injury requirement, legitimizing class action suits |
| 1973 | Ford Foundation: provides grants to establish public interest law firms |
| 1973 | Oregon statewide land use system: has primary goal of citizen involvement |
| 1974 | Portland's neighborhood system implemented: provides citywide rules and structure for citizen involvement |
| 1974 | Housing and Community Development Act: requires citizen participation for local block grants |
| 1974 | Energy Reorganization Act: includes extensive citizen involvement procedures |
| 1979 | President Carter's Executive Order 12160: calls for extensive participation in many federal programs |

SOURCE: Original

office. There were several well-established agencies involved, including the Greater Council of Churches, YMCA, YWCA, Albina Neighborhood Council, and Portland Housing Authority.

The plan originally adopted by the ACWPC was mostly developed by the interagency group established by the community council. In establishing the first official board of directors, 10 members were a part of the original committee, representing agencies, 10 members were elected as representatives who lived in the target area, and 10 more members were elected from across the city to bring experience and expertise to the board. Five member slots were left open in order to potentially increase the residential representation.

On March 2, 1968, elections for board members were held under League of Women Voters supervision. This was a milestone event in the civic history of Portland: an election of everyday citizens to oversee spending federal funds, actions that in the past had been managed behind closed doors by Portland's elected officials and civic elite. The election was announced on television and radio and in newspapers. Even a sound truck circulated through the neighborhood urging voters to cast ballots. Two candidates canvassed their district. By day's end, 1,781 residents out of a total of about 28,000, or 6.4%, had voted. Of the 16 elected from the neighborhood, 9 were black. The mayor then appointed 6 whites and 5 blacks. The final composition of the board was described as 5 unemployed women (two black women from community organizations), a black contractor, a white roofing contractor, 2 white bankers, 2 black businessmen, 2 black social workers, a black deputy sheriff, a white lawyer, a white printer, 4 clergymen (2 black), 3 elementary school teachers (2 black), a white educational administrator in a suburban school district, a black housing director (in Albina), a black job placement counselor at the Albina Neighborhood Center, and a white assistant commissioner of the Oregon Bureau of Labor. Twenty-three of the 27 were residents of the model neighborhood.

At about the same time, under progressive mayor Neil Goldschmidt, the City of Portland institutionalized the emergent neighborhood movement by creating the Office of Neighborhood Associations (see Chap. 4, Witt). This action legitimized direct democratic action at the grassroots level by allowing organized neighbors to directly influence city policies. The general policy was that recognized neighborhood associations should have a voice in "any matter affecting livability of the neighborhood, including, but not limited to, land use, zoning, housing, community facilities, human resources, social and recreational programs, traffic and transportation, environmental quality, open spaces and parks." In a few years, neighborhood associations went from unofficial status (at least outside Model City areas) to semiofficial status with a stake in land use and social services issues, and then to a legitimate stake in almost any activity in the association's geographic area of town. The number of neighborhood-based organizations grew rapidly until by the 1970s there were over 75 neighborhood associations, and a small army of activists was now armed with legitimacy and authority. During this time, through the new direct face-to-face democratic venue of neighborhoods and through more citizen advisory committees, the City of Portland created an open-door policy that changed the expectation of citizens' relationship to their local government.

In 1973, the State of Oregon implemented its landmark state land-use planning policy—Senate Bill 100—whose first goal was citizen involvement. To develop a statewide land zoning system the State embarked on a statewide kind of Chautauqua. The state mailed out over 100,000 invitations to citizens to attend workshops in 35 locations. During 1975, over 10,000 people participated in the workshops, helping to shape the land use system while also getting a crash course in land use and planning issues (Cogan 1999).

Citizen involvement took on a whole new meaning with the Model Cities grassroots approach to managing federal funds for impoverished areas, which included first and foremost the residents of the affected areas; implementation of Jeffersonian direct democratic governance through the Portland neighborhood system; and the statewide invitation to participate in creating a new land use system. In the 1950s, and before, citizen involvement meant bringing together the usual cast of elected officials and civic elite. After the reconstruction period in the late 1960s and early 1970s, Portlanders learned to expect much more. Citizens in Portland expected to be provided the opportunity to be involved in public policy on an ongoing basis, not just to elect politicians to represent their interests.

The key magic potion that Putnam ponders about Portland's exemplary civic path may be explained by these civic innovations that created a common experience of direct democracy and open government. While the civic order was in upheaval, as clearly indicated first by social movement unrest, and then by an organizational ecological shift as dramatic as the extinction of the dinosaurs, the emergent political leadership of Portland took advantage of the rising tide of civic activism; rather than resisting the new forms of collective behavior, the activists were incorporated into a larger civic umbrella.

Content analysis of news media during the period reflects a shift from street activism to this new form of civic life. By the mid-1970s through the mid-1980s civic news, in both the "straight" and "alternative" press, was dominated by stories of citizens working together through neighborhood associations, serving on citizen advisory committees, and creating new nonprofit advocacy groups. In the late 1970s and 1980s, three-fourths of the news about neighborhood action was positive in the form of stories about neighborhoods being saved, hosting block parties, and working cooperatively with city agencies to develop neighborhood visions and plans.

The City of Portland expanded its neighborhood involvement program throughout the 1970s and 1980s. By 1986, there were 23 bureau advisory committees (BACs), where citizens mucked around in the everyday business of city bureaus. The Office of Neighborhood Associations (ONA) was given the task of overseeing appointments, coordinating between BACs and their respective bureaus. Also, ONA was given the task of orientation and training. While some degree of orientation and training has always been a part of commissions, boards, and citizen advisory committees, since these citizens often had less professional expertise in bureau issues, the training needs were more intense. ONA produced background packets on city budgeting and held workshops for new members to help make their input more valuable.

The process of involving citizens through the BACs was supplemented by the Neighborhood Needs Report system, also created in the 1980s. The system allowed neighborhood associations to prioritize public works projects. The bureaus were expected to respond either with approval of the projects or explanations about why they could not currently be undertaken or might be undertaken in the future.

The BACs were labor intensive and represented the epitome of the city's investment in citizen democracy during this period. Not all bureaus responded warmly to this process, and eventually the BAC process was modified, allowing bureaus to have more control over how citizen advisory processes were established. But for the 1980s it represented the City's commitment to representative participation by more citizens.

From the 1960s to the 1970s the number of citizen advisory committees and task forces grew dramatically. While the number of boards and commissions remained more or less constant, the number of citizen advisory committees more than doubled from 27 in 1960 to 56 in 1972, and the number of task forces jumped from 5 to 25. As previously mentioned, citizen advisory groups and task forces are often short lived compared to boards and commissions. Only 8 of the 56 citizen advisory groups, and none of the task forces, were around in the 1960s. The growth of these groups represented a change in the interests of citizens, their desire to be involved in public policy issues, and the willingness of the government to offer room at the table for a broader range of citizens. While membership on commissions and boards remained relatively constant, there were almost twice as many appointments to citizen advisory committees and task forces as there were appointments to city commissions and boards (1,572 compared to 856). While civic boards and commissions tend to draw upon well-established professionals, citizen advisory committees draw from a much wider range.

The City of Portland's investment in civic engagement peaked in the 1980s and then began to decline. During the 1990s there were fewer formally sponsored citizen involvement committees and fewer appointments of "citizens at large" to participate in public policy debate and community public works projects, as illustrated by Table 5.3.

In the late 1980s and early 1990s the NIMBY (not in my backyard) phenomenon took hold in Portland and most communities around America. Instead of citizens working together from a sense of common collective goals or community vision, the period saw a rise in activists motivated by a sense of entitlement: "I've got mine, now pull up the ladder."

In the 1990s, unlike the 1970s, two-thirds of the news about neighborhood actions was negative. Headlines referred to neighborhoods as war zones: "Battle of Boise," "Long Dispute over Fire Station Resolved," "North Portland Opposes Jail," "Two Portland Victories for NIMBY Movement," etc. The neighborhood system, established to provide the city with intermediary organizations, suddenly was challenged by outside groups. Conservative lobbies such as the Pacific Legal Foundation and Cascade Policy Institute adopted techniques first developed by

**Table 5.3**

*Estimated number of citizens on City of Portland citizen advisory boards per 1,000 population*

| Decade | Portland Population | Civic Members per 1,000 |
|---|---|---|
| 1960–1969 | 373,000 | 3.1 |
| 1970–1979 | 380,000 | 4.7 |
| 1980–1989 | 366,000 | 6.6 |
| 1990–1999 | 439,000 | 4.6 |

SOURCE: Original

progressive organizations, but applied them to protecting individual property rights and limiting Oregon's land use laws. Even corporations took on the guise of citizen interest groups, forming their own "grass-roots"—or, as pundits referred to them, "Astroturf"—organizations such as the Temperate Forest Foundation.

The quantifiable changes in civic involvement in the creation of public policy can be seen as an anomaly, as a larger withdrawal from broad democratic ideals, or as an indication that citizens are once again changing their methods. Today, Portland's official civic life—indeed, much of the city's bureaucracy—is dominated by yesterday's street activists. This evolution of social activists from outside agitators to established civic players was brought home recently when a local newspaper published a series of articles about files kept by members of the Portland police force to monitor the actions of "subversives." One of the subversives they watched became the current mayor, Vera Katz, and another became one of the city's most respected commissioners, Mike Lindberg.

The outsiders are now the insiders, raising the intriguing question of how today's aging establishment will respond to young activists and newcomers (see Chap. 6, Sussman and Estes). Are the established civic organizations that displaced the civic order of the 1950s flexible and resilient enough to incorporate challenges by outsider groups, young people, and new immigrants?

New structures may provide ways to deal with these emerging challenges while still retaining the innovative character of the civic reconstruction since the 1960s.

In the early 1990s, the City of Portland invested in a strategic planning process called the Portland Future Focus. A 40-member policy committee was created, in the words of its chairperson, Hardy Myers, "to think about our city as a whole, to think about where we're heading, where we would like to head and steps we can take to get there." This kind of visioning process, also adopted by other cities and counties in the Portland region, is an increasingly popular way to bring together diverse communities of interest to develop consensus about a vision for the community. Whereas in the past this vision setting may have taken place behind closed doors amongst the civic elite, strategic planning processes like the Portland Future Focus are more open and democratic. The membership of the Future Focus reflected the changing landscape of the civic world. While business and labor interests were represented, it was also populated by citizen interest groups and social service and environmental activists. On the committee were 9 business representatives, 14 from government and schools, 1 from labor, and 16 from issue interest groups or neighborhood associations.

Watershed councils are another civic innovation with promise. There are at least 80 in Oregon, all formed in the last 10 years. The watershed councils, and less formal "friends of" watershed groups, have provided a new governance structure that has facilitated problem solving among public agencies, private businesses, land owners, and interest groups.

The story of a small urban stream in southeast Portland, beset with innumerable environmental problems that for decades defied technocratic solutions, provides a rich illustration of how the transformation of civic infrastructure contributed in critical ways to determining solutions to intractable environmental problems. Johnson Creek suffered many of the customary problems of urban streams: poor water quality, degraded habitat, and the impact of attempts to control or alter natural flooding (see Chap. 12, Ozawa and Yeakley). These conditions made the creek a thorn in the public side for decades. Several government agencies took on the issues that plagued Johnson Creek, producing 46 reports and/or plans over a 50-year period. Citizens created a storm of protest at various times, contesting the science, the cost, and government itself. One agency, Metro (Portland's regionally elected government), proposed a solution to the creek's problems, only to find itself under attack (see Chap. 2, Seltzer). A fledgling citizen group created an initiative to eliminate Metro.

It wasn't until the 1990s, when government agencies adopted a revised policy of coproducing studies and plans alongside citizens, as well as working hand-in-hand with over 175 nonprofit organizations to physically restore the watershed, that progress was finally achieved. This way of approaching public works efforts in a populist, pluralist world is tedious and time consuming. The solutions to the creek's problems have turned out to be as much social as they are environmental. Engineers and other technocrats still provide the science and engineering, but implementation is conducted within a new process regime. In many cases, citizen activists have become amateur scientists, building their civic skills of organizing and running public meetings as well as learning about the science of stream restoration. The new civic structures, such as the Johnson Creek Watershed Council, and investments by government agencies in educating the public to be better stewards of the watershed, have altered the relationship between citizens and government. This new civic infrastructure, which frames the process of policy deliberation and community service on behalf of the watershed, has taken the place of traditional civic organizations and traditional agency management practices. Working on stream restoration projects in the field as well as in innumerable workshops and public forums, citizens acquire the knowledge to be well-informed and involved citizens. People work together on public works projects across interest group boundaries.

In the mid-1990s, the Coalition for a Livable Future (CLF) formed as an alliance of 60 activist groups, including chapters of national environmental groups, affordable housing advocacy organizations, churches, and social justice organizations. The CLF conducts most of its work through seven working groups: affordable housing, economic development and urban revitalization, government investment and finance, transportation reform, urban design, national resources, and environmental justice. The CLF is a self-correcting, self-educating organization that attempts to affect the regional dialogue about urban growth through a variety of self-teaching and public education activities. It has used a variety of forms of outreach and education to meet its goals, including sponsoring speakers, hosting workshops, creating urban design charettes, sponsoring field and canoe trips, taking advantage of regional "teachable moments," slide shows, letters to the editor, white papers, conferences, presentations at conferences, coalition and working group meetings, one-on-one conversations, and testimonies. The CLF provides a vehicle for interest groups to leverage their individual power into a stronger single voice by developing shared policy statements and carrying out civic actions. The CLF allows interest groups to learn about the perspectives of other interest groups. In this way, the CLF provides a way to overcome the democratic deficiencies of single-purpose interest groups.

An even more unconventional group is the City Repair Project, formed in 1996 by a group of citizen activists who wanted to create a more community-oriented and ecologically sustainable society. The group started with an "intersection repair" project in southeast Portland where it invited neighbors to redesign a street intersection as a public square with corner kiosks, tea stations, and lending libraries all surrounding a mandala design painted in the intersection itself. City Repair has now created a half dozen such intersection projects as well as an annual weeklong celebration called the Village Building Convergence.

In all these examples of recent civic innovations it is important to understand the changing shape of the activism. To remain flexible and robust, a civic infrastructure needs to accommodate the creative energies of youth, newcomers, and challengers, and leave honorable space for civic elders.

One of the important things that Putnam and his fellow Harvard scholar Theda Skocopol point out about the character of American civic life today is that civic encounters are increasingly orchestrated by clearly defined rules of engagement but lacking in underlying social structures that allow people to overcome differences and create collective visions of community. In the good old civic days, they argue, there were more civic places and civic organizations where people met in nonadversarial settings, bridging class, political, and interest barriers.

Portland has built an exceptional civic infrastructure over the last 30 years, but as the city enters the twenty-first century the next test will be whether the collective vision can hold steady with a more diverse population and the divisive tactics of special-interest-group politics. The divides between inner-city and suburban, urban and rural, and religious and secular were narrower when Portland developed its civic life during the late 1960s and early 1970s. The continued strength of "the city that works" (Portland's motto) lies in how adroit the Portland civic establishment is at creating an innovative and inclusive approach to community dialogue. That may be dependent on how sincerely its leaders believe in what organizational theorists call the intelligence of the swarm, or in this case the citizens of the Portland region. Can the city live up to the motto inscribed on the Skidmore water fountain, "good citizens are the riches of a city"?

We believe that the ferment of civic activism of the previous generation has changed both the "vocabulary" and the "grammar" of civic life—the goals and values that are commonly accepted and the ways that decisions are made. If this is true, Portland represents a challenge not only to Putnam's thesis of a decline in civic participation but also to his concern that such declines erode the shared goals and patterns of trust that are often called "social capital."

Structural explanations do not seem to explain Portland's rich civic life. Portland is quite similar to Seattle, Denver, Austin, and Columbus in demographic structure and economic base, but it ends up with a very different style of public life. What does seem to account for Portland's distinctiveness is learned behaviors. Early successful examples of participatory action encouraged other activists and bred institutions that in turn embedded and reinforced particular styles of action. In effect, Portlanders in the last 35 years have learned the rewards and problems of active citizenship through practice.

Nevertheless, the underlying challenge for progressive Portland is whether the efflorescence of civic activism will be limited to a single generation. In places such as Birmingham and Chicago, the "civic moment" faded after a few decades as problems seemed less urgent. New groups with new issues did not find the progressive consensus open to their concerns and had little interest in celebrating past accomplishments. In effect, this is a civic version of the Halfway Covenant problem—the challenge of maintaining a mind-set across generations.

Will Portland's habit of planning, or a larger habit of civic activism carry its own momentum? Will newcomers care to learn the Portland style? Can a particular political culture or style be transmitted across generations? Will the institutionalizing of activism perpetuate or dampen the fervor of reform? Is the civic infrastructure created since the 1960s robust enough to accommodate the interests and needs of a changing community? Will what Putnam calls the "Portland anomaly" fade or continue in the twenty-first century?

REFERENCES

Abbott, Carl. 1983. *Portland: Planning, Politics, and Growth in a Twentieth-Century City.* Lincoln: University of Nebraska, p. 188.

City Club of Portland. 1967. *Report on Problems of Racial Justice in Portland.* Portland: City Club of Portland.

Cogan, Arnold. 1999. Interviewed by Ernie Bonner. March 10. http://www.pdx-plan.org (accessed 22 December 2003).

Humphrey, Tom. 1955. Housing authority boom years. *Oregon Journal,* 16 October, p. 1.

Putnam, Robert, and Lewis M. Feldstein. 2003. *Better Together: Restoring the American Community.* New York: Simon and Schuster.

Salute to Women. 1969. *Oregon Journal,* 21 October, p.5.

# 6 | Community Radio in Community Development: Portland's KBOO Radio

Gerald Sussman and J. R. Estes

KBOO community radio has been a Portland institution since its founding in the 1960s. At the time, the most celebrated urban mecca for the culturally and politically alienated was San Francisco. But Haight-Ashbury came and went. The counterculture types who migrated to Portland in those days usually stayed. Of those who founded KBOO radio, most remained in Portland; many are still active supporters of the station. What is most remarkable about KBOO is not just its longevity (older than National Public Radio) and unwavering commitment to serving the city's underserved groups but also the spirit of volunteerism that has animated the station since its outset.

This chapter explores how KBOO has contributed to sustaining and building diverse communities in metropolitan Portland. A related question is: How do these efforts affect the meaning of city, identity, urban culture and politics, and community? Urban communities are often thought of as people and places with which their denizens share a sense of affinity and belonging. At the same time, the sense of place to which people become attached is continually reconstituted through what Kevin Robins sees as the "disorderly possibilities" of the city, regularly infused and disrupted by newly arrived or invented cultures and subcultures, ethnic groups, lifestyles, architecture, spatial appropriations, and the like (Robins 1999, 56).

If a city is defined by its unique historical, social, cultural, political, and physical attributes, as opposed to being merely a reproduction of standardized "growth machine" development, then KBOO is working hard at resisting homogenization. Kevin Robins argues that cities need to embrace the antisystemic "disorderly possibilities" of an urbanism not tied to the ordered "technoculture" of capitalist virtuality, but rather, per Jacques Dewitte, to "a disposition to encounter others [in full sensation] and to accommodate the unforeseen" (Robins 1999, 56). Cities are not just for gentrified professionals who love the reliable atmosphere of Starbucks, afternoon lattes, and nouveau cuisine or who welcome new sports arenas, conference complexes, and the simulacra of retail, tourist-oriented "restoration" of the old city, harborside areas, historical landmarks, and the like. Cities as a shared space (and the media that represent them) are for all citizens—of all nationalities, ethnicities, ways of life, and outlooks—and not just those with privileged tastes and "birth rights."

Portland's community radio station contributes substantially to many people's sense of community, of place, and of disorderly possibilities in the city and metropolitan region without deference to such "birth rights." KBOO has never been formally studied, and with the exception of Berkeley, California's KPFA, there is very little written about American community radio in general. Much of our understanding about the value of KBOO in giving peripheral groups a sense of belonging to and ownership of the city and region had to be constructed through interviews. We wanted to know how the station got started, the principles under which it operated at its origins and continues to operate (in 2004) after 40 years (36 on the air), and how it relates to various aspects and qualities of urban life and culture, politics, work, citizenship, ethnic diversity, education, movement, entertainment, and a sense of place. What difference has KBOO made in the life of the city and its surrounding areas? In an era of increasing media conglomeration and homogenization of cultural and political life, community radio helps to maintain place identity and supports local civil society through critical citizen education and by encouraging active civic participation.

Part of KBOO's success has to do with its reflexive relationship with the political and artistic culture of the city in which it has been reared. Portland is well known for having attracted more than its share of "fringe" communities, and, though not nearly as cosmopolitan in its makeup as larger cities such as New York, Chicago, or Los Angeles, it also tends to be less economically stratified. The struggle for the preservation of public space and public culture, a battle largely lost in most U.S. cities, remains "contested terrain" in Portland and has given KBOO an opportunity to be a player in various efforts, from radical environ-mentalists to mall developers, to redefine the meaning of community in this medium-sized urban metropolis. As two community radio broad-casters note, "Grassroots radio stations are more than simple audio out-lets; they actually *help to create community* in their listening areas by fostering civic participation" (Durlin and Melio, 2003, 253; emphasis in original). (See Chap. 5, Johnson, for an in-depth look at civic engage-ment in Portland.)

## Public Airwaves as Public Space

From its beginnings, radio has been part of a broader struggle for popu-lar empowerment, public service, and freedom of expression. In radio's earliest years, amateur radio enthusiasts played a key role on both sides of the Atlantic in preventing the medium from becoming a permanent government monopoly. Unlike the British example, however, the U.S. government, once it decided to open up radio use, was anxious to give away frequencies, favoring commercial vendors over public or nonprofit operators. In recent years, the number of independent radio stations has drastically declined at the same time that commercial radio has rapidly consolidated, leaving less space for the airing of public interest news, information, and cultural programming.

The lack of informative radio in the United States is particularly unfortunate given that it is the most utilized medium for people over age 12, representing 44% of daily media usage by time. Only 15% of all AM and FM stations are public, and most of these are National Public Radio (NPR) affiliates (Downing et al. 2001, 181; Riismandel 2002, 427). The increasing coarseness in network broadcasting and the creeping com-mercialization of public radio have made community radio an impor-tant media alternative. And with centralizing monopoly tendencies and commercial intensification in broadcasting overall, the preservation of public space, independent political and cultural expression, and com-munity identity is increasingly defaulting to community broadcasters.

In July 1932, on the eve of the Nazi takeover of Germany, playwright Bertolt Brecht (1932) wrote a now frequently cited commentary on the broad public utilities of radio. He argued that broadcasting should be an apparatus not merely for distribution but for social communication. In his view, radio had a great emancipatory potential, if only broadcasters

knew how to receive as well as to transmit, how to let the listener speak as well as hear, how to bring him [*sic*] into a relationship instead of teaching him [*sic*]. On this principle the radio should step out of the supply business and organize its listeners as suppliers. Any attempt by the radio to give a truly public character to public occasions is a step in the right direction. . . . .[I]t must follow the prime objective of turning the audience not only into pupils but into teachers.

In general, American radio as an informational, educational, or cultural medium historically has been undermined by weak governmental regulatory policy. In contrast to many European and Latin American countries, U.S. commercial stations have a near commercial monopoly over the use of the airwaves and have singularly ignored public service obligations (Sussman 2003). Moreover, in more recent years, corporate networks have taken over most independent radio stations (Durlin and Melio 2003, 253), especially in the larger urban markets. In Portland, as in other metropolitan areas, national chains (CBS/Infinity, Clear Channel, Entercom) and regional media moguls (Paul Allen, Robert Pamplin) now dominate the AM and FM spectrum in terms of number and power of radio frequencies.

Challenging corporate commercial control of radio media in the metropolitan area are four public radio stations (all FM): KOPB (NPR); KMHD, an all-jazz station run out of Mt. Hood Community College; KBPS, an all-classical music station licensed to the Portland Public Schools (also managing at the moment an AM station); and KBOO. Each receives some Corporation for Public Broadcasting (CPB) support. Providing by far the broadest range of programming, KBOO is the only station whose mission is explicitly dedicated to expanding the enfranchisement of minority group programmers and listeners and offers the only progressive news perspective in the metropolitan listening area. In this way, it contributes to making Portland a place known for celebrating its difference and edgy political, social, and artistic culture.

## Growing Portland's KBOO Radio Community

In 1964, a group of Portlanders, joined by outside community radio activists, began plans for a community radio station (Portland Listener Sponsored Radio), adopting the call letters KBOO. The initiative was influenced by the 1960s political and social "movement" that encouraged talented people to take up public-oriented projects, including women's health clinics, Black Panther–sponsored breakfast centers, community newspapers, and other grassroots activities. Lorenzo Milam, known as the "Johnny Appleseed" of community radio, had worked at

KPFA, the country's first (1949) and now oldest and nonprofit, listener-sponsored radio station, and went on to organize a community radio station in Seattle, KRAB. Blessed with a significant personal inheritance and a penchant for humorous station names, he also helped start a "KRAB Nebula" of 14 community radio stations (Engelman 1996, 66), including KTAO in Los Gatos, California; KCHU in Dallas; WORT in Madison, Wisconsin; KUSP in Santa Cruz, California; KPOO in San Francisco; KDNA in St. Louis; and KBOO in Portland.

Located in a tiny basement studio in downtown Portland at a cost of less than $4,000, KBOO began broadcasting irregularly in 1968 with a barely audible 10-watt repeater (now called translator) signal from KRAB in Seattle. Primitive as it was, KBOO's staff and dedicated volunteers began accumulating equipment, and the station became a haven for local and visiting singers and musicians. The monthly budget at the time was $50. As of February 1971, KBOO had a checkbook balance of a mere $26.19, but the broadcasters persisted. Today, the annual budget is in the range of $700,000 (Silverman interview 2003).

In 1970, as both commercial and noncommercial interests were rapidly acquiring FM frequencies, KBOO acquired a 1,000-watt transmitter that allowed its signal to reach much of northwest Oregon. Within a few years, KBOO moved to a house in inner southeast Portland and purchased additional equipment with the aid of $80,000 in federal grant money. In the late 1970s, KBOO moved back downtown and was broadcasting at 12,500 watts with some 2,000 subscribers then supporting the station. Urban renewal forced KBOO to relocate once again, this time to its current location in a renovated warehouse in the inner eastside, from which it transmits at 25,500 watts. Volunteer efforts in its building, staffing, operations, and maintenance were core to KBOO's survival and growth.

In 1975, the same year the National Federation of Community Broadcasters (NFCB) was formed, KBOO elected its first board of directors and became independent of its parent station, KRAB. By the early 1980s, KBOO began taking on a progressive identity and introducing a range of multicultural programming in several languages and tastes. Again supported by federal grant money, the station purchased more modern studio equipment, a remote transmitter, and a satellite dish. At a time when other community radio stations' listeners were dwindling, KBOO's audience was on the rise. Currently, KBOO has an estimated 70,000 listeners, over 6,700 paid subscribers, a staff of nine, and close to 450 volunteers (Kowalczyk interview 2002).

KBOO (heard on 90.7 FM within metropolitan Portland) is one of the most respected community radio stations for its commitment to supporting alternative and diverse community interests and for relying on the community as the principal source of its financial and staffing support.[1] As the station has pursued higher production standards, it has eschewed professionalism in the commercial sense and the more institutional, government- and corporate-associated alliances that NPR has formed. KBOO carries out this mission without advertising, though with some small-scale underwriting (by local shops).[2] And, unlike Portland's other commercial and public stations, it produces almost all of its own programming.

## Public Culture as Grassroots Democracy

Apart from the difference between profit- and nonprofit-run radio, there is an important distinction to be made between public and community media. The former represents state-sponsored or formally endorsed, professionalized, and institutionalized activity, along the lines conceived in Habermas's bourgeois public sphere; the latter is constituted by a more heterogeneous and independent set of actors and more broadly oppositional and radical in character (Engelman 1996, 7). Honing itself closer to the Washington-centered news agenda of events and public figures, NPR, including its Portland KOPB affiliate, would be in the first category; community radio, including KBOO, focusing more on local, disempowered social elements and issues, in the second.

KBOO serves essentially four community functions. The first is that of a *public transmitter of progressive politics and diverse local culture.* Following its mission statement, KBOO serves a broad set of constituencies, often at the cost of attaining greater market share, and its staff and volunteers continually debate the value of promoting alternative politics and culture. Whereas many other public and community radio stations have been drawn into the logic of the Arbitron ratings scheme of measuring success, KBOO has taken a different road. Thus, shows are often scheduled, according to the station's program director, "against what is commercially, intuitively smart in order to serve communities. . . . Our public philosophy is to look for disenfranchised communities who have no access to radio, period, and try to get them involved at the program and administrative level" (C. Merrick interview 2003). Though this runs against the grain of mainstream broadcast wisdom, KBOO managed to achieve its highest pledge drive ever in early 2003 despite an Oregon unemployment rate of 8.5%, the highest in the country. Moreover, the station received pledges 16% above its target (Talley interview 2003).

As Portland's social and ethnic demographics change, KBOO continues to move toward greater inclusiveness. It has become a remarkable community venue for voices, and sometimes odd points of view, rarely heard in other media. On this single station one can hear reggae, Afro-Caribbean, jazz, hip-hop, gospel, blues, punk, salsa, country, bluegrass, rock, folk, electronica, "bizarre music," norteña, African, and other international music. KBOO also features African American and Islamic culture and politics; perspectives of gays, lesbians, and transsexual identities and lifestyles; language programming in Spanish, Farsi, Yiddish, Dutch, Cantonese, Japanese, Hindi, Hawai'ian Pidgin, and Italian; programming for bikers, New Agers, environmentalists, prisoners, and labor issues; left wing news analysis and talk radio; Latino and Native American news, and other nonmainstream formats.

KBOO's programmers report stories, play music, and write poetry that is socially critical; they perform with vanishing folk instruments; and their art is sometimes beyond contemporary classification. Guided by its mission, KBOO programming is an important artistic cultural influence in the greater Portland community, giving voice to literature, drama, poetry, and music that would otherwise not be on the airwaves. Its *Radio Theatre Hour* program features a drama format rarely used in American radio in recent decades. KBOO serves the dual purpose of giving its listeners uncommon cultural content and providing a platform for local artists of all types to share their work. Nurturing the city and region's diverse creative and artistic environment, KBOO helps reduce dependence on commodified forms of culture and identity.

Its musical offerings tend toward grassroots niches or selections from small or obscure labels that are not heard on other stations. "Top 40" hits are definitely out, and KBOO is very atypical of urban radio markets where DJs "are figureheads who spin a narrow and mind-numbing list of songs that have been market-tested to death, leaving stations that sound the same from coast to coast" (Staples 2003). KBOO's musical programming is diverse not only ethnically, but also stylistically, including its avant-garde, traditional, contemporary, folk, and other genres. Between *Jazz Bebop*, *The Gospel Express*, *Swingin' Country*, *Rockaholics Anonymous*, *Portland General Eclectic*, and *Music People Hate*, it is hard to pin down KBOO's cultural style. The central point it makes, however, is that it programs what listeners will not hear anywhere else on the dial, whether announcing a locally written and produced play on the "community calendar" or playing the B-side of a long-lost R&B recording. KBOO's music and arts are radical, funky, and always people-oriented in ways that defy other radio stations' standards and access restrictions. This programming approach offers community life eclectic and "disorderly possibilities."

Disregarding the commercial imperative that drives most radio stations, KBOO programmers are not bound by the constraints that playlists impose. KBOO's programmers are free to explore genres they know best and regularly engage feedback from listeners. This creates a point of contact and discourse between the station and audience. One DJ invites "shout-outs" on his hip-hop show, and callers range from children to adults, including people in prison. Another programmer comments, "We play what we want to and if the audience complains, we change it. But mostly people call and say, 'Where did you get this? I've never heard it before.' We try to focus on things you won't hear on the radio 20 times a day" (B. Merrick interview 2003). Audience response in the form of call-ins and dedicated financial support is an important gauge by which programmers evaluate their efforts.

In a manner rather Brechtian in character, its music and public affairs programming is frequently intermingled, with no strict separation between segments. One striking example involved a picketer in front of the KBOO studio, protesting the station's coverage of the U.S. invasion of Iraq in 2003 as not supportive of the American troops. A jazz DJ on the air at the time invited the protester inside and put him on his live show to discuss the issue with the call-in audience (Springer interview 2003). Many, though not all, music show hosts do not hesitate to discuss political issues, and talk show formats often play music of resistance. In general, KBOO makes great efforts to put voices on the air from a wide range of backgrounds and tastes in the metropolitan and surrounding areas. And although KBOO leans politically toward the left, it is nonsectarian in character and includes voices on the right that meet the station's mission statement (Kowalczyk interview 2002).

Its second function is its *provision of radio training*. Formal training is offered by KBOO staff and outside professionals (sometimes from KOPB) for all interested community radio volunteers. Training includes interviewing techniques, reporting, voicing, writing for radio, and technical preparation, such as engineering and digital editing. KBOO also provides political workshops on understanding Portland public policy and other community issues for potential reporters and show hosts. Catherine Komp, former evening news and public affairs director at

KBOO, now a reporter at an NPR affiliate in upstate New York, notes, however, that it is the volunteers themselves who pass on much of the technical knowledge:

> One of the great things about KBOO is this "each one-teach one" philosophy that we have, so it's not just professional paid staff people training the volunteers. You train volunteers to train other volunteers. That not only instills confidence and empowers them, but it passes information along a whole chain of people that I think is really healthy. So that everybody is better informed and knowledgeable and skilled, as opposed to just a very small group of people that you have to go to. It doesn't consolidate power. (Komp interview 2003)

And there is evidence that KBOO indeed is successfully passing on radio skills.[3] For those without a regular show of their own, KBOO's training allows volunteers to contribute by producing public affairs or music segments that may be played during scheduled programs. The training sometimes provides a useful segue for volunteer programming at the Portland Community Access cable channel. Experienced programmers often recruit or train new volunteers who are interested in hosting their own programs. The host of a weekly hip-hop show, Corey Loggins (known on radio as "DJ Audio") brings in high school–aged individuals interested in learning what is involved in radio production and lets them know that KBOO is there for them. This is important to Loggins because, as he explains, KBOO was the only station in the area willing to offer a black teenager his first experience in radio (Loggins interview 2003). He wants other teenagers to know that KBOO is there for them. Other programmers, such as 72-year-old John Talley, who is part Mohawk and host of *Indian World*, also take their mentoring role seriously. Talley has been on the air since 1976 and is concerned about his show's continuity (Talley interview 2003). Radio veteran Bruce Merrick (on the air as "Uncle B"), who cohosts *Swingin' Country*, says he enjoys training new, young programmers because of the innovative ideas they bring to the genre (B. Merrick interview 2003).

A third KBOO function is *political education and mobilization*. With in-depth on-the-air analysis of local, national, and international affairs and cosponsorship of political talks and community events, usually with other nonprofit or grassroots activist groups, KBOO encourages its listeners to take an active role in public affairs. The station has conducted live interviews with numerous national and international political speakers, including Vandana Shiva, Noam Chomsky, Howard Zinn,

Jim Hightower, and Medea Benjamin. Street activism is difficult for the station to sponsor or even openly endorse, inasmuch as encouraging illegal (i.e., without a permit) demonstrations could lead to the loss of its broadcast license. Nonetheless, when street protests occur, such as the 2003 marches in Portland in opposition to the U.S. invasion of Iraq and the campaign fund-raising visit of George W. Bush, KBOO was at the scene providing live remote coverage. On more local issues, KBOO has hosted forums for candidates in school board and city council elections and aired live election day coverage from party headquarters.

KBOO's news and public affairs programming is the core of its political education and mobilization efforts. Based on a news and public affairs approach that is intended to inform and educate rather than simply grab public attention, KBOO doesn't report school shootings, fires, murders, car crashes, other sensational stories, sports, or extended weather reports—all of which is left to the commercial stations—unless there is a specific community angle to it, such as the issue of police brutality (Komp interview 2003). It is the only public station in Portland, and one of the few nationally, that offers listeners a full hour of locally produced evening news, plus a half-hour of morning news, Monday through Friday. Unlike other stations, KBOO provides news of interest to gays and lesbians, antiwar groups, environmental activist organizations, labor unions, and other marginalized groups.

For instance, the evening news includes a five-minute nightly segment specifically on Native American news. Other material is pulled down and reedited from New York–based Free Speech Radio News, the Associated Press, Internet sources, and Oregon State News Service reports, which augment locally produced stories and occasional live call-ins from "experts" (Komp interview 2003). During the past 15 years, the amount of locally produced news and public affairs programming at KBOO has doubled, and the station now relies less on syndicated sources. The morning news director admits, however, that limited resources and the lack of outside reporters constrain the station's ability to cover more national or international news, and as a cost-saving measure certain stories, such as those from the *New York Times,* have to be extensively rewritten to avoid paying service subscriptions—and mainstream news biases (Stephenson interview 2003).

The overall purpose of its news reporting follows the station's charter for progressive social change and relies on culturally diverse staff, volunteers, members, and listeners to shape the telling of events. The morning news director calls it "activist journalism" (Stephenson interview 2003).

KBOO news and public affairs programming help listeners define a position around such issues as U.S. military intervention, civil liberties and the Patriot Act, and antigay ballot measures placed on the Oregon ballot in recent years. With a very tight but growing budget on which to operate such a complex set of program and community objectives, it is understood internally that KBOO will need to grow financially to provide better on-air presentation of news and public affairs. Partly as a result of a hands-off style of management, "maxed out" training resources, and a heavy reliance on volunteers, KBOO news reporters and public affairs programmers have a high degree of autonomy (Komp interview 2003). As far as preparing for the changes needed in the future, some think there is too much autonomy and too much time given to marginal programming in the name of diversity (Nielsen interview 2003, Uris interview 2003).

KBOO achieved an important community broadcasting and free speech victory in February 2003, when, after a long struggle with the Federal Communications Commission (FCC), the federal regulator reversed a 2001 ruling and $7,000 fine charged to the station for violating federal indecency standards in broadcasting. At issue was a song, "Your Revolution," in which Sarah Jones samples rap music played on commercial stations to criticize their misogynist lyrics. Although court costs considerably exceeded the FCC fine, KBOO's successful defense of political speech gained national attention and respect among community broadcasters (Kosseff 2003). The station's determined effort to pursue the case demonstrated its strong commitment to the defense of independent radio. Indeed, the First Amendment precedent established by the decision was a victory for *all* radio and other media—community, public, and commercial.

Related to political education and mobilization is the station's fourth function, *community building/sustaining and outreach*. KBOO's mission is about serving the underserved. Even as 87% of the Portland metropolitan area is white, a third of KBOO's on-air programmers are people of color who produce 35% of its local programming (KBOO 2003, 6). Diverse cultural and language programming makes it possible for Chinese, Latino, Italian, and other recent immigrants to feel a little more welcome and connected to the city. Women and African Americans will find a number of different programs targeted to their interests throughout the week, including such special events as the annual 24-hour coverage of International Women's Day on 8 March and programs on Black History Month. From unpublished poets regularly reading on *The*

*Talking Earth* show to local bands produced on independent recording labels, KBOO nurtures Portland area arts and talents that do not get air time on other stations.

Music and arts are central to KBOO's community building/sustaining and outreach program. On no other radio station will Portlanders hear about the "Native American Youth Association Benefit Concert," cosponsored by KBOO, featuring Native American musicians playing contemporary Native American music at a small, local venue. A Native American staff member at KBOO attributes his own awakening to the historical roots of national and ethnic oppression and discovery of a wide range of Latin American, African American, Asian, and American Indian music and songwriters in part to the multiethnic exposure in his KBOO experience (Moccasin interview 2003). Among the events KBOO cosponsors are street fairs of different ethnic communities, a "Peace Quake" with the Oregon Peace Institute, Mercy Corps, and Oregon Physicians for Social Responsibility, a number of music festivals, a breast cancer awareness event and other public health forums, an "Earth Charter" benefit, "Bands Against Bush," the San Francisco Mime Troupe, and other charitable or nonprofit groups engaged in peace, justice, community, and human rights causes. An event cosponsored by KBOO must meet the station's mission, and in 2002 the mission supported over 70 events in the metropolitan area. KBOO cosponsorship means frequent on-air promotion and listing on the station's Web site and more publicity than any grassroots organization could ever expect to receive or purchase from a commercial or public radio station.

As part of its efforts on behalf of social justice issues, each year the station carries continuous national "Homeless Marathon" programming. This consists of 14 hours of live broadcasting from the event's host city, wherever it may be, to help raise awareness of the plight of America's dispossessed citizens. In 2003, KBOO cosponsored "The World's Largest Guitar Band," a community musical event organized as a fundraiser for a locally run nonprofit diner, Sisters of the Road Café, dedicated to serving inexpensive meals to homeless and low-income Portland residents (see Chap. 13, Prince for a discussion of the homeless). To draw attention to the work of Sisters, the goal was to establish a Guinness world record (achieved) and to stage an event in the city's main outdoor public plaza "that was community oriented and brought people together across class lines," according to Sisters development director Debbie Fox (Fox interview 2003). The two-day "Pickathon," an American Roots Music Festival, is KBOO's annual station benefit concert.

This family-oriented event, held on farmland just outside Portland, features national and local country, bluegrass, and folk musicians, a square dance, and free camping.[4]

## Volunteerism versus Media Professionalism

The key to what has sustained KBOO over the 40 years of its existence is its large and highly committed base of volunteers drawn from the ranks of its listener-members. KBOO has long operated under a highly decentralized, if not anarchist, approach to governance. Its idea of democratic power, says KBOO's program director, Chris Merrick, is "to give it away," relying on the successful recruitment of volunteers and increased subscription, especially strong since 9/11, to keep the station afloat (C. Merrick interview 2003). The station's volunteer coordinator, Ani Haines, also cites the importance of KBOO's radically democratic governance structure: "In my contact with other community radio stations, we are the only one, to my knowledge, that allows members to elect the entire board of directors. Most community stations have a mixture of appointed by staff, appointed by the board, and elected by members. We really want to walk the line that we're democratically controlled and operated by anyone who cares." She adds that "All of our committees are open without a limit on size, so that they remain open. We try to carry transparency and accessibility to the limit" (Haines interview 2003).

Rejecting the notion that commercially professional radio represents the pinnacle of quality production, KBOO's core staff embrace some of the unpolished qualities that come with a volunteer-driven station—reminding listeners that its programmers are no different from them. This, they believe, is what their subscribers, who own the station,[5] and loyal listeners actually want—not the more polished and tightly packaged version of news and music they can get on commercial radio. At the same time, the station staff do seek to transmit a well-engineered sound that is as good as can be heard on radio (Komp interview 2003).

Haines (interview 2003), however, holds the view that the standard sound of radio is a product of the commercial interests that construct it, which is not what KBOO is about:

> We have very exacting standards for our news and public affairs. We have the philosophy that you don't need to be a paid professional to be an expert in something. If you have the interest and passion to learn something, anyone can learn to be a journalist, one can learn to be a DJ,

to chair a committee. We are very much trying to put forth that spirit of do it yourself. If you always leave things to the monied interests, then they're controlled by the monied interests.

She also thinks the station's morning and evening news and public affairs directors hold themselves to high standards and "are really looking for quality." The volunteers pursue that objective as well, she says, because they want to be taken seriously as broadcasters, and they care that "when their name is associated with something, it is good information. I think there is almost a peer pressure to hold ourselves to the highest standard" (Haines interview 2003). With regard to music programming, she comments,

Sometimes you hear people say "Oh, they had dead air," and that does happen sometimes, but still the program advisory committee gives constant feedback on how to improve shows. And I've noticed that volunteers give each other that feedback almost before the staff gets a chance to intervene, because the volunteers take such pride in the station that they feel they have ownership in. (Haines interview 2003)

Who are the volunteers? They range in age from youth to a few in their 70s. They are white, black, Latino, Asian, Pacific Islander, and Native American, gay and straight. A large percentage comes from places other than Oregon—the east coast, the Seattle area, Northern California, and other regions of the world. Many who volunteer at KBOO, including those with prior community radio experience, were previously activists who came to Portland because of its reputation as an activist-friendly city. Some on-air people have been broadcasting there for over 25 years, while others are engaged for only a few weeks (Haines interview 2003).

KBOO's extensive volunteer force performs a range of tasks, from sound engineering, answering telephones, fund-raising, news editing, and hosting programs to serving on the board of directors. About 160 volunteers are involved in broadcast activities, while the rest work behind the scenes. A program volunteer, Bruce Merrick, who has been with KBOO since the early 1980s, tells a story about the gutting of the building that would become their current studio almost entirely by volunteer labor. Some 140 people showed up to help strip the old building down to the walls, and up to 200 volunteers worked over four months to remodel the space—based on the plans of a volunteer architect (B. Merrick interview 2003).

The level of volunteerism at KBOO distinguishes it both from Portland's other public radio stations and from other community radio stations around the country. As one study of community radio noted, "In the 1990s, community radio has come to depend less on volunteer labor, has been more careful about targeting its listeners through a small selection of their demographic characteristics, and has become increasingly invested and incorporated in mainstream public broadcasting" (Fairchild 2001, 157). KBOO deliberately avoided the commercial tendencies they saw in public broadcasting by relying less on CPB's reduced funding, expanding its volunteer base, increasing the level of listener financial support, and broadening the diversity of its staff and programming. KBOO's volunteer coordinator says that volunteers work out of "a passion for the community they are here to represent," and that community, therefore, "gets defined in any of a number of ways . . . traditionally [in terms] of ethnic communities, and, yet, there are ideological communities and then there are musical communities . . . the one thing our volunteers have in common is their desire to share community." What inspires them is what "they feel they're representing . . . what they're bringing to the community" (Haines interview 2003).

For former KBOO outreach coordinator, Spider Moccasin, a Wasco Indian of the Warm Springs Confederated Tribes of Oregon, the question of governance is a particularly sensitive issue. He asserts that "As an indigenous person of this region, Portland is [for me] a DMZ [demilitarized zone]. This is occupied territory, a dictatorship imposed on my society, my culture, my people by foreigners." But he also speaks of the special role that community radio plays in helping to sustain his ethnic identity: "Only KBOO has the courage to acknowledge the indigenous tribal people of these territories—and not only acknowledge them but let us volunteer, let us train here, and eventually even become hired professionals here. I adore this grassroots media outlet because of that" (Moccasin interview 2003).

## Conclusions: Putting Community into Community Radio

Community radio defines itself by including and serving sections of the community not accommodated by mainstream or even public radio (NFCB Web site 2003). As its station manager commented, KBOO is not about saving the world, it is more about representing the underrepresented who live in it (Kowalczyk interview 2003). Beyond that, it is a voice of change, an advocate for a kind of community where peace replaces war as society's dominant ethos, where diverse cultural and ethnic points of reference are internalized as the norm, where a democratic public sphere and values of social justice prevail, and where grass-roots governance of everyday life is the mainstream way of thinking about politics and culture. Long-time KBOO volunteer Barbara Bernstein, remarks that "When I go to a new town, I try to find on the dial a community radio station. When I find it, I feel I'm plugging into the community. And I can tell an awful lot about the health of the community by the way that station sounds" (Bernstein interview 2003).

Over the past four decades, KBOO has matured from its primarily white "hippie" identity to a more self-confident, open, and inclusive community institution. These changes did not come without conflict: ethnic, racial, and gender barriers had to be confronted and broken down. It could hardly have been otherwise, as one public intellectual has observed, inasmuch as "[c]ommunity control, as an unthinking localism, [inevitably] masks conflicts within and between communities" (Liora Salter, one of the founders of Canadian community radio, cited in Lewis and Booth 1990, 131). Yet, KBOO's internal struggles, unlike some other community radio stations, did not give way to a top-down consolidation of power. Instead, what has evolved is a more volunteer-based, self-conscious multiculturalism, and a mind-set of collective resistance and radical self-government.

KBOO community radio is not without its detractors, inside and out. In the view of one former commercial broadcast professional, KBOO's news perspective is too strongly attached to activism and advocacy, "too locked into preset ideas, too narrowcast, and too well-read" to reach the working class and the issues that affect their lives. Working class people, he asserts, are more disposed toward country-western music and right wing talk show hosts than KBOO (Frederick interview 2003). Speaking from a different angle, a current KBOO programmer complains that the station allows its diversity commitments to obstruct the needed objectives of audience and membership expansion and higher levels of broadcast professionalism. "It's very hard," he says, "to be part of a democratic organization with as many tendencies as this one" (Uris interview 2003).

KBOO's programming runs against the grain of the commercial imperative precisely to serve the interests of less enfranchised communities (C. Merrick interview 2003). Its mission is not to win the ratings game, and the rough edges of its live programming can not compete on the same terms as the slick, prerecorded, tightly edited, postproduction packaged programming of commercial radio or NPR. To do so and still presume its independent status would play to the illusion that the mass media is autonomous from dominant structures of cultural (re)production in a capitalist economy. Mario Tronti describes the socializing power of such dominant structures in his 1962 polemic, "The Factory and Society." He argues that, over time, capital relentlessly drives every sector of society toward economic exchange and industrialized social relationships:

> The more capitalist development advances, that is to say the more the production of relative surplus value penetrates everywhere, . . . the relationship between capitalist production and bourgeois society, between the factory and society, between society and the state, become more and more organic . . . and the whole society becomes an articulation of production. In short, all of society lives as a function of the factory and the factory extends its exclusive domination over all of society. (Cited in Cleaver 1992, 137, n. 13; Cleaver's translation)

In theorizing about tendencies resident within capitalism, Tronti sees class antagonism permeating more and more the dynamics of everyday life, including mass culture. Applying political economy specifically to media, Leslie Good finds that "social relations of communication are inseparable from social relations of power" in general (cited in Engelman 1996, 3). An important question for community radio is the extent to which it allows itself to internalize commercial pressures as the normal rules of the game. KBOO staff tend to believe that, unlike the approach taken by public and commercial radio, local arts, news, and public affairs means that urban media are not simply one-size-fits-all distribution networks or local franchises of big city headlines and culture. Instead, without being parochial, radio should first fulfill the needs and interests pertinent to the least empowered people in its signal area. KBOO has long endured and grown with this principle in mind.

As a relatively low cost and spatially accessible means of mass communication, community radio has great potential for democratizing the airwaves and empowering citizens, and, unlike television, it is a medium to which people frequently tune in and call in outside the home, on the road, or at work. In 1986, a tenuous time at KBOO, its Program Guide conceded that should listener funding dwindle, the station would by necessity become more reliant on federal and private grants, underwriting, and funding events. In the face of this challenge, KBOO opted to "stay primarily listener-supported." The Guide argued that:

Listener support is the freest way we can support ourselves. Ignoring our declining listenership puts all our programming in jeopardy [and, therefore, the] key is to design programming which we have good reason to believe will appeal to listeners. We have made significant strides in serving new audiences over the last few years (Children, Seniors, Latinos, Blacks, Gays, Disabled People). [The Guide added that] most of our listeners aren't looking for media salvation, they just want an oasis in the wasteland of Portland radio. Let's get them to the oasis and then try to change the way they think about the media. (Quoted in Lewis and Booth 1990, 123)

KBOO does represent an oasis of resistance against politics as usual and mass culture. The outreach coordinator at KBOO sees the station as an antidote to the ideological spin coming from mainstream media. He says that "even if we freak people out or upset people, and they don't agree with [KBOO], they know that it isn't bought and dominated and controlled and hypnotized—that it isn't the same old propaganda" (Moccasin interview 2003). In this view, community radio offers refuge for people yearning for a more democratic society and against the hegemonic, homogenizing, and authoritarian tendencies of the state.

Community radio faces a more immediate challenge—the pressure coming from CPB to use market-based "programming economics" (subscriber demographics) to determine a public station's program and staffing needs. CPB's public radio audience research study, "Audience 98," found that more affluent and educated professionals were more likely to subscribe to public radio than the rest of the populations served. Following the study's logic, a number of public radio stations across the country have begun to drop their commitments to serving broad ethnic, cultural, income, age, and identity groups in favor of more upscale listeners—trumpeting one more triumph of market determinism over public service policies. In the summer of 1998, the station management of KUOP, until then an independent affiliate of NPR and Public Radio International (PRI) in California's Stockton–Modesto area, made a sudden announcement that, based on its audience profiling study, it was dropping most of its musical and local programming and switching to a primarily news and information format. In the words of one author, KUOP abandoned "its spatial community . . . seeking an audience comprised entirely of members of the professional-managerial class" (Hurley 2003, 95).

The KUOP story is not likely to be repeated at KBOO any time soon. KBOO's listenership and subscribers have been growing in the post-9/11 political environment. Asked about the impact on the Portland region were KBOO to go under, all respondents concurred that the city's community spirit would be greatly diminished. "KBOO helps it [the region] to have a vibrant, progressive community, because there is so much opportunity for interaction that is missing if you don't have a station like KBOO. It really gets information out there that people can share, and various groups can cross-pollinate each other that wouldn't have otherwise" (Stephenson interview 2003). KBOO's volunteer coordinator spoke about her vision of the station: "I would like to see us get tuned into by more and more folks who aren't used to alternative news and more people have the opportunity to get turned on to these ideas and question areas of our society. . . . And in the future we can really question commercial media's ability to entertain or inform you to see if we can combine efforts to become the mainstream" (Haines interview 2003).

Portland is widely regarded as a city that has resisted submission to the forces of economic integration, copycat commercialism, and cultural homogenization. Its intact neighborhoods, strong civic values, locally owned restaurants, coffee shops, and movie theaters, relaxed social interactions and informal dress codes, and many grassroots activist organizations all contribute to its unique identity among American cities. Within the urban public arena, KBOO community radio has given voice to a wide array of ethnic communities, musical talent, political opinion, social justice and support organizations, radical youth and counterculture, and other groups and individuals that are part of the city's diverse, often disorderly, social and cultural milieu. For cities in this globalizing age to remain places of vibrant social and political exchange, they need to preserve public spaces for spontaneous, experimental, independent, and free expression of ideas and values. These objectives have been part of KBOO's mission statement from the beginning, which is what has made it a long-enduring, volunteer-based, and vital organization in the Portland scene and the city's most authentically local media outlet for grassroots politics, public affairs, arts and culture, and community action.

NOTES

1. KBOO's organizers determined at the outset that the station would be entirely listener sponsored, although it has received some grant funds from the Corporation for Public Broadcasting (CPB), the parent of the Public Broadcasting Service (PBS) and National Public Radio (NPR). John Ross, station manager in the 1970s, urged the CPB to allocate its funds to smaller, low-powered stations

to help community radio proliferate, but CPB insisted on a policy of supporting the better-equipped, better-funded stations (Milam 1975, 272–275). KBOO's founders also decided from the beginning that the station would be primarily a volunteer organization, moving farther in this direction than the National Federation of Community Broadcasters (NFCB), of which it is a member, had advised.

2. KBOO accepts limited underwriting from small-scale shops. One staff member notes, somewhat facetiously: "We specialize in insulting our underwriters. We've had several underwriters withdraw their underwriting because we've done critical stories on them" (Stephenson interview 2003). Another staff member adds: "Our underwriter coordinator is very upfront [with underwriters]—that if you're underwriting, you're underwriting free speech and supporting community, and that's a good thing, isn't it? That's part of his sales pitch. I think we're really committed to our ethic; that this is one place where money doesn't influence [content]" (Haines interview 2003).

3. Volunteers, with or without a radio program of their own, are encouraged to learn "how to run the boards," and many long-time volunteers report a steady improvement in the station's production quality over the years. A number of people trained at KBOO have moved on in the media world, including Emily Harris, who worked with Bill Moyers at PBS and is currently NPR's Berlin correspondent. Former KBOO people also include Robert Smith, an NPR New York correspondent; Robert Manning and Beth Hyams, respectively, KOPB's *Morning Edition* anchor and assistant news director; Kat Snow and Harriet Baskas, respectively, editor for the *California Report* on San Francisco NPR affiliate KQED and station manager for the public radio station in Bellevue, Washington; and others who now work in commercial radio.

4. Through the efforts of Spider Moccasin, the American Roots festival program is now more inclusive of blacks, Latinos, women, and Indians on the bill and no longer, as Moccasin says, "a private white boys' drinking club. . . . What could be more Americana," he says, "than the people who have been here for more than 10,000 years?" (Moccasin interview 2003).

5. The morning news director, Kathleen Stephenson, says that together with its volunteers, KBOO's paid subscribers (members) are the "foundation" of the organization. "Whether you pay $365 or $20, which is the low-income membership rate, you still have one vote for the board of directors." Not everyone who listens is a paid member, but that number has been rising, particularly since 9/11. Between 1999 and mid-2003, the subscriber base grew by more than 76% (KBOO 2003, 3; Stephenson interview 2003).

REFERENCES

Brecht, Bertolt. 1932. Der Rundfunk als Kommunikationsapparat ("The radio as an apparatus of communication"). In *Bjitter des hessischen Landestheaters. Darmstadt*, No. 16. July. http://home.freeuk.com/lemmaesthetics/brecht1.htm (accessed 1 November 2003).

Cleaver, Harry. 1992. The inversion of class perspective in Marxian theory: From valorisation to self-valorisation. In *Essays on Open Marxism*, edited by Werner Bonefeld, Richard Gunn, and Kosmas Psychopedis, 106–144. London: Pluto Press.

Downing, John D. H., Tamara V. Ford, Genève Gil, and Laura Stein. 2001. *Radical Media: Rebellious Communication and Social Movements.* Thousand Oaks, CA: Sage.

Durlin, Marty, and Cathy Melio. 2003. The grassroots radio movement in the United States. In *Public Broadcasting and the Public Interest*, edited by Michael P. McCauley, Eric E. Peterson, B. Lee Artz, and DeeDee Halleck, 252–264. Armonk, NY: M. E. Sharpe.

Engelman, Ralph. 1996. *Public Radio and Television in America: A Political History.* Thousand Oaks, CA: Sage.

Fairchild, Charles. 2001. *Community Radio and Public Culture: Being an Examination of Media Access and Equity in the Nations of North America.* Cresskill, NJ: Hampton Press.

Hurley, Mary E. 2003. Should one size fit all audiences? A study of KUOP. In *Public Broadcasting and the Public Interest*, edited by Michael P. McCauley, Eric E. Peterson, B. Lee Artz, and DeeDee Halleck. Armonk, NY: M. E. Sharpe, pp. 95–109.

KBOO. 2003. *Annual Report.*

Kosseff, Jeffrey. 2003. FCC reverses ruling on indecency charge at Portland, Ore. radio station. *The Oregonian*, February 22. LexisNexis accessed through Academic Universe (accessed 15 December 2003).

Lewis, Peter M., and Jerry Booth. 1990. *The Invisible Medium: Public, Commercial and Community Radio.* Washington, DC: Howard University Press.

Milam, Lorenzo. 1975. *Sex and Broadcasting: A Handbook on Starting a Radio Station for the Community*, 3rd ed. Dallas, TX: Dildo Press.

National Federation of Community Broadcasters (NFCB). 2003. http://www.nfcb.org (accessed 1 November 2003).

Riismandel, Paul. 2002. Radio by and for the public: The death and resurrection of low-power radio. In *Radio Reader: Essays in the Cultural History of Radio*, edited by Michele Hilmes and Jason Loviglio, pp. 423–450. New York: Routledge.

Robins, Kevin. 1999. Foreclosing on the city? The bad idea of virtual urbanism. In *Technocities*, edited by John Downey and Jim McGuigan, pp. 34–59. Thousand Oaks, CA: Sage.

Staples, Brent. 2003. Driving down the highway, mourning the death of American radio. *New York Times*, June 8. LexisNexis accessed through Academic Universe (accessed 12 January 2003).

Sussman, Gerald. 2003. Introduction: The struggle for and within public television. In Public television in a neoliberal era, edited by Gerald Sussman, special issue, *Television and New Media* 4 (2): 111–115.

INTERVIEWS

Bernstein, Barbara. 2003. Interview with authors. 18 August. KBOO program host and former NFCB member.

Fox, Debbie. 2003. Interview with authors. 2 July. Development director, Sisters of the Road Café.

Frederick, Lew. 2003. Interview with authors. 2 April. Director of public information, Portland Public Schools.

Haines, Ani. 2003. Interview with authors. 24 February. KBOO volunteer coordinator and program host.

Komp, Catherine. 2003. Interview with authors. 26 June. Former KBOO evening news and public affairs director.

Kowalczyk, Dennise. 2002. Interview with authors. 26 November. KBOO station manager.

Kowalczyk, Dennise. 2003. Interview with authors. 6 August. KBOO station manager.

Loggins, Corey ("DJ Audio"). 2003. Interview with authors. 9 July. KBOO program cohost.

Merrick, Bruce ("Uncle B"). 2003. Interview with authors. 9 July. KBOO program cohost.

Merrick, Chris. 2003. Interview with authors. 24 February. KBOO program director.

Moccasin, Spider. 2003. Interview with authors. 19 August. KBOO outreach coordinator and program cohost.

Nielsen, Chris. 2003. Interview with authors. 31 July. KBOO program host.

Silverman, Bruce. 2003. Interview with authors. 6 August. KBOO archivist.

Springer, Kim. 2003. Interview with authors. 14 July. Member of KBOO board of directors.

Stephenson, Kathleen. 2003. Interview with authors. 17 and 24 February. KBOO morning news and public affairs director.

Talley, John. 2003. Interview with authors. 14 July. KBOO program host.

Uris, Joe. 2003. Interview with authors. 8 May. KBOO program host.

# 7 | If Zealously Promoted by All: The Push and Pull of Portland Parks History

Chet Orloff

Colonel Hawkins has now started on a far-reaching scheme, which, if zealously promoted by all, will, within a few years, give Portland the most beautiful parks in the world.

—*The Oregonian* 1902.

In the fall of 1843, on their way upriver from Fort Vancouver to Oregon City, Asa Lovejoy and William Overton climbed out of their canoe at a spot called "the clearing." For these two travelers, the clearing that autumn day may have been a place to pause from paddling, to take lunch or a necessary rest stop (there being certain things one can't do from a canoe). Whatever their reasons for stopping, before they pushed off again they made Portland's first business decision. They decided to found a town.

Even as they contemplated human hands building on their future real estate, they must have known that the hand of nature had already touched this place. Shaped by volcanoes and floods, edged by forests, lined with rivers, the new townsite was bounded by greens and blues. Its natural beauty and economic potential drew settlers in the next decade, and Portland grew quickly. The nicknames for the city in its first half-century—"Eden," "The City of Roses"—expressed its parklike nature. Even the derisive epithets that still stick—"Stumptown" and "Puddle City"—refer to Portland's natural icons: trees and rain. Nature's encompassing presence in Portland has endured.

When we consider the nature of urban America since 1851, the year of Portland's incorporation, we must consider the supporting role parks have played in sustaining the health of the nation's cities. When early social workers blamed cities for crowding and sickening their residents, planners saw parks as refuges of health and rejuvenation. Parks counted as economic assets because they raised property values and attracted development. Parks mixed populations, to good effect. Since that decade 160 years ago, cities have built parks for physical recreation and psychological refreshment, urban aesthetics, landscape preservation, and economic growth. Portland's own park history has closely followed—and recently has led—the evolution of American parks and their relationship to the design of cities. While this history has been known to Portland park advocates, it has only recently begun to be documented and analyzed (Abbott 2001, Fadely 1987, Houck 1989, Howe 1992).

The history of parks and greenspaces in general has been divided by others into various periods. Perhaps most noted is Cranz's scheme of four eras of park usage: Pleasure Ground (1850–1900), Reform Park (1900–1930), Recreation Facility (1930–1965), and Open Space System (1965–present) (Cranz 1989, 3–154).

I have organized the following chapter around what I consider Portland's own three distinct park periods: Creation: The Pleasure Grounds and the City Beautiful (1843–1910), Recreation: Jungle Gym and Jane (1910–65), and Refuge: Open Space and Greenspace (1965–the present). Woven through these layers of time is an enduring characteristic of Portland's park history: the leadership of private citizens in the creation and maintenance of its parks, a leadership sustained today by a 150-year tradition of volunteerism, public involvement, and perseverance.

What has inspired the people of Portland to put such personal time and effort into their parks? Since their city's founding, Portlanders have believed that their city is, itself, a kind of park—in its setting and access to nature, its open spaces and natural acreage. In defining their sense of place and their sense of self, Portlanders rely as much on their natural setting and parks as on their relatively short history and their distinct and widely recognized architectural and urban-design heritage.

## Creation: The Pleasure Grounds and the City Beautiful (1843–1910)

Early Portlanders fully appreciated the place they had chosen for their town: a place bounded by rivers, surrounded by green hills, lying between ocean and mountains, warmed and bathed by a temperate climate, made habitable by the bounty of its nearby fields. The first generations of settlers said it was imbued with moral, spiritual, and physical qualities that nurtured industry, sensitivity, and refinement—values necessary for a civilized and productive community. It was a romantic belief, in harmony with some increasingly influential American artists and writers in the East. Portlanders wanted to create a city combining both an urban high culture and a rural hardiness.

While Portlanders prepared their city for growth, a New York farmer was studying the world's leading garden architects. During Portland's first decade, the mid-1840s to the early 1850s, Frederick Law Olmsted began advocating for parks as tools for social reform, physical refreshment, and cultural, intellectual, and spiritual improvement. America's new parks shouldered substantial expectations. Elemental to his vision for parks— soon realized in New York's Central Park and others nationwide—were access to nature and wilderness, and the role that parks—his "wildernesses in the city"—could play in shaping people as well as cities. In Olmsted's mind, the wilderness experience—even in a park setting—imposed itself on all the senses, capturing one's attention. As a park designer and social philosopher, he saw individuals taking an active part in their environment. This experience, Olmsted and other reformers believed, led to deeper levels of personal understanding and improved social behavior among the rougher urban classes (Fadely 1987, 18; Rybczynski 1999). Olmsted, his partners, and their colleagues in the new profession of landscape architecture led dozens of communities through exercises in park and town planning, advocating the benefits of nature within cities.

While Olmsted traveled the country persuading city administrators and civic leaders to plan ahead by adding parks to their already built and increasingly crowded cities, early Portlanders were giving land for parks in a city they could only envision, not yet built and not yet crowded. Among the notable donations were James Terwilliger's land claim, William Chapman's and John Couch's additional park blocks, and Ben Holladay's eastside block. In 1852, a year after incorporation, Portland accepted a dedication from pioneer town developer Daniel Lownsdale of a row of narrow blocks west of town. Lownsdale, whose native Louisville had a similar row of "park" blocks, may have intended the blocks to serve as both a promenade and, possibly, a firebreak for the wooded hills above the new townsite (Reps 1981, 42–47). The 18 blocks today form the tree-lined spine of the city (MacColl 1988). In 1871 the Portland City Council purchased 40 acres of parkland in the hills a mile west of town, naming it "City Park." It was an ambitious achievement for a community of 8,293 inhabitants. For most of Portland's citizens it may also have been a dubious one, as the new park, high above the city, was initially inaccessible by graded road or streetcar.

Expanded more than 15-fold over the years and renamed Washington Park, the park today has a world-class zoo, an international rose test garden, Japanese and Shakespeare gardens, a green amphitheater, ball fields and tennis courts, Hoyt Arboretum, the Portland Children's Museum, the World Forestry Institute, several miles of trails, a small passenger train, and two elegant reservoirs.

In the late nineteenth century, City Park offered visitors grand views of the "emerald compass" encircling the city, interior views within the park itself, and a sense of closeness to nature, removed from the clang and cluster of the city below. It was a "pleasure ground" in the spirit of nineteenth-century cemeteries and parks. Yet, even with this large park, Lownsdale's Park Blocks, a handful of neighborhood parks, and the surrounding fields and forests, three men in particular—Rev. T. L. Eliot, L. L. Hawkins, and Ion Lewis—believed that the city could do better in providing its citizens access to nature.

Even as he managed the affairs of Portland's Unitarian Church and the needs of a growing family, the Reverend Thomas Lamb Eliot made time to help found and lead the local school district, the Multnomah County Library, the Portland Art Museum, the Oregon Humane Society, the Boys and Girls Aid Society, Reed College, and other vital institutions. While others have held more power, no one in Portland's 150-year history has matched Eliot's vision, influence, and leadership. In him, Portland's park system had one of its three greatest advocates.

Second of the three was a retired banker, Lester Leander Hawkins. Third was architect Ion Lewis, formerly of Boston. He helped produce some of Portland's most distinctive architecture of the late nineteenth and early twentieth centuries (Hawkins and Willingham 1999, 184; Wilbur 1937).

As the century came to a close, Eliot, Hawkins, and Lewis lobbied the state for legislation requiring that any city with 3,000 or more people establish a park commission. Referred to Oregon voters, the referendum passed in 1900 and the Portland City Council quickly established its own Portland Board of Park Commissioners. Even as they routinely placed parks on the city council's agenda, the new commissioners—Eliot, Hawkins, Lewis, J. D. Meyer, the mayor, and the city auditor—worried that parks were not receiving the attention and enthusiasm they had expected as they planned for the future. They wanted the kind of authoritative push that only outside, "expert" help could confer.

While Eliot and his fellow commissioners built their park board, a group of leading merchants, manufacturers, and bankers began in 1902 making even bigger plans for Portland: its own world's fair to celebrate the 1905 centennial of the Lewis and Clark expedition. It was confidently predicted that this Portland extravaganza would propel the city and region into the new century with a boldness equal to the demands of the emerging American economy. Eliot and his colleagues had neatly married their own needs for a park planner to the fair board's desire for a fair planner. Eliot went east looking for a park-planning firm with experience in designing world's fair grounds, like that created in Chicago by Daniel Burnham, Charles McKim, and Frederick Law Olmsted (Abbott 1981, MacColl 1988).

While Oregonians pondered parks and fair grounds, America's planners, architects, and designers—with the Olmsted family and partners at the forefront—organized professionally and institutionalized a design ethic of beautifying cities. The movement's objective was to transform American cities—darkened by decades of industrialization and poor, if any, planning—into beautiful as well as utilitarian places. "Beautility" was their catch phrase. Portland's business and civic leaders embraced the principles of City Beautiful—beauty, utility, recreation, urban design, community pride—recognizing that they were precisely what the city needed to develop its economy, shake the town out of its nineteenth-century conservatism, take its mind off the pervasive reminders of vice, and keep a step ahead of Seattle, its rival to the north (Guzowski 1990, 21–32).

Eliot ultimately went to Brookline, Massachusetts, to negotiate for the services of America's "cutting edge" landscape architecture firm whose principals—Frederick Law Olmsted Jr., and stepbrother John Charles Olmsted—were also key figures in the City Beautiful movement. Eliot had helped to raise $10,000 (half for a park plan, half for the fairgrounds) for the Olmsteds' expertise. John Charles Olmsted agreed to come to Portland (Lutino and Merker undated, 2–12; MacColl 1988, 269).

Arriving in early April 1903, Olmsted immediately went to work on the design for the fairgrounds. He then turned to Portland's terrain, park inventory, real estate prospects for future parkland, and park personnel. Hawkins took Lewis and Olmsted for tours by carriage while the latter took copious notes of all he saw on five-inch index cards and snapped hundreds of photographs of the Portland landscape. He spent his evenings at the Portland Hotel writing up his notes in longhand, which were then typed by hotel stenographers (Guzowski 1990, 43). Predicting a recurring problem that would haunt the Portland system, he wrote his wife on 29 April, "I have enjoyed my park reconnaissance very much as the landscape is fine and the possibilities for parks, as far as land is concerned, are excellent. But I fear the money will be deficient" (Olmsted 1903b).

Strategic, visionary planning was at the heart of the Olmsted Report of 1903. Olmsted wanted Portlanders to look far into the future—50 years or more—especially when it came to purchasing land while it was still within the city's means. Typical of Olmsted plans, it was comprehensive, including advice on land acquisition, the qualities of good parks and park systems, parkways and boulevards, park governance, and administration.

Olmsted outlined a "comprehensive system of parks and parkways for Portland." It began with a large forest reservation between Riverview Cemetery and the southern suburb of Lake Oswego, partially achieved today with Tryon Creek State Park. An informal "picturesque" parkway would run from Riverview Cemetery along the eastern foot of the West Hills, connecting the downtown park squares and Washington Park and passing by Macleay Park up to what is now Forest Park. Terwilliger Boulevard today is part of this proposed city-length parkway as are Skyline Boulevard above and Leif Erikson Drive through Forest Park. On the river itself, at the south end of town, he suggested the City acquire Ross Island for park purposes. East of the river, he proposed a river bluff parkway. McLoughlin Boulevard is a partial realization of this planned road. Another parkway would run north along the river bluff above the rail yards and Mocks Bottom to the University of Portland. A great meadow park in the Columbia Sloughs would preserve the bottom land scenery near the river. He then proposed running a series of boulevards (more formal than parkways) from Sellwood Park to Ladds Addition, out to Mt. Tabor Park and then north, up to Columbia Slough Park and back over to the proposed parkway on the bluff above Swan Island, which he also recommended for inclusion in the park system. Like Boston's Emerald Necklace, designed by his stepfather Frederick Law Olmsted, John Olmsted's proposed park system—elongated and connected—would provide a greenbelt around and nearly across the city. He left it to the people of Portland and their park board, staff, and city council to make the plan real (Olmsted 1903a).

There was less will and little way, however, for Olmsted's plan to proceed. The city's leadership was focused on the Lewis and Clark Exposition and the prospects for postfair economic growth. L. L. Hawkins had died and Rev. Eliot had resigned from the Parks Board. While parks commissioners Hawkins and Lewis had expressed total support for the plan, Mayor George Williams, in a 1904 *Oregonian* article with the tentative title "Is Portland Ready for a Park System," probably represented the sober reality that the plan faced: "While we must all agree that an elaborate system of parks and boulevards such as he has planned would greatly enhance the beauty and attractiveness of the city, we must cut our garment by our cloth and cannot afford such an outlay" (*The Oregonian* 1904). Perhaps the greatest "lost opportunity" was the Lewis and Clark fairground itself. Olmsted had wanted to see this area become a park, but even before he arrived it had been sold for future development and then leased back for the fair's temporary use.

Olmsted may have been discouraged by the City's reluctance to proceed, but steady progress was made over the succeeding decades, at Portland's own deliberate pace.

## Recreation: Jungle Gym and Jane (1910–1965)

With the exception of one new playground in the North Park Blocks, in the first four years after Olmsted's first visit, Portlanders built homes, not parks. Olmsted himself returned several times to consult on private landscaping projects, often commenting on the progress—or lack thereof—of his plan. While excitement over the fair died down, the city's business affairs and housing starts came to life. Portland grew by as much as 50% in the decade after the Exposition (Abbott 1981). The Olmsted Report languished, annually buried deeper and deeper under subsequent Park Board reports. In an apparent effort to inject life into Olmsted's plans, *The Oregonian* published occasional articles on the need for more parks and improved park services. The 24 February 1908 issue discussed the particular need for a parks administrator. The newspaper argued that the kind of park improvements described in the 1903 Olmsted Report required a skilled superintendent with wide experience in American and European park systems. "We must have this man," the paper argued, "if Portland is to keep pace with the city's growth and if that system is to be a worthy expression of the city's taste and liberality, and of this generation's forethought for the next." Waiting in the wings, already chosen by Olmsted if not yet the city council, was "this man."

While ably managed over the preceding four years, the Portland Parks Department had not found a superintendent equal to Olmsted's vision. Two days after *The Oregonian* article, however, the city council hired Emanuel L. Mische, already twice recommended by Olmsted, Mische's former employer. Following formal training at the Missouri

Botanical Garden, Boston's Arnold Arboretum, and Kew Garden, Mische had spent eight years working as a horticulturist and designer for the Olmsteds. Hired as Portland's fourth park superintendent, Mische spent much of his first year, 1908, negotiating for land on Terwilliger Boulevard and Mt. Tabor. In order to gain some control over public spaces, Mische recommended that he be given authority for the design and placement of fountains, monuments, statuary, sculpture, and architectural works. Already, overall design matters related to street widening, grades, street trees, subdivisions, and construction fell under the Parks Department's authority.

With the Olmsted Plan's foci on connecting urban dwellers with nature and increasing interest in playgrounds and exercise programs, Emanuel Mische found himself charged by his board and the city council with balancing the diverse recreational needs of Portland citizens. During the six years (1908–1914) of his superintendency, Mische began to turn Olmsted's descriptive vision into landscapes and plantings. He also began to build the recreational infrastructure of playgrounds and athletic, cultural, and educational programs that would be the theme for Portland's park growth. In spite of his short tenure, Mische laid the foundation for the balanced and integrated park system that Portland has today (Guzowski 1990, 110).

Mische applied his experience in horticulture to creating intentional designs within parks that previously had been planned with little sense of order or relationship with parks elsewhere in the city. Acting on Olmsted's dictum to create a comprehensive plan and "look" for the city's parks, he put his groundsmen to work transforming the Park Blocks into a showplace for shrubs and flower beds, planting colorful ornamentals and roses, and improving the walkways and benches. Such formality and color, he deemed, were appropriate to a park that still edged the city's downtown core. On the other hand, he avoided such a formal style in Washington Park, developing instead the more naturalistic look encouraged in Olmsted's report. Mische next turned his attention to the new neighborhood parks that the city was acquiring in response to increasing neighborhood requests. (The demand for parks would be among the earliest organized efforts by Portland's neighborhoods.) He followed the advice of his mentor in mixing native species and exotics from the east coast, and in creating a sense of separation from the surrounding streets and homes. He was able to accommodate the competing needs of solitary pedestrians and groups of noisy children. No provisions were made for carriages or cars that would intrude on visitors' serenity or play or jeopardize their safety (Guzowski 1990, 111–128).

Olmsted had been particularly taken with the potential for Portland's three "scenic reservations"—Washington, Macleay, and Mt. Tabor—parks of 100 acres or more that were large enough for interior views and exterior panoramic vistas. In Washington Park, Mische built or rebuilt paths to take advantage of this topography. He shared Olmsted's opinion that the wilderness aspect of Macleay Park should be maintained, with as few intrusions as possible; at the same time, recognizing the need for security and fire prevention, he hired two guards to patrol the trails. He rid the park of hunters, evicted a dairy that was polluting the watershed, and succeeded in removing an unsightly flume. In 1909 the Wildwood Trail—early on one of Portland's most heavily used and popular forest paths—was laid down between Macleay Park and the Forestry Center, the last remaining major building on the grounds of the 1905 Lewis and Clark Exposition (Portland Parks and Recreation 1998, 6). Across the city at Mt. Tabor Park, Mische completed an ambitious design that reforested the west slope, opened vistas toward Mount St. Helens and Mount Hood, and constructed a shelter, bandstand, and comfort station near the summit. His proposed series of cascades and pools connecting city reservoirs number 5 and 6 was never realized, however, due to financial limitations (Guzowski 1990, 129–137).

Although Mische today is remembered for his horticultural skills and for sensitively responding to what some now describe as "Olmstedian" qualities of urban wilderness, he also gave considerable attention to the needs of children at play and adult athletes. Portland has always been a city of exercisers. Almost as soon as they trudged in from the 2,000-mile hike across the Oregon Trail or stumbled stiff-legged off the ships that brought them up the Pacific Coast, Portlanders took to the town's hills and nearby mountains, its rivers, bicycle routes, horse tracks, and walking trails.

Two years before Mische took up his work of implementing the vision of the City Beautiful movement, Portland had embraced yet another trend, the Playground Movement (Guzowski 1990, 104). Despite, or because of, the mud, children by the hundreds swarmed into the North Park Blocks in December 1906 to inaugurate Portland's first playground. Swings, a climbing rope, sand boxes, seesaws, a great slide, and horizontal, parallel, and vaulting bars gave outlet to young energy. Boys and girls each had their own area, and it was soon deemed necessary to build a fence around the boys' playground to keep out the men who were setting up boxing matches and betting and having a generally "pernicious influence." Beyond merely strolling through greenways, Portlanders were discovering new uses for their parks and Mische proved that he could integrate the increasingly diverse users of the city's forests, picnic and playgrounds, fields, formal gardens, and pools. With the exception of Macleay Park, all other parks incorporated programs and facilities such as fields, courts, and playgrounds to support organized sports and play. In 1911, the Parks Board created a committee to plan a system of playgrounds with the Board of Education, the first major interaction between the schools and the Parks Board (Portland Parks and Recreation 1998, 5–7).

After 13 years of giving shape, leadership, and support to the creation and maintenance of parks, the Portland Parks Board was dissolved in 1914 when voters established a commission form of government. Existing city boards were abolished, giving their responsibilities to elected city commissioners. Superintendent Mische then reported to a commissioner of public works. In his first annual report after the change, Mische complained that the lack of a general plan under the new system would spell failure for the parks. The following year, he resigned. With Mische's departure Portland lost the experience and informed perspective that connected it directly with the guiding principles and inspiration of the ambitious 1903 Olmsted plan.

"Without Eliot, without Mische, . . . and Eliot above all, . . . Portland would not have achieved a notable recreation system." So Portland's early park years were summed up by Paul Keyser, who replaced Mische as superintendent in 1917 (Keyser 1958, 4). In his first year, Keyser, an engineer by training, added golf to the system's programs. The first golf course was sited in the southeast neighborhood of Eastmoreland. Through the 1920s, the new superintendent added two more golf courses and expanded the city's recreational programs. The Community House Program began offering gym, dance, handicraft, and home economics classes. The program established daycare services for working mothers. Part of the city zoo was moved from the lower part of Washington Park (Marconi Street) to the current site of the Japanese Garden. Just below the location of the tennis courts, the parks department established the National Rose Test Garden, "for the scientific testing outdoors of new roses and the cultivation and development in the open of existing varieties." The city was given hundreds of varieties of roses from across the United States and Europe for planting in the new garden. During this decade the park system also received several new sculptures, fulfilling the bureau's role as the city's public-arts manager. Heroic statues of George Washington, Theodore Roosevelt, Abraham Lincoln, Joan of Arc, and the elegant, diminutive "Rebecca at the Well," were donated and installed in parks (Portland Parks and Recreation 1998, 11–13).

Like his predecessor, Keyser maintained a balance of establishing recreational programs while preserving and adding greenspaces in the city's larger parks. During the mid-1920s, he worried that large tracts of land recommended for purchase by Olmsted and Mische had still not been acquired by the city. While citizens supported small neighborhood parks, Keyser believed that diminished interest in larger city parks such as Washington and Macleay was due to the automobile, which was now taking growing numbers of Portlanders to open space and forests outside the city. Even as he enriched Portland's recreational park programs, Keyser sought to expand the city's large forest reserves to lure residents back into Portland's own large parks. He began efforts to expand Macleay Park along Balch Creek, from a new wildflower garden beneath the Thurman Street Bridge up the creek to the Audubon Society's planned 40-acre bird sanctuary along Cornell Road. During the 1928 National Forestry Week, with the encouragement of the Chamber of Commerce, the city council agreed with Keyser that the city should establish an arboretum—a long-held dream of Mische—in Hoyt Park above Washington Park. Multnomah County deeded the city 145 acres for this purpose. Not content with these successes, Keyser turned his eyes on even more land in what is now Forest Park, noting prophetically—and paraphrasing Olmsted—that "Portland could easily attain one of the largest and, I daresay, one of the most notable parks in the country containing . . . a forest primeval, trails, viewpoints and glens, not miles away but within our urban borders" (Portland Parks and Recreation 1998, 12).

The Depression stalled Keyser's ambitions, as it did those of park systems in other cities. During the economic downturn, Portland's Parks Bureau relied heavily on federal relief funds, which supported trail construction; built and restored picnic shelters, fire pits, roads, bridges, and stone buildings; and developed playground facilities. In addition to their construction projects, the newly employed men and women of such New Deal agencies as the Civil Works Administration, the Civilian Conservation Corps, and the Works Progress Administration staffed recreation programs as coaches, teachers, artists, and playground supervisors. In 1938, Dorthea Lensch was appointed playground supervisor to manage the bureau's recreation division. Nearly one-half of her staff were federally funded relief workers. Responding to the realities of the

Depression, with adults having more leisure time and children being offered limited activities in schools, Lensch implemented several new recreational and cultural programs, sometimes using school buildings in neighborhoods not served by park community centers. The bureau offered classes in drama and dance, exercise and bridge, photography, sculpting and painting, nature lore, first aid, archery, badminton, and field hockey. Lensch endeavored to open the parks to the public during a time of heightened demand for public recreational services, which private agencies were not able to adequately address (Portland Parks and Recreation 1998, 14–15).

World War II initially resulted in the closure of Portland's largest parks. Following the attack on Pearl Harbor, the city closed Washington and Mt. Tabor Parks in fear of sabotage to the reservoirs—Portland's immediate water supplies—and deferred new construction for five years. The war created challenges for a park bureau not yet recovered from the Depression. With juvenile delinquency increasing, as children were left on their own with parents working for local wartime industries or in the military, the bureau was pushed to expand its recreation programs into schools, community centers, churches, and the new wartime housing projects. The Parks Bureau worked with schools and neighborhoods to plant "victory gardens" that provided young Portlanders a productive out-of-school activity as well as fresh summer and fall produce. Symptomatic of the stress felt in the city as increasing numbers of minorities arrived to work in Portland's wartime shipyards and factories, baseless complaints about "Asiatics" and African Americans monopolizing tennis courts and other facilities prompted Superintendent Keyser to issue plans (never implemented) for a community center in Albina to serve ethnic minorities. Indeed, minorities in Portland bore the brunt of wartime anxiety. Japanese citizens were forcibly moved from their communities and interned in camps in eastern Oregon and beyond. African American laborers were denied access to many kinds of jobs and had to resort to federal action to open union positions for them (Portland Parks and Recreation 1998, 16).

Throughout the first third of the century, little development took place on the hills northwest of Portland and even less during the succeeding Depression and war years. It was here that John Olmsted recommended the city establish a "forest park."

"The investment," he advised in 1903, "of a comparatively moderate sum in the acquisition of these romantic wooded hillsides for a park or reservation of wild woodland character would yield ample returns in pleasure to taxpayers and to those dependent on them, while to a large part of the poorer classes a visit to these woods would afford more pleasure and satisfaction than a visit to any other sort of park" (Olmsted 1903a, 41–42).

A group of citizens under the chairmanship of retired forester and Portland Audubon president Thornton T. Munger put action to Olmsted's eloquence and in November 1946 formed the Committee of Fifty to promote the city's acquisition of the forested hills and ravines above the former site of Guild's Lake. The committee began raising money, consciousness, and recruits in an effort to convince the Oregon legislature to allow counties to transfer to cities for park purposes lands that had come into public ownership due to tax default. By July 1947 the city council was able to proceed with plans for Forest Park. It dedicated 2,000 acres and approved plans to acquire an additional 6,000. Notwithstanding a fire four years later that burned 80% of Forest Park, the City made further headway toward Olmsted's "forest reservation" in 1951 when Multnomah County transferred land to the City for the new park, and Portland high school students launched what would become a multiyear reforestation effort by planting 30,000 trees (Portland Parks and Recreation 1998, 17).

In the two decades following the Depression and World War II, the Portland Parks Bureau not only multiplied its landholdings severalfold to over 6,000 acres, it also enlarged the range of its recreational offerings. Responding to substantial increases in recreation participation (a 35% increase in 1951 alone), the bureau added community centers; greatly enlarged its volunteer corps (3,500 by 1957); moved and enhanced the zoo (commencing the era of the baby elephant); created trail maintenance, "aquatheater," and weightlifting programs; and added to its inventory of buildings such historic structures as the rustic Pioneer Church in Sellwood and the elegant Pittock Mansion. As the city grew with the postwar economy, especially during the 1960s, the park bureau continued to make great strides in providing recreational services, along with the space in which to provide them. And, inspired by new governor Tom McCall's pressure to create a waterfront park where the Willamette River flows through the city, plans and provisions for open space began to command increasing attention from the public, their political leaders, and park officials (Portland Parks and Recreation 1998, 18–20).

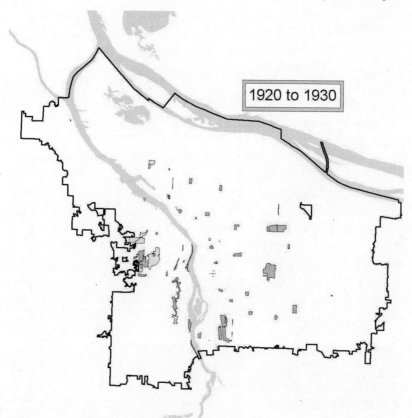

1920 to 1930

FIGURE 7.1. Portland Parks, 1920–1930. Source: Portland Parks & Recreation.

## Refuge: Open Space and Greenspace (1965–the present)

Portland was conceived in "the clearing"—an open space—by the river. A tradition of open space ensued. Daniel Lownsdale's initial deeded blocks, Terwilliger Park, and other gifts of land have preserved the open space refuge that the Olmsteds and other early park planners urged growing cities to provide. Although Portland has had infill and density as twin goals over the past two decades, the city has maintained its provisions for "breathing room" and not become a dense city. (For a discussion on density, see Chap. 10, Chapman and Lund.) So the vision of Eliot, Hawkins, and their fellow park-system founders; of their planner Olmsted; of his plan's implementer Mische; and of Paul Keyser has been sustained.

"Open space" has broad meanings. It encompasses small squares at the heart of the city as well as large spaces at its edge that are not

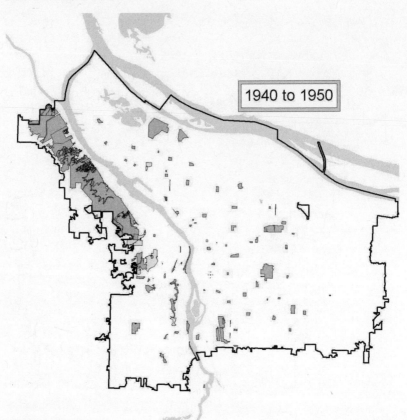

1940 to 1950

FIGURE 7.2. Portland Parks, 1940–1950. Source: Portland Parks & Recreation.

"parks" at all, but greenspaces—wetlands, stream corridors, meadows, forests, and other nearby "wild" places. When one looks at a map of downtown Portland, a linear north–south pattern of open spaces emerges. (For more on downtown, see Chap. 8, Abbott.) The North and South Park Blocks along Ninth Avenue, the Plaza Blocks on Fourth, and Waterfront Park form green stretches of open space breaking up the grid of buildings on the west side. The east side's expansive commercial and retail districts offer less such refuge, with space afforded intermittently by parks and the Eastbank Esplanade. It is the central business district that presents local and national models of urban open spaces.

The renovation of Portland's Civic Auditorium was part of an extensive urban-renewal process in South Portland during the 1960s and 1970s. Even before the auditorium's remodeling itself began, a block of

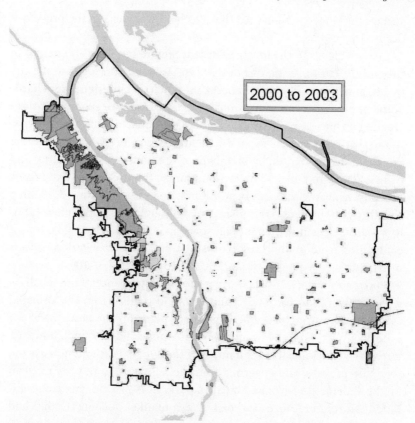

FIGURE 7.3. Portland Parks, 2000–2003. Source: Portland Parks & Recreation.

open space across the street was proposed for a park. Angela Danadjieva, a San Francisco architect with Lawrence Halprin's design firm, created the design for a nearly full-block fountain park. Dedicated in 1970, the Forecourt Fountain (since renamed in memory of founding Portland Development Commission chair Ira C. Keller) is an abstraction of northwest waterfalls cascading over columnar basalt outcroppings with sculptured terraces and pools. The waterfalls, ledges, pools, and surrounding stairs, benches, and grass provide space for sitting and wading, and for audience members taking a break from auditorium performances. The fountain quickly became a landmark park and, with a bit of exuberance, was called by *New York Times* architectural critic Ada Louise Huxtable "perhaps the greatest open space since the Renaissance" (Portland Parks and Recreation undated). This from a writer who, seeing Portlanders thoughtlessly replacing their historic buildings with surface parking lots, remarked that Portland was a city in the process of destroying itself.

Sixteen blocks to the north, O'Bryant Square began as an attempt in the early 1970s to regain one of the "lost" Park Blocks. A gift to the city by Mr. and Mrs. William E. Roberts, the square was designed as a hardscape to create an outdoor "brown-bag" performance space with trees creating an enclosure. Near the center of the square is a bronze fountain in the shape of a rose. The park opened with concerts but soon became increasingly frequented by members of the homeless community and drug culture. In 1984, Pioneer Courthouse Square opened and drew potential concert audiences away. Efforts are now under way to heighten visibility into the park by removing trees, though O'Bryant Square's ability to succeed as downtown open space may depend upon its possible connection to additional park blocks that may appear as Park Avenue is restructured (Portland Parks and Recreation undated, 9–10).

Portland's waterfront was covered for nearly a century and a half by wharves, warehouses, retail buildings, and roads. From the Olmsted Plan of 1903 through several subsequent plans for the downtown, the waterfront was targeted for park space. Money and civic will, however, were always lacking. Through much of the 1960s, Portland newscaster, secretary of state, and governor Tom McCall prodded the city to clean up the Willamette River and create a park. In 1971 a citizens group initiated efforts to remove Harbor Drive, a blanket of concrete that had long separated the city from its river. (See Photos 1 and 2 in Chap. 2) With support from Mayor Neil Goldschmidt and the Portland Development Commission in the mid-1970s, Portland architects Wolff, Zimmer, Gunsul, Frasca Partnership developed a master plan for a new park. With the dedication of Waterfront Park in 1978, Portlanders for the first time gained access to the west bank of the Willamette. It was an immediate success, but by 2000 popularity had degraded the park, frustrating citizens beneath the crush of high-attendance events (carnivals, concerts, and food festivals). In 2002 the Parks Bureau initiated a master planning process designed to balance the conflicting demands of diverse users upon the park's long and narrow landscape. As had been the case 30 years before, the process elicited substantial public involvement in planning the future of Portland's "front yard." Guided by a citizens advisory committee, the public participated in numerous workshops to envision and debate potential uses and designs. Architects, landscape architects, and planners provided technical support and advice. The result was an ambitious vision for Waterfront Park, one that will take many years to finance and achieve.

Six blocks west, on a block that Portlanders have dubbed their community "living room," citizens have consistently maintained an intense interest and protectiveness for what architect Pietro Belluschi called at its opening in 1984 "one of the best moves Portland ever made." Taking the place of a parking lot that had replaced the Portland Hotel (once the city's most popular meeting space) Pioneer Courthouse Square—immediately adjacent to Pioneer Courthouse—quickly became a year-round, day- and night-long gathering ground. The Square's brick pavement—built with bricks sold to raise funds for the project—terra cotta walls, and classical columns are a neighborly reflection of the Square's surrounding buildings, which date from among the city's oldest to its newest. Whimsical sculptures, such as an umbrella-holding man hailing a cab, a "Weather Machine," a waterfall, space for events and exhibits, a public-transit and city information center, plus a Starbucks coffee shop and Powell's book store place the Square comfortably into the city's culture. Its creation, led by architect Will Martin, depended on the diverse team he brought together: landscape architect Doug Macy, historian Terence O'Donnell, sculptor Lee Kelly, writer Spencer Gill,

PHOTO 3. Pioneer Courthouse Square at SW Broadway and Yamhill St., 2004. Dubbed the city's "living room," this innovative public space replaced a parking structure in the mid-1980s.

and designer/artist Robert Reynolds (Portland Parks and Recreation undated, 11–12). Urban observer William Whyte considered Pioneer Square among the nation's finest programmed open spaces (Whyte 1988, 152).

The first section of the Eastbank Esplanade, directly across the river from Waterfront Park, was opened in 2001 and illustrates the challenge, and one successful solution, of creating open space in a closed, congested, and cacophonous location. Tucked between the Interstate 5 freeway and the Willamette River, this narrow, mile-and-a-half-long park includes the longest floating walkway in the country. The habitat demonstration and riverbank restoration project uses several large "root wads" to provide habitat areas for fish along with bioengineering techniques employing native vegetation to treat freeway runoff before it enters the river. Graphic designers from the landscape architecture firm Mayer/Reed included cultural history in the Esplanade through a series of illustrated and text panels providing information about the river and Portland history. Four pieces of public art, *The Running Gate, The Stackstalk, The Alluvial Wall,* and *The Ghost Ship,* were created and installed by RIGGA, a group of local artists working with the support of the Regional Arts and Culture Council's Percent for Art program.

From an airplane approaching Portland, the landscape shows great contrast. Passing over the city, small squares and larger parks leap out with colorful plazas and green open space. Further out, however, one is struck by the sheer expanse of land covered by trees and water and open land. From the airplane passenger's perspective, the larger cityscape looks not like a patchwork of green but like strips of green connecting metropolitan Portland's parts into a regional whole. These are greenspaces that, through good luck and great vision, have (in most cases) been intentionally preserved between and within communities. As with all things of permanence, the vision took some time to become reality.

In 1903, John Charles Olmsted had discussed with Portlanders his notion of naturalizing the city with large parks connected by parkways, winding a ring of greenspace around and through the city. "While there are many things," Olmsted wrote in his 1903 Report to the Portland Park Board, "both small and great, which may contribute to the beauty of a great city, unquestionably one of the greatest is a comprehensive system of parks and parkways" (Olmsted 1903a, 14). From 1903 into the 1970s, connecting parks and greenspaces, as Olmsted had advised and some Portlanders appreciated, remained an almost unimaginable, even utopian, strategy. First of all, there was the sheer cost of the land.

Further, with the notable exception of Forest Park, once Portland had established its large early parks it put increasing emphasis on playgrounds and sports fields, and small, highly programmed open spaces in the downtown.

Independent suburban communities in the 1970s and 1980s followed Portland's lead in their own parks and recreation programs—preserving and connecting greenspaces was not part of local park districts' agendas. Then, in 1971, the Columbia Region Association of Governments (CRAG) presented an ambitious scheme for regional open-space planning titled, "Proposals to the Portland-Vancouver Community for a Metropolitan Park and Open Space System." Integrating Olmsted's proposals with urban philosopher Lewis Mumford's vision for a regional community, the CRAG plan suggested a way to navigate toward a regional, comprehensive park system. With no public input, the plan stalled for two years until two events took place under the leadership of Governor Tom McCall that would restart the process and provide a new framework for park and open-space planning in Portland and its neighboring communities.

In 1973 the State of Oregon initiated state land use planning. The law stipulated that cities were to create urban growth boundaries and develop comprehensive plans with planning goals relating to the preservation of open spaces; scenic, historic, and natural resources; land resources; and recreational needs. The following year, the state issued the Willamette River Greenway Plan, which directed development away from the river, establishing a minuscule 25-foot greenway setback and requiring protection of natural elements and scenic qualities. With such state-mandated planning goals, the Portland region acquired the tools to begin building the "comprehensive system" of greenspaces and parks earlier envisioned by John Charles Olmsted. Using these tools—comprehensive regional planning, locally set land use goals, an urban growth boundary—a small number of parks and greenspace advocates, in partnership with local and regional governments, began to realize Olmsted's larger vision. Leading this persistent effort were the Audubon Society's Mike Houck and Barbara Walker, founder of the 40-Mile Loop Land Trust. With volunteers and staff of Metro and the Portland Parks Bureau, they helped initiate a planning process that, through the 1990s, would result in a regional strategy for parks, greenspaces, and greenways across metropolitan Portland.

As an urban naturalist with the Audubon Society of Portland, Mike Houck encouraged Metro, the Portland area's regional government, to take the lead in protecting natural resources and wildlife, and thereby comply with the State of Oregon's land use planning Goal 5, which protects natural and historic resources and open spaces. Working with Metro from 1989 to 1992, he convinced the agency to take the lead in building a "greenfrastructure," a connected system of natural areas and greenways across the region (Howe 1992, 2–4). Coincident with Houck's work, Barbara Walker, an articulate and long-time volunteer leader in local parks issues, had been advocating the establishment of the 40-Mile Loop Land Trust, whose goal was to create a trail system around the region. The concept for such a loop first surfaced in the Portland Parks and Recreation Bureau's 1983 master plan and benefited from the subsequent struggles for the Oaks Bottom Wildlife Refuge and the Marquam and Powell Butte nature parks. "When I first saw Barbara's slide depicting the Loop," Houck reported in 1989 to the City Club of Portland, "it was impossible to ignore the striking coincidence of the trail and natural areas that it passes through. . . . It was a marriage of tremendous recreational and wildlife viewing opportunities too good to pass up. The concept to link these two efforts is also in keeping with the philosophies espoused by Olmsted, Mumford, and the CRAG report" (Houck 1989, 5).

Consummating this "marriage" in 1992, Metro adopted a "Metropolitan Greenspaces Master Plan," aimed at purchasing, managing, and protecting natural resources. The plan's vision was "to balance an urban landscape with wildlife habitat in the midst of a flourishing cosmopolitan region." Voters were convinced and quickly authorized Metro to acquire, develop, maintain, and operate a system of parks, open space, and recreational facilities of metropolitan concern (Metro 1997, 84). In 1994, the same year Multnomah County's parks division merged with Metro's greenspaces program creating Metro Regional Parks and Greenspaces, the regional government adopted the Regional 2040 Growth Concept to guide future decisions about land use, transportation, urban design, and natural resources. A year later metropolitan residents further embraced the greenspaces agenda and passed a $135.6 million bond measure for open spaces, parks, and streams. The funds have allowed Metro to acquire over 8,000 acres of wetlands, riparian areas, forests, and meadows and more than 50 miles of stream and river frontage; and to strengthen its park programs, including school classes, restoration projects, public tours, and other environmental education activities. If one combines the metropolitan region's open space inventory (parks, greenspaces, and the regional trail system) with individual park districts' recreation programs, the elements that Olmsted envisioned for Portland 100 years ago are now in place.

In 1988 Charles Jordan (a former Portland city commissioner) became director of the Portland Parks Bureau. Despite property-tax limitation measures and the frustrations of budget cuts throughout much of his 15-year tenure, Jordan started to build on the city's own 1992 park plan. The plan was based on a five-year Parks Futures Project that identified $100 million worth of capital improvements to the nearly 100-year-old park system. Ultimately, the 1994 general obligation bond provided $59 million for much-needed improvements in lighting, irrigation, and paths in parks as well as heating, plumbing, and electrical systems in buildings. Later bond measures provided further capital funding for the bureau. Throughout the 1990s, while Metro's regional parks department was adding land and establishing its environmental education offerings, the Portland Parks Bureau improved its capital facilities—tennis courts and community centers, pools, and fields—and added new classes in athletics and the arts. Parks director Jordan also led the bureau in providing enhanced programs to underserved parts of the community. As with most municipal park agencies in Oregon by the mid-1990s, Portland's was increasingly relying on nonprofit "friends" groups to raise funds and organize events. The decade saw increasing collaboration between the Parks Bureau and the school district in school recreational programs.

Following two years of work by many of the same individuals and staff who contributed to Metro's plans, Portland crafted its own updated park vision. The "Parks 2020 Vision," adopted by the City Council in 2001, was an effort to recommit the city to Olmsted's vision of 1903: more land for parks, a regional approach, able and informed park leadership, access to parks by all, well-maintained facilities, and excellent and diverse programs throughout the city. A Portland Parks Board was reestablished to provide public input into park policies, operations, and plans. And, in recognition of the realities of government funding in twenty-first-century Oregon, a private park foundation was organized to raise money for land acquisition, operations and maintenance, scholarships, and new facilities (Portland Parks and Recreation 2001).

The city of Portland has changed dramatically since Lovejoy landed in "the clearing," since Lownsdale laid down his park blocks, and since the first generations of Portlanders began to boast of their community's parklike features: the forest and mountain views, open space, and outdoor activities that have engaged its residents and visitors ever since.

Within 50 years of Portland's incorporation, John Charles Olmsted gave it a vision for the future based on parks and the city's unique natural setting. Notwithstanding the reluctance of early-twentieth-century Portlanders to provide public dollars to implement Olmsted's plan, succeeding generations demonstrated their commitment to parks through levies and bonds, participation in parks programs, and volunteer services to build a solid, if not quite "Olmstedian," system. Today, there are over 700 parks within the metropolitan region—from 18-inch Mill End Park to 4,683-acre Forest Park—and more than 15,000 acres of natural areas with more than 150 miles of trails linking together many of these green and open spaces. Even as demanding a landscape architect as Olmsted might concede that his sometimes-reluctant client has made progress toward his vision.

In the final analysis, of course, it is not the vision of such planners as Olmsted that accomplish the plan, but the catalytic leadership of those like Eliot, Lewis, and Hawkins; like Thornton Munger, Barbara Walker, or Mike Houck; the intelligent work of committed staff; and the countless hours of thousands of volunteers. Especially over the past 30 years, citizen participation has been basic to the Portland story. (See Chap. 5, Johnson, for a discussion on citizen involvement.) Through parks, citizens have contributed to the development of the region's overall urban design, helping shape its growth and the vision for its future. Citizens have also preserved their community's past in parks and greenspaces (Fadely 1987, 32).

Olmsted had it right when he opened his report to the Portland Parks Board with an expression of the duty of citizens to their city: "It is becoming more clearly realized," he wrote, "that every inhabitant owes to his or her city certain duties. . . . Among them is that of making the city more beautiful to live and work in. [And,] while there are many things which may contribute to the beauty of a great city, one of the greatest is a comprehensive system of parks and parkways." Greenspaces are the places where Portlanders can appreciate nature's sounds, touch, sights, and smells within the confines of the city—in other words, where they achieve the values espoused in the Olmsted Plan in 1903. They are places where, in Portland, people have invested their civic pride and drawn their civic identity. It is through parks and greenspaces that Portlanders, 100 years after Olmsted's report, find their place in the natural and human history of their region and, perhaps most deliberately and enthusiastically, express their character as citizens.

REFERENCES

Abbott, Carl. 1981. *The Great Extravaganza: Portland and the Lewis and Clark Exposition.* Portland: The Oregon Historical Society.

Abbott, Carl. 2001. *Greater Portland: Urban Life and Landscape in the Pacific Northwest.* Philadelphia: University of Pennsylvania Press.

Cranz, Galen. 1989. *The Politics of Park Design: A History of Urban Parks in America.* Cambridge: MIT Press.

Fadely, D. G. 1987. *The Role of Urban Parks.* Portland: Bureau of Parks and Recreation.

Guzowski, Kenneth J. 1990. Portland's Olmsted vision (1897–1915): A study of the public landscapes designed by Emanuel T. Mische in Portland, Oregon. M.A thesis, University of Oregon, Eugene.

Hawkins, William J. III, and William F. Willingham. 1999. *Classic Houses of Portland, Oregon, 1850–1950.* Portland: Timber Press.

Houck, Michael C. 1989. *Protecting Our Urban Wild Lands: Renewing a Vision. Portland, Oregon.* City Club of Portland Speech.

Howe, Deborah. 1992. *The Environment as Infrastructure: Metropolitan Portland's Greenspaces Program.* Portland: Metro.

Keyser, Paul C. 1958. *History of the Portland Park Department.* Unpublished manuscript.

Lutino, Cielo, and Blaine Merker. Undated. *The City Beautiful Movement and Park Planning in Portland, Oregon, 1897–1928, Portland, Oregon.* City of Portland Bureau of Planning.

MacColl, E. Kimbark. 1988. *Merchants, Money and Power: The Portland Establishment, 1843–1913.* Portland: The Georgian Press.

Metro. 1997. *Regional Framework Plan: Portland, Oregon.* Portland: Metro.

Olmsted, John Charles. 1903a. *Report of the Park Board, Portland, Oregon.* Portland Parks.

Olmsted, John Charles. 1903b. 29 April 1903, Item #344, The Olmsted Correspondence. Frederick Law Olmsted National Historic Site, Brookline, MA.

*The Oregonian.* 1904. Is Portland ready for a park system? 12 June.

Portland Parks and Recreation. 1998. *A Chronological History.* Portland: Portland Parks and Recreation.

Portland Parks and Recreation. 2001. *Parks 2020 Vision.* Portland: Portland Parks and Recreation.

Portland Parks and Recreation. Undated. *Open Space Inventory—Urban Parks.* Portland: Portland Parks and Recreation.

Reps, John W. 1981. *The Forgotten Frontier: Urban Planning in the American West before 1890.* Columbia: University of Missouri Press.

Rybczynski, Witold. 1999. *A Clearing in the Distance: Frederick Law Olmsted and America in the 19th Century.* New York: Touchstone Press.

Whyte, William H. 1988. *City: Rediscovering the Center.* New York: Doubleday.

Wilbur, Earl M. 1937. *Thomas Lamb Eliot, 1841–1936.* Portland: Privately printed.

**8** | *Centers and Edges:*
*Reshaping Downtown Portland*

Carl Abbott

In 2003, the City of Portland engaged in a vigorous competition
to obtain a big league baseball team. Eager to relocate the Mon-
treal Expos for the 2004 season, major league baseball invited
Washington, D.C., northern Virginia, and Portland to make their
case as the landing place for the highly mobile Expos (who played
many of their home games for 2003 in San Juan, Puerto Rico).
Aided by a vocal group of local sports promoters and baseball
fans, Portland simultaneously pitched itself to baseball officials,
pushed a stadium funding bill through the Oregon legislature,
and commissioned an evaluation of sites for a new stadium.[1]

It quickly became apparent that siting a ballpark in Portland
is a problem very different from that faced by other cities. In
Cleveland, Baltimore, Seattle, and even Denver, new baseball sta-
diums have been built on vacant or underutilized land on the
edge of the central business district (CBD) in the hope of priming
the downtown land market and stimulating spinoff business and
housing. Portland's leaders likewise want a new stadium to be in
the urban core—for both economic and symbolic reasons—but
the problem is to find land that *needs* the stadium. Most of the
proposals involve displacing an active function (a downtown
high school, the main post office, the school district headquarters
building) or require building on top of an inner loop freeway or railroad tracks (Hunt 2003). Downtown Portland might see positive
economic side effects from baseball, but it has been doing just
fine without a big league ball park.[2]

164

This chapter explores the results, character, and reasons for the successful downtown planning and investment efforts that make professional sports a luxury rather than a necessity for downtown revitalization. I start by reviewing evidence for the success of Portland's central districts.[3] The next section reviews key steps in the downtown planning process, especially the Downtown Plan of 1972 and the Central City Plan of 1988, and analyzes these efforts as both products and generators of a downtown orientation in city and regional politics. The third section addresses some of the problems that have arisen with success— particularly the physical planning challenge of linking together a horizontally expanding urban core and the political problem of blending historically separate districts into this growing core.

## Everybody's Neighborhood

A sunny weekend—March, May, July, September—draws thousands of people into central Portland. They come by car and light rail. They visit the new Classical Chinese Garden that covers an entire downtown block. They bring their children and grandchildren to splash in the walk-in fountains that decorate old and new parks and plazas. Energetic visitors walk or jog a three-mile loop across the Willamette River created by a long Waterfront Park, two bridges, and a new Eastbank Esplanade. Others frequent a huge independent bookstore and a restored Central Library, buy cappuccinos and microbrews, stand in line at multiplex movie theaters, shop for clothes, household goods, crafts, and art. They attend home and garden shows at the Oregon Convention Center and— if the season is correct and the stars are properly aligned—take in a Portland Trail Blazers playoff game.

The description may sound contrived—it *is* a composite of various times and places—but it reflects the range of central Portland's attractions. More so than in many cities, downtown Portland and adjacent districts are "everybody's neighborhood"—space that is shared and used by people from throughout the metropolitan area. The city's core claims nearly all of the cultural institutions, civic facilities, and gathering places that serve the region as a whole. In or adjacent to the historic downtown on the west side of the Willamette River are a multitheater performing arts center and civic auditorium, art and history museums, Portland State University, and Oregon Health and Sciences University. Pioneer Courthouse Square in the heart of the retail core hosts political rallies and community events. Tom McCall Waterfront Park is the place for food-and-fun festivals, including the deeply retro Rose Festival that dominates the month of June. Political protest marches start at the waterfront and wind through the downtown streets. Hugging the east side of the river are the Oregon Museum of Science and Industry, Oregon Convention Center, Memorial Coliseum, and Microsoft billionaire Paul Allen's Blazerama (officially the Rose Garden Arena), a new privately funded arena for the Trail Blazers of the National Basketball Association.

This public face of the city impresses Portland's visitors. Writers for *Time* and the *Atlantic Monthly,* the *Economist* and the *Los Angeles Times, Architecture* and *Landscape Architecture* have all reported on the strength of downtown design, the careful conservation of a sense of place, friendliness to pedestrians, and the enhancement of the downtown with public art. Berton Roueche in *The New Yorker* pointed to "closely controlled new building, the carefully monitored rehabilitation of worthy old buildings, [and] the vigorous creation of open space" as key factors creating a city of "individuality and distinction." Downtown design earned a City Livability Award from the U.S. Conference of Mayors in 1988 and an Award for Urban Excellence from the Bruner Foundation in 1989 (Canty 1986, *Economist* 1990, Henry 1988, Kaplan 1989, Langdon 1992, Peirce and Guskind 1993, Roueche 1985).

The worst response that outside critics can summon is a skeptical recharacterization of downtown Portland as a Disneylike theme park rather than a "real" place (Bruegmann 1992, Shibley 1993). Robert Kaplan's comment is typical: "With its neat trolley lines, geometric parks, rustic flower-pots beside polymer-and-glass buildings, crowded sidewalk benches . . . Portland exudes a stagy perfection" (Kaplan 1998, 58). The whiteness of Portland's population and its downtown workers and shoppers certainly contributes to the theme park appearance, as does the willingness of many Portlanders actually to use corner trash cans rather than dropping candy wrappers on the curb. Even locals occasionally wonder if we have created a toy town rather than a city whose rough edges strike cultural sparks, but it is still possible to put a positive spin on Portland as a microcosm of American design, as did Portland writers Gideon Bosker and Lena Lencek (1985, xiv) in calling it "an intelligently curated architectural museum . . . a magisterial modern metropolis in which ancient spaces and futuristic skyscraper-sculptures were brought together on miniature, two hundred foot blocks."

Beyond its "European feel" and attractions of place, central Portland has retained economic and institutional dominance in the metropolitan area. Local, regional, state, and federal office buildings are interspersed on both sides of the river. The central office core has increased its job total and upgraded average job quality over the last 25 years. The number of jobs in five core census tracts increased from 63,000 in 1970 to 108,000 in 1995; jobs in adjacent tracts grew from 40,000 to 50,000.[4] The central city has maintained its share of regional office space, and office vacancy rates during the recession of 2001–02 were lower for downtown than for competing suburban office clusters.

As one might expect, central area workers concentrate in government, retailing, finance, and business services. One major employment cluster is "content producing" activities such as software, multimedia, printing, broadcasting, advertising, and academic research. A second is "financial and transaction services." The largest is "management, legal and engineering services." Downtown Portland is where people from Oregon and portions of Idaho and Washington go for large law firms, accounting firms, architecture firms, public relations advice, and advertising agencies. However, only one *Fortune* 500 firm had a downtown Portland headquarters by 2003, down from four in 1975 because of corporate consolidations.

The continued presence of high-end jobs brought new housing on the western edge of the CBD, along the riverfront, and on the near east side of the Willamette. The most prominent change, however, is the transformation of a rail-spur warehouse district dating from the early twentieth century and located on the north edge of downtown (Jones 1999). Within a decade, art galleries, cautious loft conversions, and new three-story condos in this "Pearl District" have been followed by expense-account restaurants, pricey furniture and antique stores, and new 10- and 12-story condo towers with million-dollar views from the top floors (see Chap. 9, Howe). The market of empty nesters and yuppies has allowed developers to push this new construction northward onto old rail yards that have been replanned as the River District with the expectation of 5,000 or more new housing units.[5]

As a result of this, the central area housing inventory is substantially newer than it was in 1970. Flophouses and cheap single-room occupancy hotels have been replaced—in part—with subsidized and physically superior apartments, special needs housing, and supervised transition housing. What we have of affordable housing is newer and of better quality. Similarly, much of the housing currently being consumed by affluent households has been built in the last 20 years. The central districts gained roughly 1,000 new units in the 1970s, 2,000+ in the 1980s, and 4,000+ in the 1990s, with no signs of letup into 2003.

Population trends track housing starts. Census tracts can be used to approximate four core area residential zones: the long-established CBD,

PHOTO 4. The Pearl District brewery blocks in transition, 2000. "The Pearl" is a major urban renewal district at the north end of downtown. Formerly an industrial area, it now includes high-density residential units, retail outlets, and several public open spaces. The former Blitz Weinhard Brewery building was directly integrated into new construction. Part of its structure and tower still stands.

PHOTO 5. Close-up of the historic Weinhard building, which now houses retail offices and a restaurant, shot from across 12th Avenue.

PHOTO 6. The Pearl District in 2004, loft housing at NW Irving Street and NW 11th Avenue.

the Pearl/River District to its north, the Goose Hollow neighborhood immediately west of the CBD, and the near east side areas bracketed within two interstate freeway bridges. The data show a general erosion of core area population in the 1970s, small gains on the west side in the 1980s, and across-the-board increases in the 1990s, especially on the west side (see Table 8.1). Not surprisingly, the bulk of core area residents fall at two ends of the income scale. Many are poor and nearly poor people living in single-room occupancy hotels, subsidized apartments, and student housing. Many of the rest are affluent occupants of new or

### Table 8.1
*Central Portland population (census tracts)*

| Neighborhood | 1970 | 1980 | 1990 | 2000 |
|---|---|---|---|---|
| CBD (43, 53, 56, 57) | 6,803 | 6,694 | 7,938 | 9,290 |
| Pearl/River District (51) | 1,487 | 1,390 | 1,590 | 3,612 |
| Goose Hollow (52, 55) | 4,738 | 4,845 | 4,773 | 5,958 |
| Near East Side | | | | |
| (11.01, 11.02, 21, 22.02, 23.02) | 8,423 | 6,466 | 6,405 | 6,941 |
| Total | 21,451 | 19,395 | 20,706 | 25,801 |

NOTE: CBD, central business district.
SOURCE: U.S. Census

nicely rehabilitated condos and apartments. Continued erosion of affordable housing from demolition, conversion, and rent inflation has steadily tilted the balance toward folks with the disposable income to support the entertainment and cultural institutions of the downtown.[6]

## Two Generations of Planning

This strong urban core is the product and beneficiary of three decades of concerted planning that has engaged city government and downtown business interests in a strong political coalition that also recognized the claims of environmental and neighborhood activists.

The key period was the early 1970s, when civic leaders and politicians constructed a powerful alliance between downtown business interests and residents of older neighborhoods. Portland in the mid-1960s faced many of the same problems as other cities in the era of "urban crisis." Downtown parking was inadequate, the private bus company was bankrupt, and a new superregional mall in the affluent western suburbs threatened downtown retailing. At the same time, older neighborhoods were at risk from schemes for large scale land clearance and redevelopment, concentrated poverty, and racial inequities. Many cities understood the situation as a zero-sum competition in which downtown businesses and homeowners battled over a fixed pool of resources. Portland is one of the few cities where the "growth machine" business leadership of the 1950s made a graceful transition to participation in a more inclusive political system. We can characterize the resulting political marriage as the mobilization of the open-minded middle.

The chief architect and beneficiary of the political transition was Neil Goldschmidt, a young poverty attorney elected to the city council in 1970 and as mayor in 1972, at age 32. He would serve until he became secretary of transportation in the Carter administration in 1979 and would later serve as governor of Oregon from 1987 through 1990. By the start of his first mayoral term, Goldschmidt and his staff had drawn on a ferment of political and planning ideas and sketched out an integrated strategy involving the coordination of land use and transportation policies. They were strongly influenced by the 1970 census, which showed the effects of a declining proportion of middle-class families on neighborhood diversity and city tax base. During 1973, 1974, and 1975, Goldschmidt's team of young policy specialists and planners brought together a variety of policy initiatives that were waiting for precise definition and articulated them as parts of a single political package that offered benefits for a wide range of citizens and groups.

This so-called population strategy emphasized public transportation, neighborhood revitalization, and downtown planning. Better transit would improve air quality, enhance the attractiveness of older neighborhoods, and bring workers and shoppers downtown. In turn, a vital business center would protect property values in surrounding districts and increase their attractiveness for residential reinvestment. Middle-class families who remained or moved into inner neighborhoods would patronize downtown businesses, and prosperity would support high levels of public services. Neighborhood planning would focus on housing rehabilitation and on visible amenities to keep older residential areas competitive with the suburbs. Three decades later, these principles continue to guide regional land use and transportation policy.

Preservation of a user-friendly downtown was the strategy's cornerstone. Business worries about suburban competition and parking problems coincided at the end of the 1960s with public disgust over a blighted riverfront. The catalyst was a battle over the future of Harbor Drive, a multilane expressway from the early 1940s that divided the CBD from the Willamette River. Under pressure from a group of young activists organized as Riverfront for People, local and state politicians abandoned plans to redesign the expressway in 1969 and opted instead to remove it to make way for a waterfront park (see photos 1 and 2 and Chap. 7, Orloff).

The success of citizen action fired imaginations about radical responses to other downtown problems. Between 1970 and 1972, the city worked on a comprehensive downtown plan. A younger generation of technically sophisticated citizen activists worked with city officials, downtown retailers, property owners, neighborhood groups, and civic organizations to treat the interrelations of previously isolated issues such as parking, bus service, housing, and retailing. The manager of the planning process remembered the importance of getting the investors involved (Baldwin 1994): "They were called the Downtown Committee, made up of about thirteen people in the downtown area. We called them the 'Powerful Downtown Committee.' . . . It included some pretty powerful people—the leaders of Portland. Anybody who was a leader who wasn't in this group felt left out, so they wanted to get in."

The Downtown Plan of 1972 offered integrated solutions to a long list of problems that Portlanders had approached piecemeal for two generations. It was technically sound because its proposals were based on improvements in access and transportation. It was politically viable because it prescribed trade-offs among different interests as part of a coherent strategy. In tune with national thinking about urban centers, the Downtown Plan also analyzed and treated downtown as a set of distinct but mutually supporting districts rather than a uniform CBD (Abbott 1993). It therefore offered different suggestions for high density retail and office corridors crossing in the center of downtown, for a university district, for historic districts, and for medium density housing. Most of its specific project suggestions were in fact implemented during the next two decades. These included new parking garages bracketing the retail core; a large waterfront park and three new public spaces within the fabric of the downtown; districts for special housing incentives; and design review to keep new downtown buildings pedestrian friendly.[7]

A good example of planning into action is transportation policy (see Chap. 11, Adler and Dill). The 1972 plan called for a downtown bus mall to speed service, facilitate transfers, and tie together a downtown that was growing rapidly along a north–south axis. Opened in 1978, the mall was crossed by light rail from the east suburbs in the 1980s and light rail from the western suburbs in the 1990s. For two decades, use of public transit to reach the downtown has grown faster than use of automobiles, especially for rush hour trips. A survey in 2001 by the Portland Business Alliance (Portland Business Alliance 2002) found that 49% of downtown workers drive to work, 20% take light rail, 25% take buses, and 6% walk or bike, a substantially higher portion of nonautomobile trips than in comparable cities.

Portland revisited downtown planning in the mid-1980s with the Central City Plan, adopted in 1988. The plan was conceived as an extension of the 1972 plan, intended in part to update the list of implementation projects and priorities. The plan retained the earlier emphasis on subdistricts and on design, calling for "an exhilarating environment" with engaging architecture, green spaces, river vistas and access, historic preservation, and other elements to "enhance the Central City as a livable, walkable area which focuses on the river and captures the glitter and excitement of city living."

Although the design rhetoric was important, the biggest decision was to recognize and promote the horizontal expansion of central uses. In addition to the downtown of 1972, the new plan dealt with two adjacent west side districts and three districts across the Willamette.[8] It identified which areas in the downtown frame to appropriate for intensified development for information industries and information workers and which to stabilize for blue collar jobs. This choice of lateral growth over intensification of the CBD reflected the fact that Portland, with a small and dwindling supply of corporate headquarters, is not likely to develop a tall skyline dominated by 30- and 40-story office buildings (indeed, only one office building with more than 500,000 square feet of leaseable space was built in the 1970s, one in the 1980s, and none since then). Instead, the market is for buildings with 200,000 to 300,000 square feet. Similarly, Portlanders have shown little interest in tall, wafer-thin apartments of the sort that now tower over much of Vancouver, British Columbia.

Comprehensive downtown planning retained the vital support of the downtown business community through the 1980s and 1990s. There were tough battles in the 1980s over the character of Pioneer Courthouse Square, developed on the site of a parking structure in the heart of the CBD, and over the location of services and shelters for homeless people (see Chap. 13, Prince). In each case, the results were politically acceptable compromises that confirmed the value of an inclusive political process. In the first instance, the outcome is an open plaza but with systematic programming of activities to keep it from being dominated by derelicts and spike-haired teenagers. In the second, the result was a "treaty" in which social service agencies that are concentrated in the skid road area agreed not to expand and development interests agreed not to push for their closure and removal.[9]

By the 1990s, the Association for Portland Progress (APP), organized in the 1980s to represent downtown businesses, became a major participant in the city's liberal political regime. It actively engaged with politicians and citizen groups around efforts to promote an active and prosperous downtown. The epitome of this era of good feelings (stoked by a booming regional economy) was the Central City Summit in November 1998. Sponsored by the APP, Portland State University, and city, county, and regional governments, the Summit brought together several hundred politicians, businesspeople, and citizen activists to discuss the future of the central city. The resulting vision statement was remarkably upbeat. Feeling comfortable with the success of downtown itself, the participants decided to lead with calls for Portland to create the nation's best public schools and to assure the health of the Willamette River. Only then did they move to a more traditional planning agenda such as affordable housing opportunities; strong arts, culture, and higher education to support information industry jobs; and high quality public spaces (Association for Portland Progress 1999).

## Bigger? and Better?

Accomplishments often bring their own problems. In the early twenty-first century, lateral expansion of central Portland is straining the downtown transportation system. It is creating new land use conflicts with neighborhood preservation decisions made 20 and 30 years ago. And in the half-decade since the Central City Summit, lateral expansion combined with economic recession has begun to undermine the unity of the downtown business community and its ability to work in alliance with city government.

The planning challenge arises from another Portland success. Unlike many U.S. cities, Portland lacks the "dead zone" of derelict industrial districts and abandoned neighborhoods that surround the high-rise core of many cities. More than 40 years ago, Edgar Hoover and Raymond Vernon (1959) identified the problem of "gray areas" in older cities, the old transitional zones that seemed to be falling out of the real estate market. Since that time, most inner-ring districts throughout the United States have followed an up-or-out pattern in which the only options are abandonment or massive restructuring with public investments (such as sports facilities). Portland, however, has experienced little or no abandonment, scattered gentrification, and gradual reinvestment in light industrial and warehousing districts. Downtown Portland is ringed by strong industrial–wholesaling districts and viable residential neighborhoods at several economic scales.

While the core of downtown remains strong, the development and planning action is now at the edges of the central city, where areas that were once peripheral downtown activities are being eyed for substantial intensification. The expansion raises two important planning issues that are no longer adequately addressed by earlier plans. One is the need to knit together a larger and larger "central city" into a functional whole, particularly through improved transit and pedestrian facilities. The second is the desire to allow intensive downtown land uses, both for housing and employment, to expand without negative impacts on neighborhoods that were carefully conserved in previous decades.

The Portland region remains committed to a radial transit system that funnels buses and light rail cars into and through downtown (see Chap. 11, Adler and Dill). At the same time, the continued spread of central uses requires more and more work to keep the various districts linked into a functional whole. A streetcar line that opened in 2001 connects the southern end of downtown to the Pearl/River District and beyond to the densely occupied neighborhood to the northwest. The streetcar will soon be carried another mile southward from Portland State University into the South Waterfront District, where land used for metal fabricating and barge building is generally viewed as the city's

Photo 7. Streetcar at NW 11th Ave. and Lovejoy St. in 2004. This line, opened in 2001, connects northwest Portland to the University District. Plans are in the works to extend the line at its southwest end to the redeveloping waterfront district.

PHOTO 8. The Urban Center at Portland State University on the southern edge of the central business district in 2004. Opened in 2000, the streetcar crosses over the plaza, connecting the campus with northwest Portland. The building houses the College of Urban Affairs, which includes the School of Community Health, the Hatfield School of Government, and the School of Urban Studies and Planning.

next big development opportunity. Discussion is under way to build a streetcar loop between the west and east sides of the central city core. With a new northside light rail line opened in May 2004 and two southward lines under active planning, there is real concern about how to fit all necessary tracks for streetcars and light rail cars onto downtown streets.[10]

Another—and very different—transportation connector has also been a focus of controversy. Oregon Health and Sciences University (OHSU) perches on a hilltop less than a mile south of downtown. With little room left for growth, it plans to develop a satellite campus for biomedical research in the South Waterfront, about three-fourths of a mile east and 600 feet lower, and to join the two sites with an aerial tram. The city backs the tram (without it, says OHSU, they might have to expand in the suburbs) and a recent design competition offered visually exciting options. With the tram and the streetcar extension, the South Waterfront would gain trendy transit ties to both Portland State University and the medical school.

But the aerial tram is a neighborhood issue as well as a transportation issue because it will have to pass over portions of the Lair Hill and Corbett neighborhoods. These old Jewish and Italian immigrant neighborhoods were recycled by hippies in the 1960s and saved from urban renewal in the 1970s by vigorous grassroots resistance that helped to make neighborhood associations important players in city politics (Abbott 1983).[11] Their new rowhouses and small, restored workingman's cottages house both veterans of the urban renewal wars and newer information workers. Both groups value the slightly funky feel of mixed housing and the steep streets. They do not want tram loads of doctors and researchers swinging and swaying over their rooftops, and they do not want their pocket of single-family housing to be squeezed between a looming medical university and dense development on the old waterfront industrial lands below them. Corbett and Lair Hill fought off the lateral expansion of downtown a generation ago, and residents organized to fight the same battle against longer odds.

By late 2003, it was clear that proponents of core area expansion were carrying the day. Funding for the tram was in place and plans were going forward after an international design competition. The city officially launched the South Waterfront redevelopment effort on October 13. "Welcome to Portland's next great neighborhood," said Mayor Vera Katz. Plans call for new office and laboratory buildings to serve OHSU and provide the nucleus for bioscience industries. Tall thin apartment towers, Vancouver style, are to provide great vistas from expensive apartments without completely blocking view corridors from the West Hills (Manning and Rivera 2003).

Lateral expansion is having a different sort of impact on the Central Eastside Industrial District. One of Portland's most interesting planning actions in the 1980s was to adopt an industrial sanctuary policy. A zoning overlay protects inner manufacturing and warehousing districts in Northwest Portland and the Central Eastside from incompatible uses such as big box retailing and residential development. This is a powerful tool for avoiding the mismatch between the location of jobs and housing that afflicts many metropolitan areas, and can take at last partial credit for preserving tens of thousands of close in jobs in transportation, manufacturing, and trade. In effect, the policy recognizes that a seaport and regional trade center needs to push both payloads as well as paper.[12]

However, pressures are now mounting on the Central Eastside Industrial District, which is only a 10-minute walk from downtown across any of three bridges. The area counts roughly 20,000 jobs, but close-in warehouses and light industry may be anachronisms, especially as tourist attractions are appearing at the riverside and retail is encroaching from residential neighborhoods to the east. Can existing industrial structures be adapted to business and industrial uses? Or is the area ripe for transition to live-work spaces for artists and information workers? Is it a target for mixed-use projects similar to those appearing in the Pearl District? For housing towers with super views of downtown? In short, is the industrial sanctuary a policy of the 1980s that fails the changing circumstances of a new century, with the Central Eastside destined to serve the "creative class" that is now driving many urban economies?

In political and institutional terms, this expansion is reflected in the recent, problematic merger of the APP and the Portland Chamber of Commerce into the Portland Business Alliance. APP, which had expanded to include the east side Lloyd District in the 1990s, effectively absorbed the Chamber in 2002. The merger might have introduced new efforts to combine the livability concerns of downtown and neighborhood business districts. Despite a supposed citywide purview, however, new Portland Business Alliance leadership chose to confront city government on a narrow set of "business climate" issues, focused on the development interests of particular downtown subdistricts rather than the larger downtown or city as a whole, and quickly forfeited its important role in civic leadership. The change stemmed from a variety of factors: personality conflicts, new leaders who take the political compromises of the previous generation for granted, and concern that the city government's "livability agenda" is ignoring the needs of business during hard economic times.[13]

## Balancing Acts

Downtown planning in Portland has been a series of balancing acts. The landmark plans of 1972 and 1988 attempted to carefully balance the needs of retailing, office employment, light industry, cultural and educational institutions, low-income and high-income residents, and casual users. The preferred technique was to allocate subdistricts to different functions and activities and to tie the pieces together through transportation improvements and urban design. Implementation required political compromises to balance the desires of downtown property owners and developers against the needs of poor people and social service providers.

By accelerating the lateral growth of the central city, the strong real estate market and optimism of the 1990s have brought a new set of tensions that will require striking a new balance. The cherished city goal of promoting a prosperous and expansive downtown now conflicts with equally valued goals of neighborhood preservation, which date from the same era of policy innovation as the original downtown plan.[14] Activists in other close-in neighborhoods are watching the future of Corbett and Lair Hill for clues about their own future, while neighborhood business groups have a stake in the fate of the Central Eastside Industrial District. To date these tensions are being addressed as individual problems. However, the context suggests the need to revisit the balance between "central" and "neighborhood" functions and districts and to carefully tend the political alliance between downtown and neighborhoods (see Chap. 4, Witt).[15]

In turn, these questions of downtown growth and planning are embedded in a regional balancing act between the values of urbanity and environmental protection (Abbott, 2001). Portlanders like a vibrant downtown and neighborhoods with viable commercial districts, but they also love streams, trees, mountains, and views. Since the 1970s, they have tried to maintain the desired balance through regional planning, using a state-mandated urban growth boundary to limit the territory available to suburban development—a policy that protects farm- and forestland and raises demand for developable and redevelopable land within the boundary. The result, of course, is to maintain the attractiveness of downtown and its surrounding districts for residents and investors.

This regional context for downtown development virtually guarantees that the planning challenges arising from core area expansion will not go away. They played a small role in the 1972 plan, a much larger role in the 1988 plan, and will continue to be prominent during future cycles of growth. Planners and policymakers will need to deal with the resulting land use conflicts directly, and, we can hope, systematically. Indeed, the time seems ripe for planners and civic leaders to begin thinking about creating a "Bigger and Better Central City Plan."

NOTES

1. Until a new stadium might be built, the new team would use Portland General Electric (PGE) Park, a city-owned facility on the west edge of downtown that seats roughly 20,000 for minor league baseball, Portland State University football, soccer, touring concerts, and similar events.

2. One site is being considered adjacent to a freeway approximately six miles from the center of the city, but only through the insistence of one city council member (out of five) elected in November 2002.

3. Portlanders have a variety of ways to speak of their city's central area. "Downtown" sometimes refers to the retail/office core that was established during the first half of the twentieth century (the "vernacular downtown") or to the somewhat larger area between the Willamette River and I-405 that was treated by the 1972 Downtown Plan (the "planners' downtown"). I use central business district (CBD) for the former and "downtown" for the latter. The 1988 Central City Plan introduced the idea that Portland's "central city" included the downtown plus adjacent districts on both sides of the Willamette River, which more than doubled the land area under consideration. In the early twenty-first century, moreover, the "central city" is pushing against and sometimes overrunning the boundaries used in 1988. Readers familiar with the standard terminology used for referring to the largest city in census-defined metropolitan areas should note that residents mean this set of core districts, and not the entire City of Portland, when they hold, for example, a Central City Summit.

4. Data from Metro and Portland Development Commission, summarized in Abbott et al. (1998).

5. Downtown housing trends in Portland are similar to those in other U.S. cities as reported in Birch (2001).

6. The inventory of affordable downtown housing fell from 5,183 units in 1978 to 3,539 in 2002. See Northwest Pilot Project (2002). In addition, city policy has capped the number of homeless shelter beds in the historic skid road district north of the CBD.

7. Detail on both the Downtown Plan (1972) and the Central City Plan (1988) can be found in Abbott (1991). For another analysis of the Central City Plan, see Krumholz and Keating (1991).

8. The west side districts are Goose Hollow (residential/office) and South Waterfront (industrial land with high redevelopment potential). The east side areas are Lower Albina (industrial), Lloyd Center (retail/office/sports arena/convention center), and the Central Eastside Industrial District (warehousing/light industry).

9. For a detailed discussion of the political dynamics of these and similar decisions, see Bello 1993. In the mid-1990s, housing advocates obtained a similar compromise over the inclusion of subsidized units within the River District, gaining acceptance of the principle of a mixed-income neighborhood but promises for fewer units than hoped for.

10. The problem is exacerbated by Portland's 200-by 200-foot downtown blocks. They are great for pedestrians, but they necessitate short trains and relatively slow train speeds through the central city. An institutional adaptation of transit to the expanding core was the extension of the fareless transit zone from downtown (where "Fareless Square" was implemented along with the bus mall) to include the Convention Center, Rose Quarter, Lloyd Center shopping mall, and adjacent office buildings.

11. For the neighborhood's view of its battle, see Penny Allen's independent feature film *Property* (1978).

12. Maritime uses and riverfront industrial districts downstream (north) from central Portland remain an active part of the cityscape and economy. Grain ships still load within a few hundred yards of the Trail Blazers' arena.

13. In return, the city awarded a lucrative contract to manage city-owned downtown parking garages to a new bidder representing minority businesses rather than renewing the contract with the Business Alliance, taking away a source of revenue that APP/PBA had enjoyed for nearly 20 years.

14. See Abbott (1983) for a full discussion of Portland's "neighborhood revolution" and Johnson (2002) for the changes in political culture that framed neighborhood activism. See Berry et al. (1993) for a discussion of the positive effects of the resulting neighborhood association system.

15. This alliance, which I term "progressive Portland," embraces roughly two-thirds of the neighborhoods and voters within the City of Portland, as discussed in Abbott (2001). It still dominates city politics after 30 years and it sets the tone for metropolitan area political decisions—again as it has since the 1970s. Metro, the area's elected regional government, covers Multnomah County and the heavily populated parts of suburban Washington and Clackamas counties. In May 2002, voters within Metro elected a proplanning candidate as Metro Council president and rejected an antiplanning measure by nearly identical margins of 58–42 and 57–43. The votes are a reasonable approximation of the regional strength of the progressive voting alliance.

REFERENCES

Abbott, Carl. 1983. *Portland: Planning, Politics, and Growth in a Twentieth-Century City*. Lincoln: University of Nebraska Press.

Abbott, Carl. 1991. Urban design in Portland, Oregon, as policy and process. *Planning Perspectives* January: 1–18.

Abbott, Carl. 1993. Five downtown strategies: Policy discourse and downtown planning since 1945. *Journal of Policy History* 5 (1): 5–27.

Abbott, Carl. 2001. *Greater Portland: Urban Life and Landscape in the Pacific Northwest*. Philadelphia: University of Pennsylvania Press.

Abbott, Carl, Gerhard Pagenstecher, and Britt Parrott. 1998. *Trends in Portland's Central City, 1970—98*. Portland: Association for Portland Progress.

Association for Portland Progress. 1999. *A 25-Year Vision for Central Portland*. Portland: Association for Portland Progress.

Baldwin, Robert. 1994. *Interview by Ernie Bonner*. www.pdxplan.org/BaldwinWeb.html (accessed January 2004).

Bello, Mark. 1993. *Urban Regimes and Downtown Planning in Portland, Oregon, and Seattle, Washington, 1972-1992*. Ph.D. diss., Portland State University.

Berry, Jeffrey, Kent E. Portnoy, and Ken Thomson. 1993. *The Rebirth of Urban Democracy*. Washington, DC: The Brookings Institution.

Birch, Eugenie. 2001. Having a longer view on downtown living. *Journal of the American Planning Association* 68 (1): 5–21.

Bosker, Gideon, and Lena Lencek. 1985. *Frozen Music: A History of Portland Architecture*. Portland: Oregon Historical Society.

Bruegmann, Robert. 1992. New centers on the periphery. *Center: A Journal for Architecture in America* 7: 25–43.

Canty, Donald. 1986. Portland architecture. *AIA Journal* 75 (72): 32–47.

*Economist.* 1990. Where it works. *Economist,* 1 September, 24–25.

Henry, William III. 1988. Portland offers a calling card. *Time,* 12 December, 88.

Hoover, Edgar, and Raymond Vernon. 1959. *Anatomy of a Metropolis.* Cambridge, MA: Harvard University Press.

Hunt, John. 2003. Location, location. *The Oregonian,* 19 January, C1.

Johnson, Steven Reed. 2002. *The Transformation of Civic Practice in Portland, Oregon, 1960–1999.* Ph.D. diss., Portland State University.

Jones, Robert. 1999. *Re-presenting the Post-Industrial Neighborhood: Planning and Redevelopment in Portland's Pearl District.* Ph.D. diss., Portland State University.

Kaplan, Sam H. 1989. Portland sets example in urban design. *Los Angeles Times,* 12 September.

Kaplan, Robert. 1998. Travels into America's future. *Atlantic Monthly,* August: 37–61.

Krumholz, Norman, and Dennis Keating. 1991. Downtown plans of the 1980s: The case for more equity in the 1990s. *Journal of the American Planning Association* 57 (2): 36–52.

Langdon, Phillip. 1992. How Portland does it. *Atlantic Monthly,* November: 134–141.

Manning, Jeff, and Dylan Rivera. 2003. City launches south waterfront. *The Oregonian,* 14 October, A1.

Northwest Pilot Project. 2002. *2002 Downtown Portland Affordable Housing Inventory.* Portland: Northwest Pilot Project.

Peirce, Neal, and Robert Guskind. 1993. *Breakthroughs: Re-creating the American City.* New Brunswick, NJ: Center for Urban Policy Research, Rutgers University.

Portland Business Alliance. 2002. *The 2001 Downtown Portland Business Census and Survey: Executive Summary.* Portland: Portland Business Alliance.

Roueche, Berton. 1985. A new kind of city. *The New Yorker,* 21 October, 42–53.

Shibley, Robert. 1993. Commentary. In *Breakthroughs: Recreating the American City,* edited by Neal Peirce and Robert Guskind, 76–81. New Brunswick, NJ: Center for Urban Policy Research, Rutgers University.

# 9 | The Reality of Portland's Housing Market

Deborah Howe

There can be no disagreement that the Portland metropolitan region's housing prices have increased dramatically since the early 1990s. The median sale price for existing, single-family homes in the Portland metropolitan region rose over 50%, from $104,743 in 1990 (in 2000 dollars) to $160,217 in 2000 (JCHS 2001, 35). In the first quarter of 2000, the National Association of Home Builders ranked the Portland region as having the 165th least affordable housing market in the nation, a sharp contrast to the first quarter of 1991 when the rank was 55th (Chaluvadi 2003).[1]

Critics of Oregon's state, regional, and local planning policies claim that the urban growth boundary (UGB) and an array of regulatory restrictions are raising housing costs and eliminating affordable housing (NAHB undated, Pozdena 2002, Staley et al. 1999). The UGB is said to overly restrict the land market causing values to increase, limiting the feasibility of building traditional single-family homes on large lots. Supporters counter that the planning framework proactively encourages higher density and housing alternatives through permissive zoning, streamlined decision making, and public investment in infrastructure (Manvel 1999).

An econometric analysis suggests that the impact of the UGB on housing costs has been small and that "popular perceptions of a UGB-induced land shortage have helped fuel [a] bull market riding on the back of an initial demand surge" (Phillips and

184

Goodstein 2000, 342). An analysis of 85 large metropolitan areas shows that the relationship between the UGB and higher housing prices in Portland was statistically significant only in the first half of the 1990s (Downs 2002). William Fischel (2002) maintains that Portland has not been successful with infill, otherwise housing price inflation would have been lower.[2] He further asserts that "[U]nless Portland has become a much nicer place to live than it was before 1975, in which case demand shifts would explain the inflation, it seems most probable that Oregon's growth-boundaries plan does cause high housing prices as a result of its constraints on supply" (48). Nevertheless, a review of academic literature on the relationship between growth management and affordable housing suggests "market demand, not land constraints, is the primary determinant of housing prices" (Nelson et al. 2002, 6).

Public and academic dialogue about housing and the implications of planning policies is framed by the immediacy of the current trend of rising prices. However, the rapid increase in prices in the 1990s was preceded by a period of significant deflation in values, which in turn was preceded by a boom period when housing prices also increased dramatically. Furthermore, a large part of the housing price increase during the 1990s came from substantial investments in housing rehabilitation and renovation. What is missing from the current debate is an understanding of the historical context of Portland's housing challenges. Such a perspective will shed light on the nature of housing price rises and the role of planning policies in addressing needs.

This chapter examines housing affordability within the city of Portland since 1970. The focus here is on the city rather than the regional housing market because as a central city, Portland has experienced a number of factors that are unique to the region but common to other central cities, such as depopulation, disinvestment, and gentrification. This city also has a history of proactive involvement in housing issues with demonstrated results in ensuring the provision of a variety of housing alternatives.

Attention will be given to (1) housing costs and relative affordability since 1970 for both homeownership and rentals, (2) rates of homeownership, (3) the nature of public concerns and debate about affordability over time, (4) housing policies and initiatives, (5) the evolution of the housing market with respect to development of housing alternatives, and (6) what can be learned from this historical context. These considerations are of particular relevance to those states that have implemented or are considering implementing UGBs as a growth management tool and are concerned about the relationship between these boundaries and housing costs. What will become evident is the importance of public commitment to encouraging the preservation and development of a variety of housing alternatives in conjunction with limiting the extent of urban growth.

### Housing Costs and Relative Affordability

Homeowner-reported values for the city of Portland doubled between the 1990 and 2000 censuses from $74,696 to $149,863.[3] Figure 9.1 indicates, however, that the relative affordability of housing in 1990 was the end result of a one-third decline in homeowner values during the 1980s. Thus the overall increase in homeowner values was 35.3% from 1980 to 2000 and 142% from 1970 to 2000. The highest rate of increase occurred in the 1970s, when the median rose nearly 80%. The 1970s was a period of explosive growth in Oregon. The state's population increased 25.9% preceded by a rate of 18.2% in the 1960s (in contrast, the United States grew 13.4% in the 1960s and 11.4% in the 1970s).[4]

The rental housing market has been more stable over time. Median rents rose 8.8% in the 1970s, seemingly not affected by the rapid rise in home values. Rental rates during the 1980s were relatively flat, increasing only 2.2% after accounting for inflation. The greatest increase occurred during the 1990s when median rents rose 19%.

Table 9.1 provides a comparison between housing values in Portland and the United States. The table shows the percentage of houses in Portland with homeowner-reported values that fall below the 20th and above the 80th percentiles of homeowner-reported values for the nation as a whole. The same comparison is provided for gross rents. These data

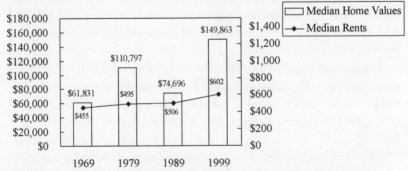

FIGURE 9.1. Portland home values and rents in 1999 dollars. Source: U.S. Census Bureau, http://www.census.gov.

### Table 9.1
*Percent of Portland housing values falling within lowest and highest quintiles of U.S. housing values*

|  | 1970 | 1980 | 1990 | 2000 |
|---|---|---|---|---|
| **Homeowner values** | | | | |
| % in lowest national quintile | 14.9 | 6.8 | 25.1 | 1.9 |
| % in highest national quintile | 9.9 | 20.3 | 5.4 | 24.5 |
| **Gross rents** | | | | |
| % in lowest national quintile | 21.2 | 17.9 | 20.1 | 12.8 |
| % in highest national quintile | 14.2 | 19.8 | 7.3 | 19.9 |

SOURCE: U.S. Census Bureau http://www.socds.huduser.org.

underscore the volatility of the city's housing market with the percentage in the lowest quintile nearly quadrupling in the 1980s and then dropping from 25.1% in 1990 to 1.9% in 2000 as housing prices rose. The percentage in the highest quintile has followed an opposite path, falling by nearly three quarters from 1980 to 1990 and then dramatically increasing to 24.5% in 2000. Table 9.1 also shows the growth in high rents with 7.3% in 1990 and 19.9% in 2000 falling within the upper quintile of rents nationwide. Only 12.3% of rents fell within the lowest quintile of rents nationwide in 2000, down from 20.1% in 1980.

Around 1982, the U.S. economy entered a recession. Oregon took longer to recover than the nation as a whole because of the economy's dependence on natural resources. Many Portland homeowners who purchased their property in the late 1970s and early 1980s experienced large losses as values declined. In the mid to late 1980s, it was possible to buy houses in Portland that were in sound condition for under $30,000. In 1988, for example, 1 in 20 houses in metropolitan Portland sold for $25,000 or less; 17% were $40,000 or less (Mayes 1990).

As home values started to rise in the 1990s, the transformation of whole neighborhoods was dramatic. Long-needed repairs and improvements were made. Using data from the American Housing Survey, Julia Reade determined that during the 1990s, the Portland metropolitan region ranked second in the nation in annual remodeling expenditures at $2,080 per homeowner (with an estimate range of $1,664 to $2,496) (2001). This can be compared against a national average of $1,430. Nearly half (46%) of expenditures by metropolitan Portland homeowners was for replacement projects relating to "major system upgrades and substitutions that are required during the lifetime of most homes." At $960 in annual expenditures for these upgrades, Portland ranked first in the nation; the national average was $570. Discretionary expenditures that "improve, add, or reconfigure space" amounted to $830 annually (Portland ranked fifth in this category) (Reade 2001, 6).[5]

Another way to consider these expenditures is that during the 1990s, metropolitan Portland homeowners invested on average between $16,640 to $24,960 in their homes. Thus, a considerable component of the increase in housing values during the 1990s is related to additional investments including both deferred maintenance and enhancements of space and amenities.

Housing affordability is a function of both housing costs and the capacity of people to pay these costs. Portland is not a high salary area. In 1999 20.4% of households had incomes that fell within the lowest quintile of national household incomes; 17.1% fell within the highest quintile (see Table 9.2). Median family income in 1999 dollars actually declined from 1969 to 1989.[6] Median household income grew 31.9% from 1969 to 1999, far outpaced by the 142% increase in homeowner-reported values during the same period.

### Rates of Homeownership

Portland's population grew from 382,619 to 529,121 between 1970 and 2000. The number of households increased from 152,065 to 223,737. However, Portland added 113,460 new residents and just over 48,000 households through an aggressive annexation program in the 1980s

### Table 9.2

*Percent of Portland household and family median incomes falling within lowest and highest quintiles of U.S. median*

|  | 1969 | 1979 | 1989 | 1999 |
|---|---|---|---|---|
| Median family income | $44,483 | $44,750 | $43,563 | $50,271 |
| % in lowest national quintile | 18.4 | 19.9 | 20.6 | 18.6 |
| % in highest national quintile | 19.8 | 18.9 | 15.8 | 18.9 |
| Median household income | $30,437 | $33,921 | $34,384 | $40,146 |
| % in lowest national quintile | 23.3 | 23.6 | 23.1 | 20.4 |
| % in highest national quintile | 16.7 | 16.6 | 13.8 | 17.1 |

SOURCE: U.S. Census Bureau http://www.socds.huduser.org.

### Table 9.3
*Household and population change holding*
*2000 boundaries constant*

|  | 1970 | 1980 | 1990 | 2000 |
|---|---|---|---|---|
| Households | 179386 | 198825 | 206118 | 223737 |
| Difference |  | 19439 | 7293 | 17619 |
| Ownership units | 105819 | 108717 | 110877 | 124767 |
| Difference |  | 2898 | 2160 | 13890 |
| Rental | 73567 | 90108 | 95241 | 98970 |
| Difference |  | 16541 | 5133 | 3729 |
| % Ownership | 59.0 | 54.7 | 53.8 | 55.8 |
| Ownership as % of household change |  | 14.9% | 29.6% | 78.8% |
| Population | 489404 | 474700 | 486025 | 529121 |
| Population change |  | −14704 | 11325 | 43096 |
| Average household size | 2.73 | 2.39 | 2.36 | 2.36 |

SOURCE: Hough, Jr. (2003).

through the 1990s. A recompilation of historical census data using Portland's 2000 boundaries as a given provides a better understanding of absolute changes over time (Table 9.3 and Figs. 9.2 and 9.3).[7]

Portland lost population in the 1970s and did not regain its 1970 population levels until sometime after 1990. The net increase in population

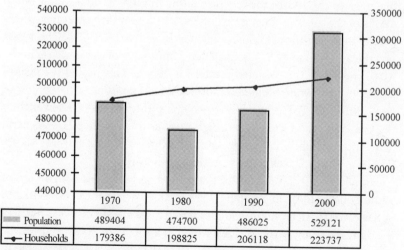

| | 1970 | 1980 | 1990 | 2000 |
|---|---|---|---|---|
| Population | 489404 | 474700 | 486025 | 529121 |
| Households | 179386 | 198825 | 206118 | 223737 |

FIGURE 9.2. Portland population and household change over time holding 2000 boundaries constant. Source: Hough, Jr., 2003.

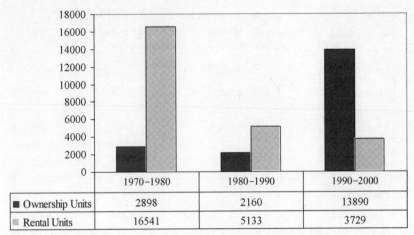

| | 1970–1980 | 1980–1990 | 1990–2000 |
|---|---|---|---|
| ■ Ownership Units | 2898 | 2160 | 13890 |
| ▨ Rental Units | 16541 | 5133 | 3729 |

FIGURE 9.3. Absolute changes intenure holding 2000 boundaries constant.
Source: Hough, Jr., 2003.

from 1970 to 2000 was 39,717. The number of households increased
steadily over this time period, increasing in total by 44,351. The average
household size fell during the 1970s from 2.73 in 1970 to 2.39 in 1980,
stabilizing at 2.36 in subsequent decades.

By assigning changes in the number of owner-occupied housing units
to the households added per decade, it is possible to observe the components of change in tenure rates. In the 1970s, the city added 19,439
households with only 14.9% owning their home (see Table 9.3 and
Fig. 9.3). In the 1980s, the increase in the number of households fell to
37.5% of the growth during the 1970s; the percentage of homeowners
among these additional households nearly doubled (29.6%). The 1990s
saw the addition of 17,619 households, about 90% of the increase in the
1970s; however, the ownership rate was 78.8%. This pulled the overall
percentage of ownership rate in 2000 to 55.8% up from a 30-year low of
53.8% in 1990. Portland's homeownership rate in 2000 is lower than
the U.S. average of 66.2%, but higher than the average of U.S. central
cities with populations greater than 100,000, which in 2000 was 48.9%
(Office of Policy Development and Research 2001).

Homeownership rates differ depending on race. In 2000, 58.6% of
white householders in Portland were homeowners compared to 38.2%
of African American householders. These rates are slightly over 80% of
the corresponding national rates, which in 2000 were 71.3% and 46.2%,
respectively. African American proportional gains in homeownership in
Portland during the last decade were less than those of white householders. The rate of African American homeownership grew only 1.6%

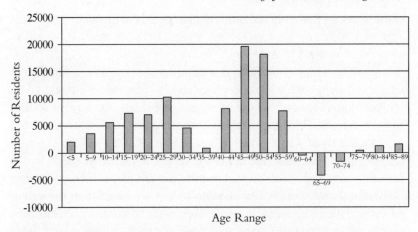

FIGURE 9.4. Differences between 1990 and 2000 age distributions for Portland. Source: U.S. Census Bureau, http://www.census.gov.

in the 1990s (from 37.6%) while the rate of white homeownership increased 6.9% (from 54.8%).

High housing prices in Portland suggest that young adults would have problems in securing homeownership. Lower savings and incomes compromise young householders; the 2000 median income for Portland householders under 25 years of age was $22,344 compared to $46,700 for those 35 to 44 years old.

Figure 9.4 shows the absolute change in the numbers within each age group from 1990 to 2000. This comparison, however, does not take into account that the 1990 residents would have aged 10 years by the 2000 census. Figure 9.5 shows the difference in the two censuses with

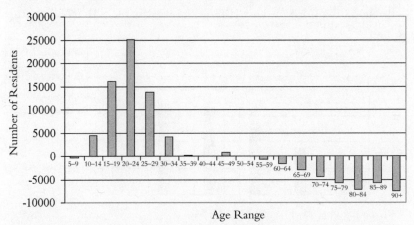

FIGURE 9.5. Portland 2000 age distribution relative to 1990 age distribution. Source: U.S. Census Bureau, http://www.census.gov.

consideration of how old the 1990 cohorts would have been in 2000. This approach builds on work by Dowell Myers (1992). It can best be understood with respect to Anthony Downs's explanation of neighborhood change in which neighborhood demographics over time is a function of who stays, along with who moves in relative to who moves out (1981).

The profile conveys that the in-migration (which in this case includes those residents added through annexation) during the 1990s consisted predominantly of young adults between the ages of 20 and 34. The relative loss of population in the upper age ranges is a result of death, moves out of the city, and the absence of in-migration of these older age groups.

Portland's rates of homeownership by age are lower than the nation as a whole for all ages (see Fig. 9.6). However, the homeownership rates increased in Portland during the 1990s for each cohort except those between the ages of 55 and 64. The 2000 rates of homeownership for those 35 and above range between 88% and 92.6% of the corresponding national rate. Although the number of homeowners 15 to 24 years old and 25 to 34 years old increased by 298 and 3,962, respectively, during the 1990s, the younger age group's rate of homeownership in 2000 was 47.3% of the national rate and the older group's was 77.6%.

## Nature of Public Concerns

As can be expected from the preceding analysis, housing has been a longstanding focus of public concern in Portland. The nature of this concern, however, has varied dramatically over the course of 30 years.

The high demand for rental housing during the 1970s led to the development of low-rise apartment complexes in various parts of the city including Corbett–Lair Hill on the west bank of the Willamette,

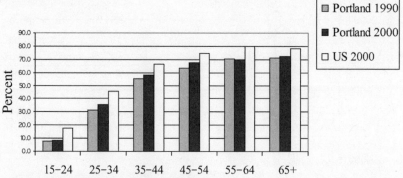

FIGURE 9.6. Homeownership rate by age.
Source: U.S. Census Bureau, http://www.census.gov.

inner-northeast Portland to house those displaced by urban renewal, and the eastern part of the city. In Buckman, an inner-city neighborhood to the east of downtown, large houses on corner lots were demolished in the late 1960s and throughout the 1970s and replaced with garden apartments. Many older houses in the same neighborhood were illegally subdivided into very small apartments to generate higher overall rent from low-income households. Degradation of the housing stock became problematic. At the same time, there was growing concern about displacement and gentrification, which was occurring primarily in Northwest Portland with the conversion of apartments to condominiums. A Bureau of Planning study (1981) touched on both issues in estimating that 15,700 persons in 6,500 housing units moved involuntarily from 1977 to 1980 (14.3% of all moves).[8] One-third of the involuntary moves were a result of reinvestment (four-fifths of which were due to the sale of a single family house that the household had been renting) and an equal proportion was the result of higher housing costs (mostly rent but also heat/utility costs). Displacement as a result of disinvestments, including lack of repairs, condemnation, and demolition accounted for one-fifth of these moves (Bureau of Planning 1981).

Gentrification was less of an issue during the 1980s, although in the latter part of the decade there was a public outcry when a developer tore down large old houses in northwest Portland to construct rowhouses. The more dominant public concern was with overall deterioration in housing and neighborhoods. Poor maintenance of rental housing was particularly problematic (Eller 1984). One of the realities of the relative affordability of the 1980s was difficulty in securing investment capital. Many banks had unwritten policies setting the minimum for mortgages at $25,000. As a result, someone who could qualify to buy a $25,000 car could not obtain a loan for a $16,000 house. It was a system of red lining without the red lines (Lane 1990). This limitation was particularly problematic in northeast Portland, which has the highest concentration of African American households due to a history of discriminatory real estate practices. This area was also hit hard by the in-migration of gangs and drug activity, which drove down housing prices. One property owner had to sell five rental houses for a total of $25,000, another signed a quit-claim deed to give away her house when tenants turned it into an automobile junkyard, and one landlord paid his tenants $500 to leave and then boarded up the property (Durbin 1989).

The lack of mortgages and the low property values limited the investments that could be made in maintaining or improving property. It was difficult to secure funds to address emergency repairs. Homeowners who did not expect to live in their house for a long time had to carefully weigh the merits of investing in repairs and renovations given that they might not recoup the costs upon sale. The absence of bank mortgages also meant that potential homeowners needed to pay in cash or look elsewhere for money. Some home sellers were willing to hold mortgages. Others borrowed from families and/or used their credit cards. This situation was ripe for unscrupulous lending practices and they did occur. Dominion Capital, Inc., purchased over 350 homes in northeast Portland at rock bottom prices. They sold the houses to individuals and held the mortgages without paying off the underlying loans. Many of the new owners faced foreclosure when the original lenders called for payment (Lane 1992).[9]

The 1980s saw a growing concern with housing abandonment. This had been an issue even in earlier decades, but drug dealing out of vacant houses added a sense of urgency to secure these properties. The city estimated that there were 2,300 abandoned houses in 1988 (VAB Task Force 1988).

The city's annexations in the 1980s and 1990s brought with them another set of housing issues. Since these areas, primarily in what is commonly referred to as "outer southeast," had been in the unincorporated parts of the county, they developed in the absence of subdivision standards, which meant substandard roads, no sidewalks, and reliance on septic systems. A U.S. Environmental Protection Agency (EPA) order to install sewers to protect the city's groundwater combined with a decline in federal resources to pay for this work resulted in significant financial hardships as homeowners were assessed for sewer installation and had to pay the costs of connections (in addition to maintaining and sometimes replacing their septic systems if problems emerged before the sewer system was in place). The housing in this area tended to be historically lower cost in part because the initial selling prices did not incorporate the cost of urban infrastructure. Furthermore, at the time of the EPA mandate, the housing was old enough to need major replacements and repairs such as new roofing. Senior citizen homeowners were particularly hard hit.

In the late 1980s and early 1990s, Portlanders blamed rising housing prices on the in-migration of Californians who were able to use their equity from a high valued housing market to buy more housing in Portland. These people had the wherewithal to pay even inflated prices and come out ahead (Stein 1990b). No study quantifying this assertion was undertaken, but there is no question that the market turned from moribund to red hot. And prices correspondingly soared. In the early 1990s, inner-city houses sold within days of being put on the market, often for more than was asked (Stein 1990a).

Beginning in the 1990s, there was a growing chorus of complaints from homebuilders about the red tape and cost of building within the city. In 1999 the Home Builders Association of Metropolitan Portland sent a letter to its members urging them to "exercise extreme caution" before building in Portland. The association cited housing design, storm-water runoff, and tree removal regulations as adding excessive costs (Oliver 1999b). Some builders decided against building in Portland because of the regulations (Oliver 1999a).

## Housing Policy and Initiatives

The early history of Portland's approach to housing concerns placed a heavy emphasis on public housing, housing code compliance, and the provision of loans and grants for housing rehabilitation. The city also relied on the trickle down theory (in which upwardly mobile households move into new and better housing in turn enabling less well off households to gain better housing in the vacated dwelling) as an important means of providing affordable housing.[10]

Over time, however, Portland has developed a strong, multifaceted commitment to housing. The city's *Comprehensive Plan Goals and Policies* includes the following housing goal:

> Enhance Portland's vitality as a community at the center of the region's housing market by providing housing of different types, tenures, density, sizes, costs, and locations that accommodate the needs, preferences, and financial capabilities of current and future households. (Bureau of Planning 2003, 35)

This statement is followed by 15 policies, with associated objectives, strategies, and implementing agencies that address housing supply, safety and quality, opportunity, and affordability. This is the culmination of the first comprehensive review of city housing policy since 1978. The addition of new policies reflects the evolving nature of the city's approach to housing, addressing such issues as balancing communities with respect to mixed income and diverse housing types and tenure, affordability across the range of incomes, the housing continuum from temporary shelter to transitional and permanent housing, regulatory costs and fees as barriers to affordability, no net loss of housing potential through comprehensive plan and zoning amendments, and removing financial and regulatory barriers to "humble housing" (i.e., small houses with basic amenities).

The city has worked within the context of state and regional planning to strengthen its housing focus. The Metropolitan Housing Rule (OAR660-07) mandates a minimum 10 units per acre housing density potential for vacant and redevelopable, buildable land. The city's 1989 periodic review analysis revealed that rezonings resulted in the city dropping below this standard (Bureau of Planning 1989). The city council subsequently adopted a no net loss policy for zoning changes affecting residential properties. This standard was further strengthened when the city amended the zoning ordinance to respond to Metro's requirement that development be required to achieve at least 80% of maximum allowable density. Metro regional planning requirements mandating accessory apartments as a permitted land use underpinned the city's development of liberal accessory dwelling requirements, which now allow units detached from the main dwelling and do not require owner occupancy.

Portland has proactively sought to capture a significant portion of the region's housing growth through support of downtown housing development and zoning regulations that favor higher densities, such as accessory dwellings and row houses. In the five-year period ending in June 2000, the city captured over 30% of the housing units built within the region's UGB, exceeding the city and regional planning goal of 20% (Office of the City Auditor 2002). Portland's voluntary regional five-year affordable housing production goal is 1,791 units for households making less than 30% of the median income (AFT 2000).

The city's commitment to supporting very low income housing is directly related to the strong and enduring advocacy of numerous individuals and organizations. Commissioners Gretchen Kafoury and Eric Sten have given voice to this perspective on the city council (see Chap. 13, Prince). The Community Alliance of Tenants, Community Development Network, Elders in Action, Northwest Pilot Project, Coalition for a Livable Future and Affordable Housing Now! have all pushed hard for greater public support of meeting the housing needs of very low income households. The Portland Organizing Project, a coalition of churches devoted to advocacy for low income residents, along with the League of Women Voters, has raised public consciousness about the level of subsidy given to downtown developments particularly given that so much of the housing is for middle and higher income households (Christ 1997; Hunseberger 1998).

The preservation and development of very low income housing has been problematic for decades. Over 1,700 units (15%) of downtown housing units were lost from 1970 to 1978. Most of these (1,345) were low-income, transient, single-room occupancy (SRO) housing. SRO housing was difficult to support since there were no federal or state programs to assist in redevelopment and maintenance (Downtown Housing Advisory Committee 1979). While the city had a goal of preserving the number of low-income housing units that existed in 1978 (5,183) they continued to disappear with an estimated loss of 1,337 in the ensuing 10 years (Bureau of Planning 1994). Housing advocates have been instrumental in setting expectations for affordable housing in return for public subsidies. In 1999, the Portland Development Commission determined that housing in the developing River District was emerging at the three targeted income ranges; the numbers of affordable units were actually exceeding the city council's 1994 goals. The city subsequently established five income ranges for new construction in the downtown, bringing the lowest targeted income from 50% of median family income to 30% (Christ 1999).

The city's affordable housing efforts are subject to systematic, formal scrutiny. The Housing and Community Development Commission formed a Housing Evaluation Group charged with annually evaluating the use of housing resources by the Portland Development Commission (e.g., Housing Evaluation Group 2002). The city auditor conducted a review of all city housing programs from June 1996 through June 2000. During this period, $100 million was spent (not including administration costs) on various housing programs assisting 11,700 households. Federal funds covered 46% of these expenditures with 32% from the city general fund and 22% from tax increment financing. Programs ranged from housing development finance to service district exemptions, homebuyer assistance programs, and property repair programs. The majority of expenditures ($62.6 million) was devoted to new construction of housing for the homeless and low-income and middle-income renters and homeowners (for more on homelessness, see Chap. 13, Prince). Approximately 41% of new housing in the city was subsidized in some manner by the city. During the same period, the Housing Authority provided $119 million in housing vouchers to 5,600 low-income households (Office of the City Auditor 2002).

## *The Evolving Housing Market*

Despite well publicized complaints about the city's housing policies, development controls, and lack of readily available properties, there has been a tremendous amount of development activity. Today there are far more housing alternatives in Portland than existed in the 1980s. One can choose among traditional neighborhoods, downtown living, mixed-use developments, transit-oriented developments, houses with accessory apartments, row houses, and even large, elegant houseboats. Special needs housing can be found throughout the city.

In the early 1990s, a partnership of the American Institute of Architects, Homebuilders Association, Oregon Downtown Development Association, Oregon Housing and Services Department, Portland Bureau of Planning, and Reach Community Development Corporation sponsored the award winning City Life: Urban Show of Homes. This project was intended to demonstrate market viability, affordability, sound urban design, and innovative architectural design on a vacant site in an inner-city neighborhood. Completed in 1995, it offered a duplex, row houses, and courtyard units with alley parking. Targeted for mixed incomes, the units varied in price from $66,000 to $125,000 (Gragg 1995).

The redevelopment of the former Carnation Dairy in inner-southeast Portland into the Belmont Dairy, a mixed-use complex of subsidized and market rate rentals and homeowner row houses along with a grocery store, has transformed a moribund neighborhood commercial strip into a regional destination. Neighborhood libraries are being upgraded with facilities that include residences. The new Hollywood Library has apartments above it. The Sellwood-Moreland Library is on the ground floor of the Sellwood Lofts, which previously housed a metal plating company.

The Safeway supermarket chain's desire to expand into a residential zone ran head on into the city's requirement that zone changes result in no net loss of housing potential. As a result, the store's redevelopment involved relocating existing houses and building new housing for seniors. A second redevelopment initiative offers assisted living above Safeway and Target stores near a light rail stop in the eastern part of the city. In downtown Portland, Safeway is participating in the Museum Place Project involving market-priced and subsidized housing, a renovated YWCA, and a condominium tower all on three blocks. The store is on the first floor of a housing development. Within a four-block radius, there are several new midrise residential developments for both low/moderate-income and middle-income households. Some downtown condominium projects have been specifically targeted to moderate-income households.

The Pearl District had just a few residents in 1990 but now houses over 5,000 with development plans that will double that number (for more background see Chaps. 8, Abbott and 10, Chapman and Lund). Condominiums in this district at $330 per square foot have surpassed the City of Lake Oswego as the most expensive real estate in the region (Sleeth 2003). At $800 to $2,000 per month, rents are high relative to the rest of the city, although some are rent controlled for seniors and low-income households. The loft housing, midrise apartments, and large-scale condos pioneered in the Pearl District are increasingly available outside of downtown, such as the Lloyd District (Mayes 1996).

Property that formerly housed offices for the Oregon Department of Transportation is now a transit-oriented development adjacent to a light rail station. The property includes housing for seniors, low- and moderate-income households, fee simple row houses, and a daycare center. A subsidized low-income housing project was built next to the light rail station at PGE Park when the light rail (MAX) was extended to the west of the city. Pendergast and Associates, a major builder in the Pearl District, developed a mixed-income project on a former car sales property along Sandy Boulevard south of the Lloyd District. This project includes both housing and commercial space.

The Roman Catholic Church sponsored the development of St. Anthony's Village on a five-acre site in southeast Portland. This

PHOTO 9. New Safeway supermarket at SW 10 Ave. and Jefferson St. in 2004, recently relocated as part of a central business district urban renewal district project.

includes units for independent seniors, assisted living, and Alzheimer patients as well as a children's daycare and a church. This project was so successful that the church formed the Village Enterprise, a nonprofit development company that is working on projects throughout Oregon. One of these is in North Portland and includes units for seniors for both assisted and independent living. Three-quarters of these units are priced for low- and moderate-income households. Innovations such as zero lot line houses and development of detached homes with condo-style owner-ship designed using the Pattern Language principles of Christopher Alexander et al. (1977) can be found (Hogue 2002, 2003). Two nonprofit organizations are promoting the land trust concept, offering lower priced homes by selling the house itself and retaining ownership of the land.

Since the mid-1980s, community development corporations and other nonprofit developers have developed nearly 6,500 housing units in Multnomah County[11] (Community Development Network undated). Over 10% of these are homeownership units and most are within Port-land's boundaries.

## What Can Be Learned?

Portland used to have "affordable housing" because people did not want to live in the city. Such housing was often of poor quality and degraded. The city, however, has reinvented itself as a vibrant place where people want to live, and they continue to move here even in a depressed econo-my (Oppenheimer 2003). Neighborhoods that suffered significant dis-investment have a new lease on life as property owners rehabilitate and improve old housing and developers build new units.

In light of the reality of higher housing costs, the city, nonprofit organizations, and private developers have made significant commit-ments to producing new housing that meets the needs of lower income households. It is more expensive to develop this type of housing. But the alternative is affordability derived from a market that depresses property owners' ability (both landlords and homeowners) to capitalize on their investments (a result of reliance on the trickle down theory).

It is ironic that during the 30-year period from 1970 through 2000, the lowest rate of homeownership was reported in 1990 when Portland's housing market was considered to be affordable. The reluctance of banks to underwrite small mortgages is undoubtedly a contributing factor. This financing practice was one of the more unfortunate realities of Portland's housing history. Had the situation been different, home-ownership rates among low-income households, in particular minorities in the inner-northeast neighborhoods, could have increased, thus allowing these households to build equity with appreciating property values. It could also have helped in stabilizing neighborhoods.[12] The city also missed an opportunity to assist nonprofit developers in buying properties at low prices for eventual rehabilitation and/or development. Taking properties out of the buy–sell cycle would have enabled their long-run affordability, especially for rental housing.

The city has also missed other opportunities. An architectural critic noted that when the Portland Development Commission decided to dispose of the property associated with Terminal One to the north of downtown, the city decided not to buy the property. It was subsequently sold to a developer who intends to build 113 expensive row houses. The Commission did not place any restrictions on the sale so neither higher density nor development of affordable housing are mandated (Gragg 2002).

Portland's policies reflect the possibility that the city may once again experience the wide fluctuations in housing values that marked the last three decades of the century. For example, the city stopped maintaining a list of vacant and abandoned houses since there now are so few, but the Comprehensive Housing Plan includes this strategy should the market once again collapse (Bureau of Planning 1999, 44–45). The potential for a downturn in the housing market is real. Oregon's well publicized state budget problems and its chronic underfunding of education at all levels may emerge as a serious deterrent for families considering raising their children in Portland. There is already anecdotal evidence that some Portland families are relocating to Clark County, Washington, because of a lack of funding for Oregon public schools (Begay 2003).

Critics who focus on the impact of the UGB as a land market constraint that unfairly drives up housing prices would like to leave the impression that Portland's planners and policymakers are simply passive observers of the rising prices. The city's history of commitment to affordable housing rebuts this claim. Portland has seized numerous opportunities to proactively facilitate the development of affordable housing.

Those who claim that the price increases are attributable to market constraints resulting from planning policies should explain the 80% increase (in 1999 dollars) in homeowner-reported values during the 1970s when Portland's population declined by 4.1% (from 381,877 to 366,383) with a corresponding loss of 482 homeowner housing units. There certainly was plenty of undeveloped land readily available within the city in the 1970s. The UGB was not established until 1980 and initially had limited implications since so much developable land had been encompassed.

If anything in this history is relevant to other cities, it is the importance of "growing" a multifaceted approach to housing. This involves developing institutional capacity, fostering political commitment, allowing for the influence of advocates, taking advantage of opportunities as they arise, and using a wide variety of approaches. Constant monitoring of goal achievements is imperative.

Portland's housing future is unwritten. But the experience of the past would suggest that Fischel's (2002) question about whether Portland is a better place to live now than in 1975 would have to be answered in the affirmative. Portland's future will be guided by a legacy of efforts to create a city that provides a quality living environment even for those of limited means.

NOTES

1. See www.nahb.org for a description of the Housing Opportunity Index (HOI) and www.friends.org/resources/nahb.html for criticisms of this index.

2. Infill includes development of vacant lots and redevelopment of underdeveloped properties. The latter involves tear downs and building at higher densities, conversion into dwellings of existing nonresidential structures such as abandoned warehouses, or the addition of accessory dwellings to a single-family residence.

3. Homeowners' understanding of the current housing market influences their estimates of the value of their property. Thus the values for 1980 may be inflated and the values for 1990 lower than warranted.

4. This growth was concentrated in the 200 square miles of the Willamette Valley. The destruction of highly fertile farmland helped to generate the political will for establishing the Oregon land use system (Abbott and Howe 1993).

5. One interesting side note is that the Portland region was second in the nation in average annual spending on "do-it-yourself" projects; only Salt Lake homeowners spent more (Reade 2001).

6. The U.S. Census Bureau defines a household as including all people occupying a housing unit. A family consists of a householder (that person in whose name the home is owned, being bought, or rented) and one or more persons related to the householder by birth, marriage, or adoption (see www.census.gov).

7. This is the only historical data holding 2000 boundaries constant that will be presented in this chapter because other variables that conform to this geography are not readily available.

8. Nearly one-quarter of these households actually moved into the city due to problems in other locales (Bureau of Planning 1981).

9. Dominion Capital, Inc. went bankrupt after being charged with unfair trade practices and racketeering. The Portland Community Reinvestment Initiative, a city-backed nonprofit firm, ultimately bought Dominion's interest in these houses (averting foreclosures and evictions of at least 80 households), managing and rehabilitating the homes to maintain their affordability (Christ 1996).

10. In the late 1980s, a senior-level planner said to the author that one reason the city was reluctant to address a zoning issue in which residences were a non-conforming use in a commercial district was that to do so would mean that the housing would become less affordable. As a nonconforming use, banks were unwilling to extend loans to upgrade the housing.

11. Portland lies within three counties: Clackamas, Multnomah, and Washington. In 2000, Portland's share of Multnomah County's population was 79.8%, which represented 99.6% of the city's total population.

12. Some households may not have had the incentive to buy since their rents were historically low. When rents started to rise, these households could not afford the correspondingly higher purchase prices. Nevertheless, one African American realtor who specializes in northeast Portland noted that the rising housing values did enable many African American homeowners to sell their houses and use the capital gains to move elsewhere in the region.

REFERENCES

Abbott, Carl, and Deborah Howe. 1993. The politics of land-use law in Oregon: Senate Bill 100, twenty years after. *Oregon Historical Quarterly* 94 (1): 5–35.

Affordable Housing Technical (AFT) Advisory Committee. 2000. *Regional Affordable Housing Strategy: Recommendations of the Affordable Housing Technical Advisory Committee Accepted by the Metro Council.* Portland: Metro.

Alexander, Christopher and Sara Ishikawa and Murray Silverstein with Max Jacobson, Ingrid Fiksdahl-King and Schlamo Angel. 1977. *A Pattern Language: Towns, Building, Construction.* New York; Oxford University Press.

Begay, Jason. 2003. Enrollment explosions startles schools. *The Oregonian*, 13 October, B01.

Bureau of Planning. 1981. *Portland Residential Displacement Study: Survey Research Results.* Portland: Bureau of Planning.

Bureau of Planning. 1989. *Review Proposed Local Review Order (adopted by City Council, March 1, 1989, Resolution No. 34523).* Portland: Bureau of Planning.

Bureau of Planning. 1994. *Central City Plan Housing Report.* Portland: Bureau of Planning.

Bureau of Planning. 1999. *Adopted Comprehensive Plan Housing Policy.* Portland: Bureau of Planning.

Bureau of Planning. 2003. *Comprehensive Plan Goals and Policies: Adopted 1980, Last Revised November 2003.* Portland: Bureau of Planning. http://www.planning.ci.portland.or.us/pdf/ComprehensivePlan.pdf (accessed 26 May 2004).

Chaluvadi, Ashok. 2003. E-mail communication with author. 11 December. Senior Research Associate, National Association of Home Builders.

Christ, Janet. 1996. Dominion Capital. *The Oregonian*, 15 February, D13.

Christ, Janet. 1997. Coalition seeks delay in River District vote. *The Oregonian*, 22 July, B02.

Christ, Janet. 1999. River District housing hits income goals. *The Oregonian*, 25 May, E03.

Community Development Network. Undated. *Guide to CDCs and Nonprofit Housing Developers.* Portland: Community Development Network. http://www.cdnportland.org/cdc_guide.html (accessed 26 May 2004).

Downs, Anthony. 1981. *Neighborhoods and Urban Development.* Washington, DC: The Brookings Institution.

Downs, Anthony. 2002. Have housing prices risen faster in Portland than elsewhere? *Housing Policy Debate* 12 (1): 7–31.

Downtown Housing Advisory Committee. 1979. *Downtown Housing Policy and Program.* Portland: City of Portland Development Commission.

Durbin, Kathie. 1989. Derelict houses become more than eyesore for city. *The Oregonian,* 19 February, A01.

Eller, Jan. 1984. *Report of the Code Compliance Task Force.* Portland: Bureau of Buildings.

Fischel, William. 2002. Comment on Anthony Down's "Have housing prices risen faster in Portland than elsewhere?" *Housing Policy Debate* 12 (1): 43–50.

Gragg. Randy. 1995. Urban street of dreams. *The Oregonian,* 29 September, D01.

Gragg, Randy. 2002. End of the line for Terminal 1. *The Oregonian,* 27 November, D01.

Hogue, Kendra. 2002. Attached at the hip. *The Oregonian. New Home Monthly,* 21 March, 03.

Hogue, Kendra. 2003. Common ground. *The Oregonian. New Home Monthly,* 20 March, 03.

Hough, George C., Jr. 2003. E-mail communication with author. 31 July. Manager, Oregon State Data Center.

Housing Evaluation Group. 2002. *Fourth Annual Housing Evaluation Report: July 1, 2000–June 30, 2001.* Portland: Housing Evaluation Group.

Hunseberger, Brent. 1998. River district: Building anew or padding pockets? *The Oregonian,* 15 December, A10.

Joint Center for Housing Studies (JCHS). 2001. *The State of the Nation's Housing: 2001.* Cambridge, MA: Harvard University Press.

Lane, Dee. 1990. Blueprint for a slum: Major lenders aid decline of NE Portland. *The Oregonian,* 10 September, A01.

Lane, Dee. 1992. Agency rescues home buyers. *The Oregonian,* 17 April, A01.

Manvel, Evan. 1999. *Myths and Facts about UGBs.* Portland: 1000 Friends of Oregon. www.friends.org/resources/myths.html (accessed 26 May 2004).

Mayes, Steve. 1990. Home buying on the cheap. *The Oregonian,* 28 January, H01.

Mayes, Steve. 1996. More housing headed for Lloyd District. *The Oregonian,* 29 August, D02.

Myers, Dowell. 1992. *Analysis with Local Census Data: Portraits of Change.* San Diego: Harcourt Brace Javanovich.

National Association of Home Builders (NAHB). Undated. *Urban Growth Boundaries.* Washington, DC: National Association of Home Builders. http://www.nahb.org (accessed 26 May 2004).

Nelson, Arthur C., Rolf Pendall, Casey J. Dawkins, and Gerrit J. Knaap. 2002. *The Link between Growth Management and Housing Affordability: The Academic Evidence.* Washington, DC: The Brookings Institution Center on Urban and Metropolitan Policy.

Office of the City Auditor. 2002. *A Review of the Efforts and Accomplishments of City Housing Programs: 1996–2000.* Portland: Office of the City Auditor.

Office of Policy Development and Research. 2001. 2000 census results: Housing trends 1990–2000. *U.S. Housing Market Conditions.* 2nd Quarter.

Washington, DC: U.S. Department of Housing and Urban Development. http://www.huduser.org/periodicals/ushmc/summer2001/summary-2.html (accessed 26 May 2004).

Oliver, Gordon. 1999a. Developers are feeling squeezed between aesthetics, affordability. *The Oregonian*, 13 October, A01.

Oliver, Gordon. 1999b. Builders group warns against Portland. *The Oregonian*, 5 October, A01.

Oppenheimer, Laura. 2003. Growth of cities defies economy. *The Oregonian*, 10 July, A01.

Phillips, Justin, and Eban Goodstein. 2000. Growth management and housing prices: The case of Portland, Oregon. *Contemporary Economic Policy* 18 (3): 334–344.

Pozdena, Randall. 2002. *Smart growth and its effect on housing markets: The new segregation*. QuantEcon, Inc. Washington, DC: The National Center for Public Policy Research. http://www.nationalcenter.org/NewSegregation.pdf (accessed 26 May 2004).

Reade, Julia. 2001. *Remodeling Spending in Major Metropolitan Areas*. N01-4. Cambridge, MA: Joint Center for Housing Studies, Harvard University.

Sleeth, Peter. 2003. Prime prices reside in the Pearl. *The Oregonian*, 24 January, D01.

Staley, Samuel R., Jefferson G. Edgens, and Gerard C. S. Mildner. 1999. *A Line in the Land: Urban-Growth Boundaries, Smart Growth, and Housing Affordability*. Policy Study No. 263, Reason Policy Institute, Los Angeles. http://www.rppi.org/urban/ps263.html (accessed 26 May 2004).

Stein, Michelle. 1990a. Homes moving fast in booming market. *The Oregonian*, 6 May, A01

Stein, Michelle. 1990b. Population paranoia meets the welcome wagon Californiaphobia. *The Oregonian*, 8 April, L01.

Vacant and Abandoned Buildings (VAB) Task Force. 1988. *Vacant and Abandoned Buildings Task Force Progress Report*. Portland: Vacant and Abandoned Buildings Task Force.

# 10 | *Housing Density and Livability in Portland*

Nancy Chapman and Hollie Lund

We shouldn't be obsessed by the numbers of acres [within the urban growth boundary]. We should be obsessed with designing our communities better.
—Kitch (2002)

This observation lies at the heart of an ongoing debate among citizens, policymakers, and academics over the state of growth and livability within Portland's metropolitan region. The innovative state and regional growth management policies implemented here have been closely scrutinized for their effectiveness and relevance in other communities experiencing growth and sprawl. Thus our chapter begins with a traditional approach to evaluating the effectiveness of these growth management approaches by asking the question: Has the metropolitan region experienced an increase in density within its growth boundary? We review several difficulties encountered when attempting to measure density and sprawl (its close cousin), and present what we consider to be the most appropriate indicators and assessment of the region. We then explore how Portland residents have made the linkages between density and livability, particularly with respect to their attitudes toward changes in Portland's growth patterns in the 30 years since Senate Bill 100 (which later became the 1973 state land use law). Finally, we examine more closely the character of this growth within Portland's communities, specifically by using case studies of Portland neighborhoods. Before moving substantively into these questions, we present first a brief description of the planning context of the Portland metropolitan region.

## State and Regional Planning Principles

The regulatory framework that guides Portland development has at its core many quality of life principles. To assess growth patterns in the region, it is important to first understand these principles and the ways in which they are implemented.

Prior to the establishment of urban growth boundaries (UGBs) and other statewide growth management tools starting with Senate Bill 100, the Portland metropolitan region was relatively low in density. The inner city was characterized by single-family homes, typically on 5,000-square-foot lots; apartment complexes; and a few high-rise apartment buildings. Attached single-family housing was extremely rare. In more suburban areas, lots became larger and blended into farmland.

The statewide land use planning goals adopted in 1973 were designed in part to increase density and reduce sprawl in Oregon's cities and metropolitan regions. These goals required jurisdictions to establish UGBs and provide housing at all income levels, and set specific guidelines regarding multifamily housing and density levels. Housing density requirements were higher in larger urbanized areas with greater growth potential. According to Toulan (1994), this may help explain the relative success of the Portland region in containing growth compared to other jurisdictions in the state. The state did not mandate how these density requirements were to be achieved, allowing for creativity and flexibility among the jurisdictions.

Also contributing to Portland's growth management success is the presence of a comprehensive, long-range framework for guiding growth within the region (the 2040 Growth Concept). This framework was adopted by Metro, the region's metropolitan planning organization (MPO), and has been incorporated throughout regional and local policies. And unlike most regional governments, Metro has the legislative power to enforce its policies. The guiding framework (expanded on in Chap. 2, Seltzer) identifies the following values related to the management of sprawl (Metro 2003):

- Encourage a strong local economy
- Encourage the efficient use of land
- Protect and restore the natural environment
- Maintain separation between the Metro UGB and neighboring cities
- Provide a balanced transportation system
- Enable communities inside the Metro UGB to preserve their physical sense of place

- Ensure diverse housing options for all residents
- Create a vibrant place to live and work

To carry out this vision, city and county growth plans (required by state law) must incorporate such strategies as compact growth centers, transit-oriented development, affordable housing, and open space development. Combined, these strategies focus higher-density, mixed-use development into defined activity areas that are well served by transit, such as downtowns, regional and town centers, and main streets. They also improve access (by all residents) to public spaces, including parks and natural features, and a range of housing choices. In evaluating sprawl and other impacts of growth management strategies, however, many studies overlook these important concepts and focus solely on the density numbers—which are clearly just one piece of the puzzle.

## Measuring Sprawl in the Portland Region

Although Portland is often viewed as "the urban planners' Mecca" (Gordon and Richardson 2000), the success of its growth management strategies in reducing sprawl (defined here simply as outward growth) has received mixed reviews. Examining recent reports on sprawl and other relevant work, we find two major sources for the disagreements. The first relates to defining the term while the second relates to the wide range of scales at which sprawl is being measured.

### Problems of Terminology

The first problem relates to a lack of agreement on the definition of sprawl. Is it purely an issue of density, the descriptor that appears most frequently, or does it also imply measures of livability, such as access to jobs and open space? Since Portland's planning goals and growth management strategies emphasize not only efficient use of space but also high quality of life, we argue that any assessment of the effectiveness of those strategies must include measures of livability.

Many researchers, planners, and others interested in the shape and condition of our cities have given a great deal of attention to the question, What is sprawl? Putting aside the causes and consequences of sprawl, the most common measure is density (Freeman 2001, Pendall 1999, Phillips and Goodstein 2000, Wassmer 2000). This seems largely due, however, to the ease of attaining necessary density figures and not to a belief that density is the only relevant measure. Sprawl is also commonly identified by the separation of land uses (Freeman 2001, Galster et al. 2001, Wassmer 2000) and scattered, or leapfrog, development (Galster et al. 2001, Wassmer 2000, Weitz and Moore 1998). The most detailed definition to date, developed by Galster et al. (2001) identifies eight unique dimensions of sprawl. In addition to density, dimensions include continuity, mixed uses, concentration, clustering, centrality, nuclearity, and proximity. Although this provides a stronger methodological framework than that found in other studies, attaining all the necessary data for conducting such an analysis can be daunting. In fact, the authors themselves were able to conduct measurements for only a subset of their proposed dimensions. Ewing et al. (2002) also developed a multidimensional measure that, although the number of dimensions is fewer compared to Galster et al. (2001), may be more appropriate to this discussion because of its clear relationship to the goals and strategies of Smart Growth. The four basic dimensions are (1) residential density; (2) neighborhood mix of homes, jobs, and services; (3) strength of activity centers and downtowns; and (4) accessibility of the street network. Still missing in all of these definitions, however, is any mention of public space.

The importance of considering multiple dimensions in studies of sprawl is illustrated in Ewing et al.'s (2002) calculation of overall sprawl scores for 83 U.S. regions. Based on only two (residential density and mixture of uses) of the four dimensions already noted, Portland would be considered *more sprawling* than Los Angeles. After incorporating measures of the "strength of centers" and "accessibility of the street network," however, Portland ranks as the 8th *least* sprawling of the 83 regions while Los Angeles ranks 45th. (It is also important to note that most of those regions that ranked higher than Portland were older regions whose growth was limited by geographic barriers) (Lang 2002).

## Problems of Scale

Unfortunately, even if a definition is agreed upon, there is still the problem of scale. The two most common units of analysis for measuring sprawl—metropolitan statistical area (MSA) and urbanized area (UA)—are misleading for the Portland region. MSAs, for instance, include the entire area of each county that overlaps the city and its suburbs; for Portland, this includes not only a large share of rural lands outside the UGB but also all of Clark County, Washington, which is outside of Oregon's jurisdiction and not regulated by its statewide or regional growth management policies. This is particularly problematic because, unlike the Oregon counties, Clark County is an area where "low-density development boomed" during the 1990s (Northwest Environment Watch 2002, 5), likely leading to overestimates of the amount of sprawl occurring within the majority of greater Portland.

UAs improve the situation slightly by eliminating the rural areas of the surrounding counties, but the Portland–Vancouver UA also includes land in Clark County. It has also been argued that UAs underestimate the loss of rural land because the threshold at which land moves from a "rural" to a "suburban" classification may be too dense (Kolankiewicz and Beck 2001). In response to these issues, a number of researchers have employed new strategies for defining the Portland region; unfortunately, they are not consistent and still lead to varying results. This is an area in need of more attention, not just for improving our understanding of growth management in Portland but for studies of sprawl in all regions.

In studies of density, the boundaries traditionally used (the MSA and the urbanized area) include not only areas that lie outside Portland's UGB but also parts of Washington State not covered by Oregon legislation. If the UGB is successful, we would expect increases in density within it and decreases in development outside it, except for areas within the UGBs of the surrounding small towns. Thus its effectiveness cannot be truly evaluated using anything except the UGB as the study boundary.

## Is Portland Sprawling?

Recognizing the aforementioned limitations of past research, it appears that Portland's growth management strategies are working. Perhaps the earliest evaluation of one of these strategies—the UGB— was conducted in 1991 by ECO Northwest. The study found that in Portland, 91% of single-family development and 99% of the multifamily development between 1988 and 1990 occurred within the UGB. It also found that Portland's UGB was much more successful in containing growth than those in three other Oregon UAs. Similar conclusions were reached in a follow-up study a decade later (ECO Northwest 2001). In both studies, however, densities remained lower than allowed levels due to market constraints.

A study by Northwest Environment Watch (2002) compared growth in the three Oregon counties of greater Portland to that of Clark County (also in the greater Portland region, but located in Washington State where UGBs have been less strongly enforced). The study found that Oregon's growth during the 1990s was more likely to occur in medium- to high-density neighborhoods (more than 12 persons per acre) than was growth in Clark County. During the same period, Clark County also covered 23% more of its land with impervious surfaces and lost 40% more farmland per capita than did the three counties in Oregon. It is also important to note, however, that Clark County's weaker growth controls may have taken pressure for low-density housing off the remainder of the MSA by accommodating spillover from areas with stricter controls (Harvey and Works 2001, Lewis 1996). As growth patterns have gradually become more compact since Washington's adoption of growth management in 1994, however, the accommodation of "spillover" is likely to be more difficult.

Conder (2000) also relied on building permits to analyze the type and amount of development occurring within Portland's UGB. The study found that during 1997 and 1998, 66% of the development in the City of Portland and about 30% in the entire UGB was either infill or redevelopment (referred to jointly as "refill"), as opposed to new construction on vacant land. The study concluded, "[Portland's] present estimated refill rate is consistent with our twenty year forecast for individual jurisdiction growth" (Conder 2000, 4).

Nelson and Sanchez (2003) compared Portland's population densities (broken down by urban, suburban, exurban, and rural areas), to those of San Antonio, Columbus, Charlotte, and Orlando. The study defines "urban" as 3,000 or more persons per square mile, "suburban" as 1,000 to 3,000 persons per square mile, "exurban" as 300 to 1,000 persons per square mile, and "rural" as less than 300 per square mile. Although Portland experienced significant population growth from 1990 to 2000, it realized the smallest loss of rural lands and significantly less suburban and exurban development than the comparison cities. Orlando, which also has urban containment policies, showed significantly more outward development.

Combined, these studies suggest that Portland as a region has been successful in focusing its growth into compact centers and protecting its outlying lands, at least compared to other regions and surrounding areas. As discussed earlier, however, regional analyses only tell a part of the story; to understand issues of livability we need to come down to the community level. A study by Portland's regional government (Metro 2003) provides additional insight into where and how growth is occurring at the community level. Through an analysis of 13 communities in the Portland region, the study showed that established neighborhoods were maintaining or increasing density, that new residential developments in 2000 were accommodating more people and households per acre than those in 1990, and that by 2000 the majority of employment (62%) was located within designated "activity centers." Much of the increase in density in new development can be attributed to smaller lot sizes for single-family homes (see also Chap. 9, Howe). Between 1996 and 2000, there was a 132% increase in single-family homes constructed on lots of less than 5,000 square feet, and lots 5,000 square feet or greater *decreased* by 32 to 47%. Home sizes, on the other hand, showed little change (Conder and Larson 2001). Contributing to the increasing density in new developments was an increase in multifamily housing development. The study found that densities did not "plateau" toward the end of the decade; densities were still increasing during the last year of the analysis, from 1999 to 2000. Single-family developments, for instance, increased from an average of 5.9 dwelling units per acre in 1999 to 6.2 in 2000. Multifamily densities increased 16.4 units per acre in 1999 to 21.6 per acre in 2000.

## Density and Livability in Portland Neighborhoods

Density and livability have been issues of public debate, with a large body of research claiming that people overwhelmingly desire large-lot, suburban housing while others, such as Myers and Gearin (2001), argue that there is actually a large, untapped demand for higher-density housing close to shopping and public transit. Therefore, it is important to consider the public's response to such development in the Portland region.

At first glance, the picture is not clear. For example, consumer demand shows Portland residents looking inward rather than outward for housing, with concomitant increases in inner-city housing prices (Conder and Larson 2001), yet citizens have frequently protested increased density either as infill or on the suburban edge. Looking more closely at these protests, however, it appears that citizens are concerned not just about density but also with the quality and character of the development. Controversy has been particularly strong in the case of redevelopment and quality of infill.

For example, a recent report on density from the City Club of Portland, a nonpartisan civic organization, concluded that the "the City has dissipated too much of its planning energy on projects that contribute too few new housing units, including politically contentious neighborhood infill" (City Club of Portland 1999, 87). Contentious changes in the zoning code during the last decade include allowing accessory apartments within, attached to, or in detached structures in all residential zones except residential: farm and forest; and particularly the provision that does not limit their development to owner-occupied homes. Duplexes may be added to corner lots and transition lots in the same zones.

In the 1970s and 1980s, Portland residents protested on a number of occasions the destruction of single-family housing for new high-density housing—not just because of the increased density but because of the loss of historically significant buildings. The outcome of one such protest was a policy requiring a review and a 90-day stay before demolition of any house on the city's historic inventory.

The design of rowhouses and infill single-family houses has also generated protest. Early rowhouse designs featured garages on the ground level and stairways to the second level entry, resulting in three-story structures that towered over the surrounding houses and were removed from the life of the street and sidewalk. Single-family infill houses with garages protruding in front of a recessed entrance, termed "snout houses," have also been controversial. Portland responded by adopting community design standards in 1997 limiting the size and dominance of garages at the front of the house.

New city codes that did not include minimum lot sizes in a number of zones, intended to allow odd-sized lots to be developed, created a firestorm of protest in 2000 when developers discovered that the underlying platting of lots in some neighborhoods was smaller than the zoning classification. Small houses on double lots were replaced by "skinny houses" on 2,500 square foot lots. In response to public protests over the houses judged to be out-of-scale with the surrounding neighborhood and lacking good transition to the street, the city established a 3,000-square-foot minimum lot size for new single-family homes.

Outside of Portland's developed areas, however, residents seem more concerned with discouraging higher density as a whole and are less likely to differentiate between "good" and "bad" types of high-density development. Their concerns were recently conveyed in an initiative measure placed on the 2002 ballot by a group called Oregonians in Action. The measure would have repealed Metro density requirements and prohibited Metro from adopting ordinances to dictate housing densities in neighborhoods. The measure lost, however, due to lack of support in the more urban counties, while a countermeasure placed on the ballot by Metro passed. This measure prohibited increased density requirements in existing single-family neighborhoods but retained the density requirements for new developments.

Finally, an annual citizen survey conducted by the City of Portland and Multnomah County since 1993 finds that the number of city residents who rate the livability of their neighborhood as "good" or "very good" has increased over the past decade, from 77% in 1993 to 82% in 2002 (Office of the City Auditor 2002). The study was based on random samples of over 5,000 residents from eight neighborhood regions. This perception of livability, however, has not been consistent across time or throughout the city or region. These variations will be expanded on in the context of the case studies.

## Livability: Access to Everyday Amenities and Public Space

We used a case study method to take an in-depth look at the character of this increasing density in our neighborhoods and its impact on residential "livability," particularly in terms of accessibility of parks, retail and public uses, and access to and quality of public space. We include in *public space* the public–private transition in residential areas that includes front porches, sidewalks, and planting strips as well as parks and natural areas. Case studies for nine neighborhoods in the region are based on data from the U.S. Census, Portland's Regional Land Information System (RLIS) database and site evaluations (see Chap. 2, Seltzer, for more information about RLIS). The case study neighborhoods represent areas where new development or infill development was prominent in the 1990s, including three communities developed under the principles of New Urbanism. Each neighborhood was examined through site evaluations in order to understand the "on the ground" impact of Portland's growth management planning principles.

In conducting our case studies, we focused on two aspects of livability: access to retail, parks, and civic uses and access to and quality of public spaces. Although the value of access to jobs and retail has been well accepted and implemented in practice and academia, the importance of public spaces in local and regional growth is often overlooked. Public spaces play numerous roles, however, in combating the potential negative impacts of high-density development on both individuals and the built and natural environments and should be included in any discussion of livability.

As decades of research by social scientists have demonstrated, the deleterious effects of density are moderated by the organization of density in space as well as by cultural adaptations to it. The concepts of "social density" and "optimally manned behavior settings" for example, have been coined to capture the importance of design features that cluster people into smaller rather than larger groups (Barker and Gump 1964, Baum et al. 1979, Stokols 1976, Wicker 1969). Writers and researchers from Jacobs (1961) to Whyte (1988) and Taylor (1988), and more recently the New Urbanists (Calthorpe et al. 2001, Duany et al. 2000), have discussed the importance of public and semipublic spaces as transitional territories where people come to know each other casually and come to take responsibility for their shared spaces and community. Thus the transitions between public and private spaces, walkable neighborhoods with pedestrian amenities, and retail or public space destinations nearby might be expected to make dense neighborhoods more livable. Public spaces including park lands become even more important as density increases and residents have less access to private outdoor space. In addition to recreational opportunities, such spaces provide opportunities for relaxation, and even visual access to nature has been found to have health benefits (Ulrich et al. 1991, Ulrich 1999).

Public open spaces serve other purposes as well, preserving wildlife habitat and serving as ecologically important areas that support the environmental health of the region. Lack of park land is not unique to the present time period—in the New York metropolitan region, post–World War II tracts had one-tenth as much park acreage as neighborhoods established in the first four decades of the twentieth century (2.7% vs. 27%) (Rome 1998). It is for these reasons that we feel a more qualitative and comprehensive assessment of growth patterns is necessary—one that goes beyond measures such as density and other easily quantifiable factors.

## *Study Sites*

The nine neighborhoods chosen for intensive case study represent a sample of three communities each that experienced (1) new development on vacant or farmland, (2) development following the principles of New Urbanism, or (3) infill or redevelopment. All nine neighborhoods are located within the Portland UGB (see Fig. 10.1). Table 10.1 contains basic population and housing statistics for the nine communities.

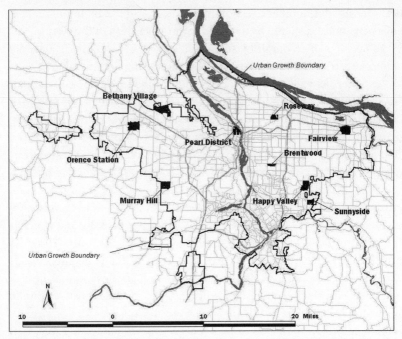

FIGURE 10.1. Location of case study neighborhoods. Source: Original

## Criteria and Regional-Level Data

Our assessment of livability was based on two organizing criteria: (1) accessibility of parks, retail, and civic uses and (2) the quality of these public and semipublic spaces. These criteria were chosen because we expect that both the accessibility and the quality of these spaces may foster social contact among near neighbors and encourage taking responsibility for the neighborhood. (Transportation accessibility and congestion, and housing affordability, also important indicators of livability, are covered in Chap. 11, Adler and Dill, and Chap. 9, Howe, respectively).

Some data about livability at city and regional level using these criteria are available. For example, Portland has been successful in maintaining access to parkland (see also Chap. 7, Orloff). According to a recent report from the Trust for Public Land (2003), which compared the quality of parkland in 55 cities, Portland ranked second (after San Diego) among medium-high population density cities in acreage of parkland per 1,000 persons (with 24.5 acres per 1,000 people, compared to an average of 16.2). Portland was also second to San Diego in the amount of parkland as a percent of city area (15.1%, compared to an average of 8.8%).

# Table 10.1

*Population and housing comparisons, 2000, case study neighborhoods*

| Study Area (Abbrev.) | Miles to Central Business District | Mandated SF Density | Current Single Family Density[a] | Population Density[b] | Household Density[c] | % Owner Occupied[d] | % Single Family Units Built since 1990[e] | % Land Single Family[f] |
|---|---|---|---|---|---|---|---|---|
| **Conventional New Development** | | | | | | | | |
| Bethany Village | 8.5 | 8/acre | 6.25 | 9.17 | 3.3 | 71.68 | 90.3 | 91 |
| Happy Valley | 9.0 | 6/acre | 3.33 | 2.62 | 0.84 | 96.53 | 83.9 | 100 |
| Murrayhill | 9.5 | 8/acre | 4.16 | 4.37 | 1.67 | 56.59 | 56.2 | 85 |
| **New Urbanist New Development** | | | | | | | | |
| Orenco St. | 12.0 | 10/acre | 5.00 | 3.80 | 2.0 | 38.43 | 59.7 | 78 |
| Fairview Village | 12.0 | 6/acre | 4.34 | 6.85 | 2.3 | 54.32 | 38.0 | 87 |
| East Sunnyside | 10.0 | 8/acre | 7.14 | 4.35 | 1.51 | 78.74 | 97.1 | 92 |
| **Refill Development** | | | | | | | | |
| Mt. Scott | 5.0 | 10/acre | 7.14 | 12.20 | 5.0 | 61.87 | 6.2 | 100 |
| Roseway | 5.0 | 10/acre | 7.14 | 10.75 | 4.60 | 77.09 | 1.2 | 99 |
| River District | 0.5 | 10/acre | 25.00 | 11.13 | 5.93 | 19.54 | 97.11 | 10 |

[a]Density on land developed as single family.
[b]Persons per acre. SOURCE: 2000 U.S. Census Bureau.
[c]SOURCE: 2000 U.S. Census Bureau.
[d]Households per acre. SOURCE: 2000 U.S. Census Bureau.
[e]SOURCE: 2002 Regional Land Information System (RLIS) database, Metro.
[f]Percent land devoted to single family. SOURCE: 2002 RLIS database, Metro.

The Trust for Public Land also identified Portland as one of four cities achieving park excellence, according to seven criteria (PRNewswire 2003). They highlighted Forest Park (in northwest Portland) as the fifth-largest city park in the nation (see Chap. 7, Orloff), the reclamation of old highways and railroad tracks for parks, the up-to-date parks master plan, advisory groups, and the availability of parks programs to people with low incomes.

At the regional level, Metro (2003) reports that 64% of the region's residents living inside the UGB are within walking distance (one-quarter mile) of a public park, greenspace, or regional trail. An important source of public open spaces in the region was the passage of a bond measure in 1995 that provided $135.6 million for the purchase of open spaces, including meadows, forests, riparian areas, wetlands, trails, and river and stream corridors (Metro 2001; see Chap. 2, Seltzer for more detail). With this work in mind, the remainder of the chapter will assess livability as it is revealed through the presence in our case study neighborhoods of (1) well-designed public and semipublic open spaces, (2) pedestrian-friendly design, and (3) neighborhood retail outlets.

### Neighborhood-Level Case Studies

Criteria for assessing the quality of public and semipublic spaces were adapted from a scale developed by Patterson (1997) to assess the degree to which neighborhoods met New Urbanism standards. Specifically, the criteria include factors that are hypothesized to make walking more pleasant and frequent; these include the presence of sidewalks, parking strips and street trees, access to retail and park destinations, a connected street network, and access to civic buildings. Other characteristics measured are thought to increase social contact in the neighborhood and include the presence of front porches and moving auto access off the street to the back of the unit.

Additional criteria used to assess the quality of public spaces and parklands include whether the space serves diverse uses and users (e.g., sports fields, paths for walking and jogging, play areas for children of varying ages) as well as the presence of natural habitat for wildlife and native plant species. The regional geographic information system (GIS) database, supplemented by field observations, was used to identify parks and public spaces within the study areas and a surrounding quarter-mile radius. Additional field observations were then used to collect data on each of the criteria.

## Redevelopment and Infill Case Studies

Three neighborhoods were chosen as case studies of residential infill and redevelopment within the City of Portland: the Pearl/River District, the Mt. Scott/Arleta neighborhood, and the Roseway neighborhood. The Pearl/River District (also known as Old Town/Chinatown) is adjacent to downtown Portland and has received considerable redevelopment and infill. The Mt. Scott/Arleta neighborhood in southeast Portland has experienced continual infill since 1970; the Roseway neighborhood in northeast Portland has received recent skinny house redevelopment. Target areas were chosen in each neighborhood, and field study identified houses that appeared to be infill/redevelopment since 1970. Year built and lot sizes were determined using property data from the City of Portland's Internet mapping server. The amount and character of infill in each neighborhood is shown in Table 10.2, the quality of the public and semipublic spaces other than parks in Table 10.3, and the size and quality of public parks in Table 10.4.

The River/Pearl District is a downtown neighborhood that has undergone planning efforts since the 1980s to redevelop it from an industrial neighborhood with housing typically in the form of single-room occupancy hotels into an upscale mixed-use neighborhood. The

Photo 10. "Skinny houses" at NE 69th in 2004. Structures like these heighten public controversy and spur refinement to planning policies in an effort to meet regional density objectives.

**Table 10.2**

*Housing units developed in infill case study neighborhoods*

| Decade | Neighborhood | | |
|---|---|---|---|
| | Pearl/River District | Mt. Scott/Arleta | Roseway |
| 1970s | 122 units[a] | 19 (18 snout) | 1 |
| 1980s | 197 units[a] | 10 (8 snout) | 1 |
| 1990s | 984 units[b] | 17 (6 snout) | 1 |
| 2000s | 2540 units[b] | 15 (4 snout) | 8 (7 skinny) |

[a]Based on 1990 census data.
[b]Based on report from PDC.

River District Housing Implementation Strategy was adopted in 1994, supported by urban renewal funding through the Portland Development Commission (PDC). Three- to five-story multifamily buildings characterized the early wave of redevelopment, but the newest housing commonly takes the form of high-rise (8- to 15-story) buildings, almost all with retail on the first floor. Of the 30 new residential buildings supported by PDC, over half are affordable only to middle- and upper-income households (Portland Development Commission 2002). In addition to parks, public, semipublic, and semiprivate transition spaces include landscaped street closures (five blocks), balconies, and occasional semiprivate outdoor spaces associated with townhouses or residential buildings. The latter are typically gated and offer little more than visual access to plantings. Trendy shops, galleries, and restaurants are common, but neighborhood retail such as grocery stores, pharmacies, and dry cleaners have been slower to develop. The shops create an active street life, so the sidewalks and cafés play an important role in local social contact. Parks include five blocks that have been dedicated as parkland since 1869 (the North Park Blocks), about 10 blocks along the waterfront (some undeveloped), and a new public square with a second planned. (See Chap. 9, Howe for more on the history of this area.)

Mt. Scott/Arleta and Roseway are working- to middle-class neighborhoods, located in southeast and northeast Portland, respectively. The housing consists largely of small, single-family detached houses developed from 1920 to 1960. They differ in the timing and amount of infill development they have received. In Mt. Scott/Arleta, infill since 1970 has followed the economy, showing a slump during the recession in the 1980s, but accelerating in the 1990s and since 2000. The identified infill units are almost entirely single-family detached homes, many of which

**Table 10.3**

*Connectivity and civic and public spaces within neighborhoods*

| | New Urbanist New Development | | | Conventional New Development | | | Refill Development | | |
|---|---|---|---|---|---|---|---|---|---|
| | Fairview Village | Orenco Station | East Sunnyside Village | Bethany | Happy Valley | Murrayhill | Mt. Scott/Arleta | Roseway | River District |
| Connectivity: intersections/sq mi[a] | 37.6 | 28.0 | 41.1 | 31.7 | 8.3 | 16.9 | 201.9 | 180.5 | 261.6 |
| Connectivity: dead-ends/sq mi[b] | 33.2 | 38.1 | 46.6 | 44.2 | 48.3 | 70.3 | 27.5 | 5.3 | 9.2 |
| Convenient transit[c] | Good | Excellent | Poor | Good | Poor | Fair | Excellent | Good | Excellent |
| Central civic[d] | Excellent | Fair | Good | Poor | Poor | Good | None | Poor | Poor |
| Neighborhood retail in or adjacent[e] | Good | Good | Excellent | Excellent | None | Excellent | Minimal | Good | Good |

[a]Four-way intersections per square mile.
[b]Dead ends, culs de sac, including looped culs de sac per square mile.
[c]Number of bus lines, access to light rail, and frequency of service.
[d]Schools, libraries, post offices, city halls, recreation centers.
[e]Grocery store, pharmacy, cleaners, hardware, health care, hair care, bank.
SOURCE: Original

## Table 10.4

*Accessibility and quality of parks, recreation spaces, and open spaces*

| Study Area | Parkland within Study Area Boundary | | | Parkland Including Surrounding Quarter-Mile Radius | | | |
|---|---|---|---|---|---|---|---|
| | Total Acres of Parkland | % of Total Land | Ratio to Population Density[a] | Total Acres of Parkland | % Developed[b] | % Natural[c] | Other Recreation |
| **Conventional New Development** | | | | | | | |
| Bethany Village | 112.58 | 14.66 | 16.80 | 181.1 | 63 | 4 | Golf, jogging trail beneath powerlines |
| Happy Valley | 142.56 | 30.72 | 93.00 | 68.37 | 63 | 31 | |
| Murrayhill | 76.78 | 15.61 | 15.48 | 28.72 | 2 | 53 | Jogging trail beneath powerlines |
| **New Urbanist New Development** | | | | | | | |
| Orenco Station | 60.66 | 8.03 | 33.80 | 0 | 4 | 5 | Golf course |
| Fairview Village | 71.62 | 12.39 | 18.04 | 53.46 | 50 | 50 | |
| East Sunnyside Village | 11.69 | 5.02 | 2.91 | 5.80 | 67 | 32 | |
| **Refill Development** | | | | | | | |
| Mt.Scott/Arleta | 0 | 0 | 0 | 33.49 | 100 | 0 | |
| Roseway | 7.92 | 3.29 | 4.88 | 67.12 | 8 | 0 | Cemetery |
| River District | 12.66 | 3.65 | 3.34 | 10.45 | 100 | 0 | |
| Entire UGB | 31,271.55 | 13.28 | | n/a | | | |

SOURCE: 2002 Regional Land Information System (RLIS) database, Metro.
[a] Acres of parkland per 1,000 residents.
[b] Percent of parkland that is developed; includes developed sports, children's play areas, picnicking, formal green space, benches. and plantings.
[c] Includes natural habitat/stream corridors.

are snout houses dominated by the garage. Infill in Roseway has been more sudden and has taken the form of skinny houses. Neighbors have protested the recent demolition of houses on 5,000-square-foot lots to be replaced by these 15-foot-wide houses on 2,500-square-foot lots.

In both neighborhoods, the mix of houses from different eras leads to a diversity of transitions from public to private space. Front porches are common on the older and newer houses, but often lacking in those developed in the 1940s and 1950s. In Mt. Scott/Arleta, some of the newer infill is shoehorned into spaces that lack connectivity with the rest of the neighborhood; a few are on lots so narrow that only the garage faces the street.

The areas also differ in access to neighborhood shopping. Mt. Scott/Arleta has only a few corner grocery stores, while Roseway has two convenient neighborhood shopping areas (although both are dominated by parking lots). Both neighborhoods have some unpaved streets and some streets lacking sidewalks and planting strips. There are no parks or public spaces within the Mt. Scott/Arleta area, but two very large public parks are located within a quarter mile. Roseway has one developed park, facilities at the elementary school within the neighborhood, and an adjacent 64-acre cemetery.

### New Urbanist Case Studies

We chose three developments within the metropolitan region that were planned according to principles of New Urbanism: Fairview Village, East Sunnyside Village, and Orenco Station. The origins of each are complex, but the driving forces included a developer (Fairview Village), the City of Hillsboro (Orenco Station), and Clackamas County (East Sunnyside Village) (Calthorpe Associates 2003). Both Fairview Village and Orenco Station were developed on open land adjacent to existing town centers dating from the late 1800s; East Sunnyside Village was built on undeveloped land. All required modifications to the zoning code or creation of a separate district to allow conformance to New Urbanism principles.

The extent to which they have fulfilled their promise for more mixed housing and commercial development as the basis for a stronger orientation to pedestrians and community building is limited. In all cases, connectivity and densities were not appreciably higher than those of the new suburban neighborhoods and did not approach those of Portland's older established neighborhoods (see Table 10.3). All three neighborhoods contain a mix of single-family homes, rowhouses, townhomes, and apartment complexes, but these are better integrated in Orenco and Fairview. Accessory apartments and mixed use housing over retail are also more common in Orenco and Fairview. The commercial core of East Sunnyside Village is the most complete; Orenco has the beginning of a good commercial core, but services outside the core tend to be auto-oriented. Fairview has found it difficult to attract a solid neighborhood-oriented commercial core (including a grocery store) within the development. Transit service ranges from excellent in Orenco (although access to destinations other than Hillsboro and Portland are limited) to poor in Sunnyside.

Fairview has been the most successful at attracting central civic spaces, including the City Hall, a library, and a post office; the other neighborhoods have only schools and a community or recreation center. Parks vary in their ability to serve diverse users, from small formal greenspaces in all three neighborhoods, to large wetland areas (Fairview and Sunnyside), to parks or schools with equipment for small children (Fairview and Orenco). Fairview has been criticized by New Urbanism proponents for its lack of attention to architectural detail, but the result has been a more affordable alternative to the typical New Urbanist community.

### Conventional New Development Case Studies

The three conventional new development case study communities are Happy Valley, Bethany, and Murrayhill. All are designated "town centers" in the Metro 2040 Growth Plan, although Happy Valley is designated for a lower density (six units per acre rather than eight). All three are currently located at the edge of the UGB, and both Bethany and Murrayhill show promise as developing town centers. Both have well-designed retail areas that are more pedestrian friendly than the suburban standard, although they tend to be oriented toward the arterial streets rather than toward the surrounding neighborhoods. The larger of Bethany's retail centers includes a street with housing over shops that echoes similar urban-scale housing in Orenco Station. Sidewalks are mandated in all new development, but parking strips and street trees are absent in most of Bethany. The quality of the transition from public to private space varies by builder within each neighborhood; some include usable porches and orientation to the street, others are more likely to provide a minimal entry-space transition. None have alleys, so garages and driveways are prominent but do not typically extend in front of the entryways. Two of the three developments have elementary schools, and two have post office outlets within their retail centers. Other civic facilities are absent. On the whole, Happy Valley is a typical suburban development on relatively large lots; Murrayhill and Bethany have incorporated more neighborhood retail and attached and apartment housing but have not integrated them into the neighborhood well. A street connection between apartment and single-family housing in Murrayhill makes the point visually—the connection is blocked with curbs on both sides and signed to allow only emergency vehicles to cross.

The natural areas in Bethany Village and Murrayhill consist largely of stream corridors and land along major power transmission lines; the latter have paved paths in the center of roughly mowed vegetation with some stands of blackberries and remnant fir forest. The public spaces in Happy Valley include open spaces along stream corridors, as well as green space buffers within some of the new housing developments. In all cases, the stream corridors and wetlands serve an ecological function but offer very little access to residents. Other active uses are located in a large, unkempt public park and at the elementary school in Happy Valley, and in Murrayhill at a recreation center for homeowners and at the elementary school. Murrayhill also provides unique landscaped boulevards with rows of trees on both sides of the sidewalk that provide a pleasant walking environment and a connection with the retail core.

## Summary and Conclusion

Although national comparative studies have not always shown the Portland metropolitan area as increasing in density and decreasing in sprawl, this may be an artifact of the incompatibility of the boundaries studied with the UGB. Comparative studies by Nelson and Sanchez (2003) and by Ewing et al. (2002) have shown significant changes, suggesting that Portland's growth management strategies are working. Densities are increasing, and sprawl outside the UGB is limited compared with similar cities elsewhere. Unfortunately, we lack a careful study of development in the areas targeted by the growth plan: town and regional centers, main streets, corridors, and transit corridors. The case studies of both the New Urbanist and the conventional new development communities showed more mixed use in and increasing density surrounding the town centers than we suspect was typical of earlier suburban growth. They still tend to lack nearby employment.

At the same time, livability surveys showed increases in livability in Portland and Multnomah County from 1993 through 2000, although the ratings have leveled or even declined slightly in the last three years. Some areas, including those containing our Roseway and Mt. Scott/ Arleta study areas, have had lower levels of satisfaction than neighborhoods in southwest, northwest, and inner northeast and southeast. Comparable data are lacking for neighborhoods outside Multnomah County. Without further study, it is difficult to pinpoint causes or assess the reliability of recent small declines in livability ratings. In addition to increasing density, the population of the metropolitan region grew by 26% from 1990 to 2000, placing the three counties in the top 4% for absolute growth nationally during the decade (Portland Multnomah Progress Board 2003).

Public and semipublic transition spaces were generally best in the New Urbanism communities. Only Happy Valley and Orenco Station reached Portland's average in acres of parkland per 1,000 residents, according to the Trust for Public Land (2003) report; all but the refill communities and East Sunnyside Village reached the Portland average in percent of land area devoted to parks and open space. Portland's overall averages are no doubt biased by the inclusion of Forest Park, which is very large but remote from much of the population. Although we might expect that increased density in new development would decrease the availability of parks and public space, the new developments are actually the best served and the inner-city development least well served with parks and public space. On the whole, development in both the New Urbanist and New Development neighborhoods reflects the emphasis that Metro has placed on purchasing ecologically significant stream corridors and natural areas throughout the region (see Chap. 12, Ozawa and Yeakley for more details). The Rock Creek Greenway through Bethany, Salish Ponds Wetland adjacent to Fairview, and the Scott View Nature Trail in Happy Valley were at least partially reserved as open spaces or developed with Metro funding. The inner east side, including the Roseway and Mt. Scott/Arleta neighborhoods, reflects development in a period when stream corridors were diverted into culverts, and park space was developed with wooded lawns, picnic tables, children's play areas, and play fields. Although they have fewer acres per resident, those acres tend to foster more active and passive uses by residents of all ages.

It will take many years to see whether development truly lives up to the promise of the 2040 Growth Concept. For the UGB to fulfill its promise of limiting sprawl while maintaining livability, redevelopment in existing neighborhoods will need to be well designed and focused on the growth areas envisioned by the 2040 Plan. The changes in density and neighborhood design have been guided by the state land use goals, Metro's principles and detailed guidance to jurisdictions, and the ability of the cities and counties within the UGB to creatively alter their comprehensive plans, zoning codes, and zoning to implement the principles. The legislative powers invested in the state's Department of Land Conservation and Development and in Metro have been critical. Important additional players have been funding sources such as the Portland Development Commission, Metro Greenspaces, state Transportation and Growth Management grants, and individual developers with a new vision. Other regions hoping to build on Portland's experience will need to find ways to coordinate policies at state, regional, and local levels, and to focus on the character of development as well as density.

REFERENCES

Barker, Roger G., and Paul V. Gump. 1964. *Big School, Small School*. Stanford, CA: Stanford University Press.

Baum, Andrew, John R. Aiello, and Lisa E. Calesnick. 1979. Crowding and personal control: Social density and the development of learned helplessness. In *Residential Crowding and Design*, edited by John R. Aiello and Andrew Baum, 141–159. New York: Plenum Press.

Calthorpe Associates. 2003. East Sunnyside Village Plan. http://www.calthorpe.com/Project%20Sheets/Sunnyside.pdf (accessed 22 July 2003).

Calthorpe, Peter, William Fulton, and Robert Fishman. 2001. *The Regional City: Planning for the End of Sprawl*. Washington, DC: Island Press.

City Club of Portland. 1999. *Increasing Density in Portland*. Portland: City Club of Portland.

Conder, Sonny. 2000. *Report on the Residential Refill Study for 97-98*. Portland: Metro.

Conder, Sonny, and Karen Larson. 2001. *Metro Single Family Home Price Trends: Donuts without Holes and Turnips without Blood*. Portland: Metro.

Duany, Andres, Elizabeth Plater-Zyberk, and Jeff Speck. 2000. *Suburban Nation: The Rise of Sprawl and the Decline of the American Dream*. New York: North Point Press.

ECO Northwest. 1991. *Urban Growth Management Study: Case Studies Report*. Salem: Oregon Department of Land Conservation and Development.

ECO Northwest. 2001. *Metro Urban Centers: An Evaluation of the Density of Development*. Portland: Metro.

Ewing, Reid, Rolf Pendall, and Don Chen. 2002. *Measuring Sprawl and Its Impact*. http://www.smartgrowthamerica.com/sprawlindex/Measuring Sprawl.pdf (accessed 18 October 2002).

Freeman, Lance. 2001. The effects of sprawl on neighborhood social ties: An explanatory analysis. *Journal of the American Planning Association* 67 (1): 69–75.

Galster, George, Royce Hanson, Michael R. Ratcliffe, Harold Wolman, Stephen Colemen, and Jason Feihage. 2001. Wrestling sprawl to the ground: Defining and measuring an elusive concept. *Housing Policy Debate* 12 (4): 681–718.

Gordon, Peter, and Harry Richardson. 2000. Defending suburban sprawl. *The Public Interest* 139: 65–71.

Harvey, Thomas, and Martha Works. 2001. *The Rural Landscape as Urban Amenity: Land Use on the Rural-Urban Interface in the Portland, Oregon Metropolitan Area.* Lincoln, NE: Lincoln Institute of Land Policy.

Jacobs, Jane. 1961. *The Death and Life of Great American Cities.* New York: Vintage.

Kitch, Mary Pitman. 2002. Let's not sell the farm. *The Oregonian*, July 28, E01.

Kolankiewicz, Leon, and Roy Beck. 2001. *Weighing Sprawl Factors in Large U.S. Cities.* http://www.NumbersUSA.com (accessed 15 August 2003).

Lang, Robert E. 2002. Open spaces, bounded places: Does the American West's arid landscape yield dense metropolitan growth? *Housing Policy Debate* 13 (4): 755–778.

Lewis, Paul. 1996. *Shaping Suburbia: How Political Institutions Organize Urban Development.* Pittsburgh: University of Pittsburgh Press.

Metro. 2001. *Six Years and 6920 Acres: Metro's Open Spaces Land Acquisition Report to Citizens.* Portland: Metro.

Metro. 2003. *The Portland Region: How Are We Doing?* Portland: Metro.

Myers, Dowell, and Elizabeth Gearin. 2001. Current preferences and future demand for denser residential environments. *Housing Policy Debate* 12 (4): 633–659.

Nelson, Arthur C., and Thomas W. Sanchez. 2003. Periodic atlas of the metroscape: Lassoing urban sprawl. *Metroscape*, Winter, 13–19.

Northwest Environment Watch. 2002. *Sprawl and Smart Growth in Metropolitan Portland: Comparing Portland, Oregon, with Vancouver, Washington, during the 1990s.* http://www.northwestwatch.org/press/portlandgrowth.pdf (accessed 18 October 2002).

Office of the City Auditor. 2002. *Service Efforts and Accomplishments: 2001-2002.* http://www.portlandonline.com.shared/cfm/image.cfm?id-=5750 (accessed 8 August 2003).

Patterson, Patricia. 1997. *New Urbanism and the Elderly in Suburban and Urban Neighborhoods.* Unpublished doctoral diss., Portland State University.

Pendall, Rolf. 1999. Do land use controls cause sprawl? *Environment and Planning B* 26 (4): 555–572.

Phillips, Justin, and Eban Goodstein. 2000. Growth management and housing prices: The case of Portland, Oregon. *Contemporary Economic Policy* 18 (3): 334–344.

Portland Development Commission. 2002. *River District Housing Implementation Strategy: Annual Report.* Portland: Portland Development Commission.

Portland Multnomah Progress Board. 2003. *Neighborhood Livability.* http://www.p-m-benchmarks.org/urban%20vitality/61.html (accessed 8 August 2003).

PRNewswire. 2003. *New Report Details Values for Nation's City Park Systems: Proposes New Standards; Offers Data on 55 Largest City Park Systems.* http://news.findlaw.com/scripts (accessed 25 July 2003).

Rome, Adam W. 1998. William Whyte, Open space, and environmental activism. *Geographical Review* 88 (2): 259–274.

Stokols, Daniel. 1976. The experience of crowding in primary and secondary environments. *Environment and Behavior* 8 (1): 49–86.

Taylor, Ralph B. 1988. *Human Territorial Functioning.* New York: Cambridge University Press.

Toulan, Nohad. 1994. Housing as a state planning goal. In *Planning the Oregon Way,* edited by Carl Abbott, Deborah Howe, and Sy Adler, 91–120. Corvallis: Oregon State University Press.

Trust for Public Land. 2003. *The Excellent City Park System: What Makes It Great and How to Get There.* http://www.tpl.org/content_documents/excellent. city.parks.pdf (accessed 25 July 2003).

Ulrich, Roger S. 1999. Effects of gardens on health outcomes: Theory and research. In *Healing Gardens: Therapeutic Benefits and Design Recommendations,* edited by Clare Cooper Marcus and Marni Barnes, 27–86. New York: John Wiley & Sons.

Ulrich, Roger S., Robert F. Simons, Barbara D. Losito, Evelyn Fiorito, Mark A. Miles, and Michael Zelson. 1991. Stress recovery during exposure to natural and urban environments. *Journal of Environmental Psychology* 11 (3): 201–230.

Wassmer, Robert W. 2000. Urban Sprawl in a U.S. Metropolitan area: Ways to Measure the U.S. and a Comparison of the Sacramento Area to Similar Metropolitan Areas in California and the U.S. Unpublished manuscript.

Weitz, Jerry, and Terry Moore. 1998. Development inside urban growth boundaries: Oregon's empirical evidence of contiguous urban form. *Journal of the American Planning Association* 64 (4): 424–440.

Whyte, William H. 1988. *City: Rediscovering the Center.* New York: Doubleday.

Wicker, Allan W. 1969. Size of church membership and members' support of church behavior settings. *Journal of Personality and Social Psychology* 13: 278–288.

## 11 | The Evolution of Transportation Planning in the Portland Metropolitan Area

Sy Adler and Jennifer Dill

Portland has sought to use land use planning techniques to reduce reliance on the automobile for several years and is often pointed to as a model for other regions. These techniques include Smart Growth, New Urbanism, pedestrian pocket, and transit-oriented development approaches, among others. A primary policy instrument supporting Portland's efforts to address transportation issues is the Oregon Transportation Planning Rule (TPR). In this chapter we first explore how the TPR evolved during the 1990s. Next, we describe the ways in which cities and the regional government have responded to its mandates. Finally, we use data from comparable regions to help determine whether Portland is achieving the intended goals of the TPR.

Traffic congestion usually tops the list of concerns for residents and politicians in urban areas. For example, a survey of locally elected officials nationwide in 2000 found them most concerned, by far, about traffic congestion, with 39% listing it as a major problem and only 22% listing it as a minor or no problem. Traffic congestion and infrastructure were the top two conditions the officials said needed to be addressed over the next two years (National League of Cities 2001). The Texas Transportation Institute's annual congestion rankings of urban areas generates significant attention in the press. These problems are not new. Cities have had congestion problems since the turn of the century, when streetcars and horses clogged downtowns. But today's problems are larger in scope and appear more difficult to solve.

Moreover, cities are increasingly recognizing that transportation issues go beyond congestion and include health, the economy, livability, and the environment.

Beginning in the 1960s, communities across the country revolted against building new freeways to meet the growing use of private automobiles. Concerns about the environmental and neighborhood impacts of expanding roadways, the energy crisis, increasing infrastructure costs, and decreasing funding all combined to lead planners and policymakers to look for other solutions. Places adopted a range of measures to reduce demand and manage the system better, such as carpool matching programs and synchronized traffic signals. While some of these programs were effective, growth in vehicle travel continued to outpace growth in road capacity and the benefits of demand and systems management programs. In the 1990s major federal legislation—the Intermodal Surface Transportation Efficiency Act (ISTEA) and the 1990 Clean Air Act Amendments—placed a greater emphasis on integrating transportation and air quality planning and created an enhanced role for regional agencies in addressing these issues. At the same time, there was a growing interest among federal, state, and local policymakers and planners in using land use planning to shape travel demand. These federal initiatives dovetailed neatly with the TPR and were reinforced by its land use orientation.

Cities and regions throughout the country are adopting land use–related approaches, though there is limited evidence that they work. This highlights the opportunity to learn from the Portland experience. In an attempt to answer a question asked by many—Do these land use approaches work in Portland?—we present evidence regarding the impacts of regional and local responses to the TPR by looking at travel trends in the region and nationwide. Since these responses have been in place for a relatively brief period of time and a great deal else has been going on as well, our findings should be taken as the first promising suggestions of longer-run changes that might occur rather than a clear indication of their success or failure.

## The Transportation Planning Rule

It is psychic pain to deal with something that is impossible, and not politically feasible. (Bianco and Adler 2001, 10)

That's how two Metro transportation modelers felt about trying to develop a plan to achieve a key goal of the original version of the Oregon

TPR: the reduction of vehicle miles traveled (VMT) per capita in the region by 10% in the next 20 years, and by 20% in 30 years.

Rule makers hadn't set out to cause pain. Indeed, the TPR, adopted by the Oregon Land Conservation and Development Commission (LCDC) in 1991, began modestly, when state land use and transportation planners and their Portland-area counterparts tried to clarify some process issues for a proposed highway to be located outside of the urban growth boundary. Adopting the final, much more far-reaching rule was, instead, meant to inspire (Adler 1994).

The TPR reflected the efforts of environmental activists, led by 1000 Friends of Oregon, to use the rule-making process to achieve an integrated set of urban form and related transport objectives. Planners supported most of these objectives in principle, especially at the state level, but found implementation in the context of local and regional government difficult. As one Metro planner put it, 1000 Friends and their allies "pushed the envelope" (Adler 1994, 134). Activists were critically concerned that all local and regional land use and transport plans conform to the directive stipulated in Statewide Goal 12, the Transportation Goal, to "avoid principal reliance upon any one mode of transportation" (Adler 1994, 129). They wanted plans that would create compact, densely developed urban regions. Such a spatial pattern would facilitate transit and pedestrian and bicycle modes of transport, reducing principal reliance on the automobile–highway system and the pressure to expand urban growth boundaries. Activists wanted land use and transportation plans integrated to achieve those objectives, and they wanted existing plans—plans that had already been acknowledged by LCDC as consistent with statewide goals, written following the 1973 state land use law—reexamined if they didn't aim at a pattern of growth that would reduce principal reliance on the automobile.

As a way of starting the very ambitious project of changing the travel behavior of large numbers of people and the investment behavior of those involved in the land development process, the TPR required that local governments adopt within two years land use and design regulations to (1) provide bikeways, bicycle parking facilities, and pedestrian ways; (2) support transit service by designating land for transit-oriented development along routes; and (3) require larger-scale developers to provide either a transit stop or a connection to a stop when the service provider requires it. In addition, local governments and metropolitan planning organizations (MPOs) were mandated to produce within four years transportation system plans that would reduce principal reliance on the automobile. These plans were required to achieve two targets that were extremely controversial during rule making, but were nevertheless included by LCDC: the reduction in VMT per capita mentioned earlier; and a reduction of parking spaces per capita in the whole MPO area by 10% in 20 years. Plans were also required to incorporate interim standards for achieving those goals.

Transportation planners argued that it would be extremely difficult to measure VMT per capita, as well as changes in VMT per capita over time. They were also mightily skeptical about reducing VMT per capita by that much—indeed, reducing it at all—since the available estimates indicated that it had been growing rapidly. State planners acknowledged the measurement difficulties and the challenges associated with accomplishing the reduction but thought it critically important to set specific targets. 1000 Friends and their allies strongly supported that approach. In light of the controversy, though, LCDC wrote a review of the VMT reduction requirement at five-year intervals into the TPR.

The TPR also mandated that governments in Metro's planning area examine alternative land use plans as a way of achieving the transportation objective; doing so was optional in other MPO areas in the state. Alternative land use options were as controversial as the VMT reduction. Local planners were extremely reluctant to reopen politically difficult-to-negotiate agreements that had been reached regarding the spatial pattern of land development in their jurisdictions. Initially, Metro was one of those governments opposed to a mandated examination of alternative land use plans. However, Metro planners were also beginning to look ahead to a Regional Framework Plan, and decided that a state-articulated set of requirements to structure the planning process might benefit this planning effort. Metro, then, moved behind the mandate to examine alternative land use plans. 1000 Friends also decided to take an unusual step to support the mandate. Its traditional role had been to monitor the implementation of regulations by government agencies—and sue when it believed the regulations weren't being adequately enforced. Instead, Friends secured a large grant from the Federal Highway Administration and contracted with a leading consulting firm, Parsons, Brinckerhoff, Quade, and Douglas, Inc., to produce the Land Use/Transportation/Air Quality Connection (LUTRAQ) study, which aimed to demonstrate that a land use plan which supported alternative transport modes could, indeed, reduce VMT.

## Early Transportation Planning Rule Implementation Experience

Following adoption by LCDC in 1991, local governments in the Portland area began to work on the land use and design regulations that planners would group under the headings of *building orientation* and *street connectivity;* these were intended to create a land development context supportive of alternative modes of transport. Ironically, given its very strong support for the TPR, City of Portland planners ran into a firestorm of opposition when they engaged commercial land developers and retailers in an ordinance development process. Developers of "big box" retail establishments and traditionally auto-dependent businesses resisted orienting their buildings to streets and transit stops and bitterly criticized the notion of reducing parking spaces. Elsewhere in the region, developers of campus-type industrial and office parks expressed similar concerns, and housing developers, both of single- and multiple-dwelling unit projects, were hostile to some approaches to street connectivity. One city, Gresham, where Mayor Gussie McRobert strongly favored the objectives embodied in the TPR, was able to pass an ordinance that went beyond what the TPR mandated regarding orientation and connectivity. The specter of Gresham increased the intensity of resistance by some developers. As a result of the turmoil surfacing around the state, LCDC changed the deadline for adopting ordinances, as well as the deadline for submitting transportation system plans, and convened a group of stakeholders in 1994 to discuss amendments to the TPR. The results of this process were a set of TPR revisions in 1995 that increased the flexibility of local planners to respond positively to developers and to scale back building orientation and street connectivity requirements.

## Amending the Transportation Planning Rule

These conflicts around land use and design regulations were minor skirmishes compared to the much more intense confrontations during the scheduled review of the required VMT and parking space reductions. LCDC hired Parsons, Brinckerhoff, Quade, and Douglas, Inc. (Parsons Brinckerhoff) to conduct the review and to propose revisions. It was during an interview with the consultant that the two Metro planners quoted previously spoke their feelings regarding the VMT reduction. Parsons Brinckerhoff found deep disagreement about whether reducing VMT per capita was an appropriate objective for the transportation system plans that local governments and MPOs were required to produce. Moreover, based on the technical work that had been done by MPOs to that point, transportation planners were unanimous that achieving the mandated VMT reduction of 10% in 20 years would require, in addition to large-scale investments in alternative modes of transport and aggressive land use changes, regional systems for pricing automobile use. No one thought such pricing systems, especially congestion pricing, were politically feasible, especially outside the Portland metropolitan area. On the more philosophical question of the appropriateness of the measure, Metro planners distinguished between reducing reliance on the motor vehicle and reducing motor vehicle use. They called attention to the fact that reduced reliance, not use, was the objective. They argued that while lowering VMT might be appropriately linked in a direct, causal sense to less vehicle use, a reduction in VMT wasn't linked in the same way with a reduction in vehicle reliance. Instead, Metro planners argued that alternative measures for achieving the reliance reduction goal, such as increasing travel shares for alternative modes of transport and increasing local and regional accessibility, were more appropriate indicators. Planners in other areas objected to the reduction of automobile use as a key goal for their transport systems plans and thought measurement of VMT a mistake. In two of these MPO areas, planners signaled their opposition by deliberately failing to include in their draft plans any interim standards to achieve VMT reduction as per TPR requirement (Parsons, Brinckerhoff, Quade, and Douglas, Inc. 1997).

Parsons Brinckerhoff found that homebuilders, commercial developers, and retailers thought that the attempt to mandate a reduction in the parking supply was seriously wrongheaded, especially in the large majority of places that were not well-supplied by alternative modes, and those that served primarily nonwork trips. Indeed, the business groups openly rebelled against the TPR as a whole. Local and regional planners were troubled as well. In the same way that they were troubled by the ambiguity of the connection between vehicle use and vehicle reliance, they questioned the link between a reduction in parking spaces and reduced vehicle reliance.

In the end, Parsons Brinckerhoff recommended that LCDC retain VMT as a measure of automobile reliance but permit local and regional governments to develop alternative measures that would focus on the use of nonautomotive transport modes. The firm also recommended that the VMT reduction standard in the TPR be decreased from 10% in 20 years to 5%. Regarding parking, Parsons Brinckerhoff recommended a shift in emphasis away from regulating the supply of spaces to the management of existing parking as well as its price, and more attention to the design and location of new parking facilities. The consultant also thought a highway pricing demonstration project ought to be collaboratively undertaken by the state and a regional jurisdiction, and that state transportation planners ought to agree to reduce acceptable levels of service regarding the flow of traffic on the highways, in recognition of the fact that congestion leads to more use of alternative modes.

Parsons Brinckerhoff retained the VMT reduction goal, although a less ambitious one, in part because of its experience working with 1000 Friends on the LUTRAQ project, and in part because of the adoption by Metro of its 2040 Growth Concept, a part of the Regional Framework Plan that would establish the context for the agency's TPR-related Regional Transportation Plan (RTP) (for more details on the Growth Concept and Regional Framework Plan, see Chap. 2, Seltzer). In the LUTRAQ study, new households and employment were reallocated from what was specified in existing land use plans. Sixty-five percent of forecasted residential units and 78% of future jobs were allocated to transit-oriented developments near existing and planned transit lines. Moderate- and high-density residential developments were reassigned to places where they could be more efficiently served by transit. LUTRAQ also included a substantial amount of transit investment, pedestrian and bicycle facilities, and parking charges for work trips, as well as certain highway improvements. The LUTRAQ package projects a reduction in daily VMT in the study area by more than 6%.

Adopted in 1995, Metro's 2040 Growth Concept committed the agency to meet TPR requirements. That policy alone differentiated Metro from the other MPOs in the state. The 2040 Growth Concept explicitly links urban form to transportation. Its strategy is to direct most future development—an expected 50% increase in population and a 70% increase in jobs by 2020—to centers and along existing major transportation corridors that are served by highways and high-capacity transit. A hierarchy of centers is set forth called design types: the Portland central business district; regional centers; town centers and station communities; and main streets, inner and outer neighborhoods. In addition to these there are industrial areas and shipping terminals, corridors, employment areas, rural reserves, and neighboring cities that are connected to the metro region by green corridors. The RTP defined the system appropriate to serve the needs of each of the above 2040 design types. Parsons Brinckerhoff noted that Metro had already taken two actions in line with the spirit of the TPR: it gave priority to transport projects that reduced reliance on the automobile and focused growth in centers. Utilizing these criteria, the flexible transportation funding available to the region was allocated primarily to nonautomotive modes. Metro had also set minimum and maximum parking ratios for developments in two different types of zones—transit- and pedestrian-accessible areas, and other parts of the region. Given Metro's power to shape the contours of local planning practice, city and county planners would not be able to exceed those ratios. Transport analyses done for the 2040 Concept estimated that per capita VMT would be reduced by 5.2% compared to 1990 levels. This was short of what the TPR required, however, and would only be achieved over a 50-year planning horizon (Parsons, Brinckerhoff, Quade, and Douglas, Inc. 1997).

LCDC agreed with most of what Parsons Brinckerhoff recommended, with some modifications. In 1998 the Commission reduced the VMT reduction standard from 10% to 5% for all of the MPOs in the state except Metro. However, it permitted all of them to develop an alternative approach to reduced automotive reliance in place of the VMT target. The alternative would have to be approved by LCDC. In addition, all MPOs were given the option of adopting new parking regulations instead of the existing TPR requirement to reduce the number of per capita parking spaces by 10%. The Commission gave examples of acceptable options, including lower minimum requirements, maximum requirements, and policy and design guidelines aiming at encouraging shared use and structured parking, and infill and redevelopment of large parking lots. 1000 Friends supported the parking-related change; lower minimums, maximums, and the other guidelines were in line with its substantive priorities. Friends wanted to hold the line on VMT reduction, though. While the organization strongly supported Metro's 2040 Growth Concept, seeing in it much of what had been proposed in LUTRAQ, including a technical innovation—a Pedestrian Environment Factor that had been incorporated into Metro's transportation planning model—Friends was far less confident of the commitment to TPR mandates in the other metropolitan areas in the state. Friends felt that the credibility of LCDC in those areas was linked to the maintenance of the VMT reduction target (Bianco and Adler 2001, Department of Land Conservation and Development 1998).

Following up on the Parsons Brinckerhoff highway pricing suggestion, Metro, in collaboration with the Oregon Department of Transportation, the regional transit district, and several other state and local governments, secured funds from the Federal Highway Administration for a two-year study of peak period pricing incentives to reduce traffic congestion. The Citizen Task Force that oversaw the study recommended in 1999 that, while no existing traffic lanes should be priced at this time, when planning for major new or expanded highway projects, peak period pricing ought to be considered, and that a pilot project to test peak period pricing ought to be identified within the next two years (Metro 1999).

## Metro's Regional Transportation Plan (RTP) and the TPR

Metro Council adopted the updated RTP in 2000. Building on the 2040 Growth Concept, the RTP is, as the state's chief land use planner said, "a significant accomplishment in integration of land use and transportation planning which, in virtually all respects is a model for other metropolitan areas" (Benner 2001a, 2). However, state planners had some concerns that they wanted addressed before LCDC would acknowledge it as fully in compliance with statewide planning goals; Metro planners and their state counterparts worked together closely to address those concerns.

One of the main concerns involved Metro's proposed alternative standard for reduced reliance on the automobile. The alternative approach set minimum mode share targets for non–single occupant vehicle (non-SOV) modes for each of the 2040 design types. These targets would have to be incorporated into city and county transportation system plans, and actions would have to be taken by the local governments to achieve them. For example, the RTP called for non-SOV mode share targets in 2020 ranging from 42 to 67% in the various districts of central Portland, from 34 to 39% in the various regional centers, 41 to 42% in the station communities, 36 to 40% in the different town centers, and 43 to 45% along the main streets. The RTP recommended doubling existing transit service to accommodate an expected 89% increase in transit riders in 2020. The patronage forecast assumed fareless zones in the central city and in all regional centers, and different levels of parking costs in most centers. It also assumed transit fare reduction programs for all trips to the central city, regional centers, and other design types that are slated for transportation demand management programs. The RTP assumed focused pedestrian improvements in the central city, regional and town centers, station communities, and main streets, and recommended substantial funding for such projects.

Metro told state planners that it would use the assumptions made in the mode share modeling process as a checklist to gauge the extent to which actions required in local transportation system plans were consistent with the work that it did to reach the non-SOV mode share targets incorporated in the Plan. Metro would analyze proposed local actions to see, for example, whether intersection density—the indicator of street connectivity—in the two categories of regional centers would average at least 10 to 14 connections per mile in 2020 as a way of measuring whether or not a pedestrian mode share target would be achieved. Factors related to parking prices, transit fares, and the presence of fareless zones would also be used to measure whether non-SOV mode share targets would be achieved.

State planners didn't have any trouble with the non-SOV mode share targets specified in the plan; they thought the percentages were reasonable. However, they were concerned about vague language on measuring local efforts to achieve the targets. State planners sought an amendment to the plan to clarify how the alternative approach devised by Metro would produce TPR-compliant plans at the local level (Benner 2001a). Metro wanted to retain as much flexibility as possible to tailor requirements to match varying conditions between and within the different design types, but acknowledged the state planners' concern regarding the devolution of responsibility to achieve the non-SOV mode share targets to local governments. Metro adopted an RTP amendment clarifying that the modeling assumptions would be used as minimum performance standards to measure local progress toward achieving the non-SOV mode share targets. LCDC was satisfied with the amendment (Metro 2002).

Metro also submitted a plan amendment to LCDC that assigned implementation responsibilities for its Green Streets program to local governments. The Green Streets effort addresses regional and local street design and connectivity, and environmental impacts of transport investments, particularly on streams and wildlife corridors in urbanizing areas, as a partial response to the addition of salmon and steelhead on the endangered species list. Best practices guidelines for protecting streams while achieving local street connectivity goals were set forth in a handbook produced by Metro, which was endorsed by U.S. National Marine Fisheries Service as consistent with its goals for habitat protection. This was seen as a major step for the federal agency, one that enhanced the status of the Green Streets work (Metro 2002).

State and regional planners continue to work toward agreement on one issue, though, ironically related to the action that triggered rule making back in the late 1980s: a procedural issue regarding proposed highways outside of the urban growth boundary. State planners agreed there was a need for the highways somewhere in the corridors identified by Metro, but they were troubled by the potential consequences if Metro placed them in the plan before protection against premature urban development of those rural resource lands was in place. Metro pledged to treat the highways as green corridors, and "hard edges" to the region, and to limit access to them, but segments of the proposed facilities were outside Metro's jurisdiction; complex coordinated actions with other governmental entities would be required, which gave the state planners pause (Benner 2001b).

## The Region, the State, and the TPR: A Political Summary

Metro's RTP and LCDC's TPR are both works in progress. Metro planners wanted to be pushed by the state, and they wanted state mandates to help them push local governments. However, when regional planners ran up against the limits of what they thought was technically and politically feasible, they asked the state to moderate some of the pressure. LCDC needed Metro to demonstrate that achieving the objectives in its TPR was possible. Metro is unique in the state, and, in certain respects, in the nation. Alone of all the MPOs in Oregon it has the authority to mandate local government compliance with both its land use and its transportation plans (for more details, see Chap. 2, Seltzer). Its technical capacities far exceed those of other regional organizations in the state. Indeed, Metro is widely recognized as one of the most technically sophisticated and innovative transportation planning entities in the country. If Metro couldn't meet TPR requirements, then LCDC would have to accommodate in order to maintain the TPR's credibility, which it did. It took a lot longer to produce a transportation system plan for the Portland metropolitan area than rule makers contemplated in 1991, but Metro has thus far done work that is applauded both by LCDC and by 1000 Friends and its allies, though much of it remains as controversial now as it was then.

## The TPR and the Cities and Counties

We turn now to an analysis of what some of the cities within Metro's jurisdiction have done to comply with TPR mandates, and analyses of travel patterns in the region that relate to the TPR's objectives. With one exception, the cities and counties within the Metro area that have adopted transportation system plans opted to develop alternative approaches to meeting the VMT reduction target. The one exception is the City of

Portland, the jurisdiction with the highest land use densities and levels of transit service in the region. The city began the planning process in 1994 and adopted its plan (more than 700 pages) in October 2002. Portland developed its plan in-house. Many other cities used consultants, resulting in similar-looking plans throughout the region. All cities adopted Metro's minimum and maximum parking ratios rather than specifically meeting the 10% parking reduction target. Again, in contrast, the City of Portland adopted the 10% reduction in spaces as an objective, along with parking ratios.

Though most transportation system plans in the region do not aim to meet the 10% VMT per capita reduction target, they all do incorporate goals and policies consistent with the intent of the TPR—to reduce reliance on the automobile. The level of commitment to this objective varies. These differences are evident in the policy goal statements of the various plans. The Portland plan supports Goal 6 of the City's Comprehensive Plan, which aims to "develop a balanced, equitable, and efficient transportation system that provides a range of transportation choices; reinforces the livability of neighborhoods; supports a strong and diverse economy; reduces air, noise, and water pollution; and lessens reliance on the automobile while maintaining accessibility" (City of Portland 2002, 2–3).

In contrast, the original 1988 plan for fast-growing Washington County included a policy goal to "provide a transportation system that maximizes the mobility of . . . residents and businesses." Washington County has since amended the policy to "provide a multimodal transportation system that accommodates the diverse travel needs of . . . residents and businesses" (Washington County 2002). And, while Portland's plan aims to reduce pollution, Washington County's policy is to "avoid, limit, and/or mitigate adverse impacts." Plans for Beaverton and Hillsboro—large and growing suburban communities to the west— also contain explicit policies to reduce vehicle trips, enhance livability, and provide a balanced, multimodal transportation system.

Even Cornelius, a town of less than 10,000 located just beyond Hillsboro and the region's high-tech area, includes some support for multimodalism. The city's transportation system is dominated by a local highway, with limited transit potential. The plan for Cornelius starts with a vision statement that first focuses on vehicle traffic flow and interconnected traffic signals. But, in the end, the statement supports the TPR goals: "Provisions are made for safe and convenient bicycle and pedestrian circulation so that one feels comfortable moving around the city without an automobile."

While all jurisdictions in the region have adopted or are about to adopt transportation system plans with goals and policies that support the TPR, the specificity of the plans varies. For example, one plan states that the TPR has a goal of reducing VMT per capita and then lists examples of transportation demand management measures, without a specific commitment to adopt such measures. Another plan states that the city is "committed to work with regional agencies . . . towards achieving the non-SOV modal targets established," but, again, includes few specific commitments on how to accomplish this. In contrast, the City of Portland goes so far as to advocate for a regional system to charge for auto trips during peak hours. Despite the varying degrees of policy and program commitment to reducing reliance on the automobile, most plans do include detailed lists of pedestrian and bicycle improvement projects. These projects respond to the TPR's requirement for bikeways along arterials and major collectors and sidewalks along arterials, collectors, and most local streets.

## Travel Behavior in the City and Region

The question on many minds is whether these plans and policies produce the intended results—reduced reliance on the automobile. Though it is too early to tell the whole story—land use changes to promote transit take more time to implement—there are some indications that the Portland region has made progress. This is revealed through projects and infrastructure on the ground and performance indicators, such as transit use. Three major alternative modes are examined here— bicycling, walking, and transit use—along with levels of traffic congestion and VMT per capita.

### Bicycling

Portland is widely regarded as one of the best large U.S. cities for bicycling. *Bicycling Magazine* twice named Portland the most bicycle friendly city in the United States and in 2001 named it the Best Overall Bicycling City in North America. When Portland adopted its current Bicycle Master Plan in 1996, there were 111 miles of developed bikeways, including off-street paths, on-street lanes, and bicycle boulevards. Five years later, that figure had more than doubled to 228 miles. Portland also amended its code to require more and better bicycle parking in new development and adopted 14 benchmarks aimed at making the bicycle "an integral part of daily life in Portland."

According to the U.S. census, the City of Portland ranks in the top five among 64 U.S. cities of at least 250,000 population in terms of the percent of workers regularly commuting by bicycle.[1] Of these cities with bicycle infrastructure data (43 of 64), Portland ranked third in miles of lanes per square mile (Dill and Carr 2003). Counts of cyclists crossing the main bridges with bicycle access into downtown went up 143% from 1991 to 2001, outpacing population growth for that time period. At the same time, the number of reported bicycle–motor vehicle crashes has remained constant, possibly indicating a reduced incidence of crashes and improved safety (City of Portland 2001).

On a regional scale, the rates of bicycle commuting are lower than within the city, but still higher than most comparable regions. Figure 11.1 shows the percent of workers commuting by bicycle as reported on the Census 2000 long form. Included are 18 regions with a total population just above and below that of the larger Portland–Vancouver region and the Oregon side of that region (labeled "Portland" in Figure 11.1).[2] Also included is Portland's neighbor to the north, Seattle, whose population is larger than any of the regions listed. The share of workers commuting by bicycle regionwide is around 0.80%, lower than only San Jose, California. The high rate of cycling is due primarily to cyclists within the City of Portland. Cycling rates in neighboring cities, such as

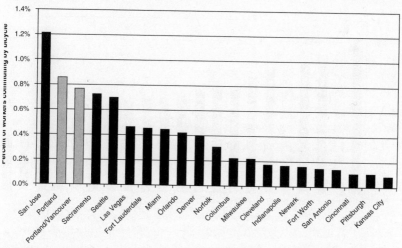

FIGURE 11.1. Percent of workers commuting by bicycle, 2000. Source: U.S. Census 2000. Summary File 3 (SF 3)—Sample data, P30. Means of Transportation to Work for Workers 16 Years and Over—Universe: Workers 16 Years and Over.

Beaverton, Gresham, Hillsboro, and Tigard are 0.33 to 0.44%, close to the national average of 0.38%.

## Walking

Paralleling its efforts to promote bicycling, the City of Portland adopted a Pedestrian Master Plan in 1998, with a 20-year timeline for improvements. When Portland began this process in 1994, it was the first major U.S. city to comprehensively plan for pedestrians. The city has designated 16 pedestrian districts, within which walking is intended to be the primary way people travel. The districts must feature a mix of land uses, appropriate densities, and a high level of transit service. The Pedestrian Plan and Transportation System Plan include lists of capital improvements to fill gaps in the system and to improve the pedestrian environment. The 2000 census indicates that more workers commute by foot in the Portland metropolitan region, particularly on the Oregon side, than in most regions of a similar size (Fig. 11.2). As with bicycling, most of the pedestrian commuting is concentrated in the City of Portland, where 5.24% of workers regularly commute on foot.

The commitment to cycling and walking can be attributed, at least in part, to efforts of two organizations—the Bicycle Transportation Alliance (BTA) and the Willamette Pedestrian Coalition (WPC). With over 3,000 members, the BTA has been involved in virtually every

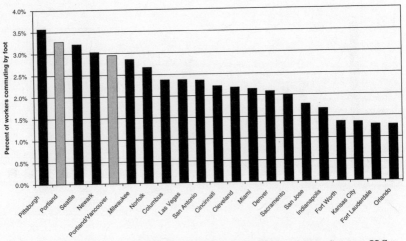

FIGURE 11.2. Percent of workers commuting by walking, 2000. Source: U.S. Census 2000. Summary File 3 (SF 3)—Sample data, P30. Means of Transportation to Work for Workers 16 Years and Over—Universe: Workers 16 Years and Over.

bicycle-related issue in the region since its founding in 1990. The WPC is the second such organization in the United States. Founded in 1991, it advocates for pedestrian safety. The WPC is credited with inventing the "pedestrian action crossing," a media event that highlights dangers at specific locations.

## Transit Use

Portland's transit system has mirrored the development of many other U.S. cities. An extensive system of privately owned electric interurban trains and streetcars began in 1890 and ended in the 1950s. TriMet, the region's main public transit agency, was created in 1969 to take over the bankrupt private bus operator. As part of the plan to redevelop downtown, increase transit ridership, and reduce air quality violations, in 1975 the City of Portland and TriMet created a fareless area covering most of downtown and opened the Downtown Transit Mall. The transit mall includes exclusive bus lanes along 18 blocks of two parallel streets. Most, but not all, of the mall includes lanes for private vehicles.

The region made a major decision to invest in a new rail system. In 1986, the 15-mile Eastside MAX light rail line opened, with funds from a controversial highway that was canceled. Westside MAX opened in 1998, adding up to a 33-mile system anchored in downtown Portland, reaching the growing suburbs of Hillsboro, Beaverton, and Gresham. In 2001, an extension to Portland International airport opened, and a 6-mile extension north to the Exposition Center opened in 2004. The City of Portland also developed and built the first modern streetcar system in North America, which opened in 2001. The streetcar makes a 2.4-mile loop connecting downtown and the Portland State University campus to the booming Pearl District and trendy Northwest neighborhoods, with extensions planned to areas of future redevelopment.

The light rail system is the focus of the Metro 2040 Growth Concept, with higher density, mixed-use centers planned around most stations. However, as most cities with new rail systems have found, higher intensity development around rail stations rarely occurs without government involvement. Metro initiated a Transit-Oriented Development program, with a $3 million grant from the Federal Transit Administration (FTA). The program was the first of its kind in the United States and uses public funds (FTA and local matching sources) to increase the intensity of development near transit by "write-downs" of land values and joint development partnerships. These incentives aim to reduce the risk and cost of transit-oriented development. Largely at the request of Metro,

PHOTO 11. The transit mall in downtown Portland running south along Fifth Avenue in 2004. (The mall runs north along 6th Avenue.) The bus mall links the Amtrak rail station and the Greyhound bus station to the MAX line, as well as providing convenient connections to other bus lines.

the FTA changed its policies prohibiting their funds from being used for such projects. In 1998, Metro purchased its first site, spending $650,000 for a joint development project in Hillsboro. Since then,

PHOTO 12. MAX light rail line at Pioneer Place in 2004. First opened in 1986 with one line, the interconnecting system now has lines to Gresham to the east, Hillsboro to the west, and Portland International Airport to the northeast. The latest addition, a line north almost to the Oregon/Washington border, opened in the spring of 2004.

Metro has funded more than 10 projects and recently committed an additional $3 million to the program.

Metro estimates that transit ridership is 10 times higher in transit-oriented developments than traditional suburban developments, and that the cost per new rider is well under one dollar—below that of building new light rail and other transit projects (Metro 2001). However, little empirical research has been conducted examining the actual transit use of residents of these developments. A graduate student at Portland State University conducted traffic counts at eight transit-oriented developments in the region and estimated that 16% of the morning and 11% of the evening peak period trips were made on transit (Lapham 2001). This is higher than the regional average share of commute trips by transit. A survey of residents of Orenco Station (Hillsboro), one of the larger transit-oriented developments in the region, found that nearly 70% claimed to use transit more often than in their previous neighborhood, though 75% still drove to work most of the time (Podobnik 2002). Eighteen percent used transit regularly to get to work, higher than the average for Hillsboro from the 2000 census (6.5%). In addition, over 86% of the residents

claimed that the feasibility of walking to neighborhood shops and services reduced their need to drive. Data from the 2000 census for the block
group that includes Orenco Station indicates that 7.9% rode rail transit to
work regularly, compared to 3.1% for all of Hillsboro. On the other hand,
the Cascade Policy Institute, a frequent critic of public spending on light
rail and transit-oriented development, observed for two clear days at
Orenco Station and found that over 70% of the light rail riders drove to
the station, thus questioning the impact of the development (Charles and
Barton 2003). This finding may be due to the timing of development
around the station. The first homes were built further away from the station, beyond what many consider a reasonable walking distance. Multifamily housing adjacent to the station was completed in 2003 and more is
under construction. In addition, 7.9% of the workers in the Orenco Station census block group walked or bicycled to work, compared to 2.6% for
Hillsboro. The development is close to a large Intel facility.

Transit-oriented developments near light rail, however, are only a
very small share of the overall housing and employment in the region.
Buses account for over 70% of all transit trips in the region. As with
bicycling and walking, the Portland region is performing well on transit
use compared to other regions. Overall transit use for commuting in the
Portland region is higher than all but two of the similar-sized regions
(Fig. 11.3). The trend over time is also encouraging for Portland. From

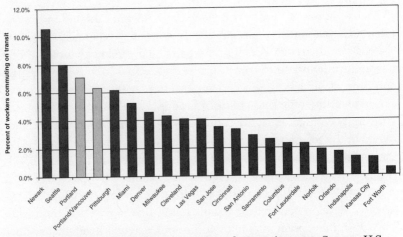

FIGURE 11.3. Percent of workers commuting by transit, 2000. Source: U.S.
Census 2000. Summary File 3 (SF 3)—Sample data, P30. Means of
Transportation to Work for rkers 16 Years and Over—Universe: Workers 16
Years and Over.

1990 to 2000, transit's share of commute trips nationwide fell from 5.27 to 4.73%. For Oregon's share of the region, commuting by transit went up over the same period from 6.01 to 7.09%. The entire region, including Washington, also went up.

Commuting is only one travel purpose, however, and makes up only about 20 to 30% of all trips. Unfortunately, comparable data on all types of trips by all modes are not available. The most recent comprehensive travel survey for the region is from 1994 to 1995, too soon to see the results of the TPR and the Metro 2040 Growth Concept. Moreover, such surveys are difficult to compare with other regions because of different time frames and methodologies. But the FTA does collect overall transit ridership figures for most systems in the United States. These data are commonly used to compare performance between systems. Figure 11.4 shows the total number of unlinked[3] passenger transit trips per capita for the same regions used in the previous figures.[4] Again, Portland outperforms most of the other regions. Transit performance is often evaluated in terms of trips per revenue mile or revenue hour of service.[5] Using these measures, Portland ranks third and fourth, respectively. Between 1985 and 2000, Portland was one of only four of these 17 areas where trips per revenue mile increased. The other three were San Jose, Sacramento, and Orlando. However, trips per vehicle *hour* in Portland fell, as they did for all but those same three areas.

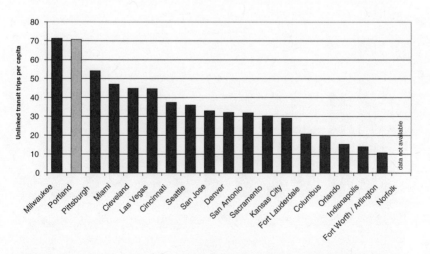

FIGURE 11.4. Total transit trips per capita, 2000. Source: Federal Transit Administration, *National Transit Database.* Included are unlinked passenger trips.

Finally, Portland is one of several U.S. cities, starting with San Diego, that invested in new light rail systems in the 1980s and 1990s. Several researchers have criticized these systems for excessive costs and low ridership. Figure 11.5 shows the number of trips made on light rail per capita for the 11 new light rail systems built since 1980. Portland exceeds all the other systems. On the other hand, Portland's system does not perform considerably better or worse than the other systems when considering the number of light rail trips per revenue mile or revenue hour.

## VMT and Congestion

The TPR uses VMT per capita as a performance measure. The federal Highway Performance Monitoring System provides VMT information for major urban areas, based on data submitted by state departments of transportation. In 1993, daily VMT per capita in the Portland–Vancouver area was 20.3 (Fig. 11.6). In 1996 it peaked at 21.6 miles per person. In 2001 it was 20.0 miles per person, a 1.5% drop from 1993 and a 7.4% drop from 1996. Over the same time period (1993–2001), only two other regions (from the list of 20 examined here) saw a drop in VMT per capita—Cleveland and Milwaukee. The 19 other areas averaged a 12.5% increase in VMT per capita. While some of the decline in Portland could be attributed to the downturn in the economy, the annual unemployment rate remained relatively steady from 1996 through 2000. In absolute terms, Portland–Vancouver ranked 18th in VMT per capita in

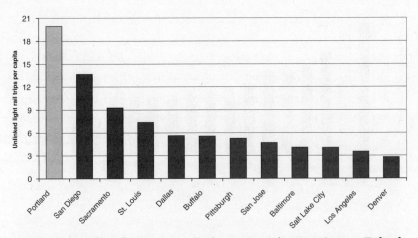

FIGURE 11.5. Light rail trips per capita (new systems), 2000. Source: Federal Transit Administration, *National Transit Database*. Included are unlinked passenger trips.

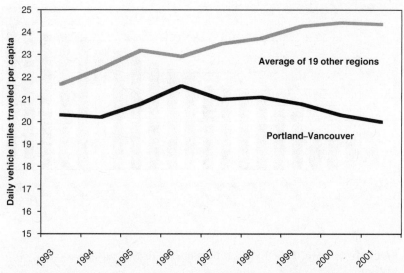

FIGURE 11.6. Daily VMT per capita. Source: Federal Highway Administration, Office of Highway Policy Information, Highway Performance Monitoring System data, *Highway Statistics, 1993-2001* (http://www.fhwa.dot.gov/policy/ohpi/hss/hsspubs.htm).

2001, with only Miami–Hialeah and New York–New Jersey showing lower VMT per capita.

Despite what seems like success in promoting alternative modes, traffic congestion in the Portland region has increased. According to the Texas Transportation Institute, the region ranked 11th nationwide in 2000 in terms of their "Travel Time Index"—a measure of congestion on highways and freeways. In 1982 the region ranked 32nd. The Institute estimated that in 2000 peak period road users in Portland spent 47 hours delayed in congestion, the 23rd highest amount nationwide (Texas Transportation Institute 2003). Figure 11.7 shows that Portland ranks 6th worst in terms of congestion (as measured by the Travel Time Index) among the comparably sized regions. Moreover, congestion increased more in Portland from 1982 to 2000 than any of the other regions (Fig. 11.8). This may be attributable to the significant increase in growth and the economy of the region compared to the other regions.

Metro projects that congestion will continue to increase. Previous RTPs sought to maintain a level of service D—about 80% of capacity— on major roads and highways. The current plan sets the standard at level of service E, about 90% of capacity, for most roadways and

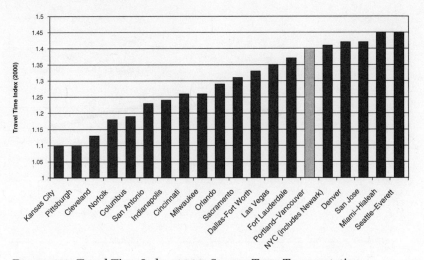

FIGURE 11.7. Travel Time Index, 2000. Source: Texas Transportation Institute.

accepts level of service F (100% of capacity) for some areas where transit and other alternatives exist. This change in acceptable levels of congestion is not unique, however, as most growing urban areas in the United States face funding and other constraints on increasing roadway capacity.

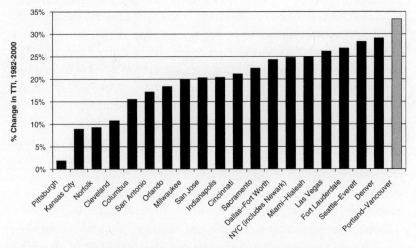

FIGURE 11.8. Percent change in Travel Time Index, 1982–2000. Source: Texas Transportation Institute.

# Conclusions

The Portland region is often looked to as a model for reducing reliance on motor vehicles and integrating land use and transportation. If the region succeeds in that, the TPR must be given major credit—at least as a key supporting actor. The TPR provided Metro with a legal tool to promote the 2040 Growth Plan, redirect transportation funding to non-road capacity projects, and convince cities and counties to adopt supportive plans. The amendments allowing alternatives to the VMT and parking reduction objectives add flexibility and reduce the likelihood of major challenges to the TPR. The TPR has prompted some cities to adopt transportation plans that consider alternatives to the automobile to a larger extent than would otherwise happen. Cities have adopted building orientation and street connectivity standards that probably would not exist without it.

Whether the region lives up to its billing as a model area for all remains to be seen. There are certainly many indications that it is. Starting with the transit mall and "Fareless Square" in the 1970s through the streetcar opening in 2001, the region has adopted many transit innovations before other areas. The region's recommitment to transit, coupled with its supportive land use policies, lead transit scholar Robert Cervero to conclude that "if an American region is poised to become a great transit Metropolis during the twenty-first century, it is metropolitan Portland. No other place in the United States has made a stronger commitment to integrating transit and urban development than Oregon's largest city and its surroundings" (Cervero 1998, 416).

The City of Portland's pedestrian and bicycle plans are certainly models for other cities. Metro's transit-oriented development program was the first of its kind in the country, now being duplicated in regions such as San Francisco. The City of Portland recently implemented a pilot "TravelSmart" project that provides individualized marketing aimed at reducing automobile use—the first use of the tool in the United States, after extensive testing in Australia and Europe. Cities all over the United States have requested Metro's Green Streets handbook. Metro was one of the first agencies to adopt street connectivity standards, now duplicated in other areas. Portland also is home to the oldest carsharing organization in the United States.

All of these innovations have undoubtedly played a role in the region's lower reliance on private vehicles. The region has a larger share of people commuting by foot, bicycle, and transit than most other comparably sized regions. Overall transit trips per capita are also higher than in most areas. But the region also faces high and increasing levels of traffic congestion, and most personal travel still is—and will continue to be—made in the private automobile.

In the future, the Portland metropolitan region will face greater challenges in its commitment to innovative transportation and land use policy. As congestion continues to increase, the debate between spending money on roadway expansion versus transit and other modes is likely to be more heated. The region has not yet succeeded in getting funding commitments to extend light rail across the river to Vancouver, Washington—considered by many a key to the region's transit system. Downtown businesses are asking for increased auto access on the transit mall. Many transportation experts assert that pricing is the key to controlling traffic congestion. That view is reflected in the LUTRAQ study, which included parking pricing, and Metro's planning studies. But, while the RTP calls for considering pricing for new facilities, the option was all but ignored in recent plans to increase bridge capacity between Portland and Vancouver. The City of Portland's success in increasing bicycle facilities stems largely from "picking the low-hanging fruit"—striping lanes on arterials with plenty of room and little opposition. The easiest, lowest-cost projects are nearly complete. The remaining projects in the bicycle plan will be more difficult to build, particularly when transportation funding is not keeping up with needs. Without an increase in funding, many of the pedestrian, bicycle, and transit projects in the region's transportation systems plans may not be built. The state has been unwilling to increase its gas tax and does not have a sales tax, which many other regions use to fund transportation projects. Funding will likely be a major obstacle to the region's fulfillment of its model role. While the results of the region's planning efforts remain to be seen, what is clear is that the region will be watched closely. And, as is already the case, critics and supporters will both find evidence to support their respective cases.

NOTES

1. The Census 2000 long form conducted on April 1, 2000, found that 1.76% of workers commuted by bicycle, ranking fifth. The Census 2000 Supplemental Survey conducted throughout the year found that 2.55% commuted by bicycle, ranking third.

2. The population for the Portland–Vancouver metropolitan statistical area (MSA) in 2000 was 1,918,009. For the Oregon side of the MSA it was 1,572,771. Included in the figure are the five regions with populations just above 1,918,009,

below 1,572,771, and the eight regions between. The range is bounded by Milwaukee at 1,500,741 and Pittsburgh at 2,358,695. Seattle's MSA population is 2,414,616.

3. An unlinked trip refers to each separate transit trip, regardless of fare payment or transfers. For example, if a person gets on one bus and transfers to another, that is two unlinked trips.

4. Newark, New Jersey, is not included because it was too difficult to separate its transit service area from the rest of the New York region. Total population is defined by the FTA as the agency's service area and may not be the same as the census MSA population. Multiple transit agencies may be included in one region. For Portland, only TriMet is included, not C-Tran, the Vancouver, Washington, transit system.

5. *Revenue mile* and *revenue hour* refer to miles or hours traveled when the transit vehicle can collect fare-paying passengers. Therefore, traveling from the last stop to the bus barn, for example, is not included.

REFERENCES

Adler, Sy. 1994. The Oregon approach to integrating transportation and land use planning. In *Planning the Oregon Way*, edited by Carl Abbott, Deborah Howe, and Sy Adler. Corvallis: Oregon State University Press.

Benner, Richard. 2001a. Memo to Land Conservation and Development Commission. 12 April.

Benner, Richard. 2001b. Memo to Land Conservation and Development Commission. 8 June.

Bianco, Martha, and Sy Adler. 2001. The politics of implementation: The corporatist paradigm applied to the implementation of Oregon's Statewide Transportation Planning Rule. *Journal of Planning Education and Research* 21 (1): 5–16.

Cervero, Robert. 1998. *The Transit Metropolis*. Washington, DC: Island Press.

Charles, John, and Michael Barton. 2003, April. *The Mythical World of Transit-Oriented Development*. Portland: Cascade Policy Institute. http://www.cascadepolicy.org/pdf/env/I_124.pdf (accessed 10 February 2004).

City of Portland. 2001. *Bicycling in Portland in the 21st Century: Bicycle Master Plan Five-Year Update*. http://www.trans.ci.portland.or.us/Plans/BicycleMasterPlan/Update2001.htm (accessed 19 June 2003).

City of Portland. 2002. *Transportation System Plan*. Portland: Department of Transportation.

Department of Land Conservation and Development. 1998. *Highlights of September 1998 TPR Amendments*. Salem, OR: Department of Land Conservation and Development.

Dill, Jennifer, and Theresa Carr. 2003. Bicycle commuting and facilities in major U.S. cities: If you build them, commuters will use them—another look. *Transportation Research Record Journal of the Transportation Research Board* 1828: 116–123.

Lapham, Michael. 2001. *Transit Oriented Development—Trip Generation and Mode Split in the Portland Metropolitan Region*. Master's thesis, Portland State University.

Metro. 1999, Fall. *Traffic Relief Options Study News*. Portland: Metro.

Metro. 2001, March. *Transit-Oriented Development Program, Improving Accountability through Enhanced Measures of Service Efforts and Accomplishments*. A Report by the Office of the Auditor. (20014-10710-AUD). Portland: Metro.

Metro. 2002, 27 June. *Ordinance No. 02-946A, Green Streets Amendments—Parts 1 and 2, and Staff Report*. Portland: Metro.

National League of Cities. 2001, January. *The State of America's Cities*. National League of Cities, Washington DC. http://www.nlc.org/opsurvey.pdf (accessed 28 May 2004).

Parsons, Brinckerhoff, Quade, and Douglas, Inc., with ECONorthwest. 1997. *Transportation Planning Rule Evaluation, Draft Report*. Portland.

Podobnik, Bruce. 2002. *The Social and Environmental Achievements of New Urbanism: Evidence from Orenco Station*. Lewis and Clark College, Portland. http://www.lclark.edu/~podobnik/orenco02.pdf (accessed 7 November 2002).

Texas Transportation Institute. 2003. *2003 Urban Mobility Study: The Mobility Data for Portland-Vancouver, OR-WA*. Texas A&M University, College Station. http://mobility.tamu.edu/ums/mobility_data/tables/portland.pdf (accessed 23 February 2004).

Washington County. 2002. A-Engrossed Ordinance No. 588. Exhibits 1 and 3. October 9, 2002.

# 12 | Keeping the Green Edge: Stream Corridor Protection in the Portland Metropolitan Region

Connie P. Ozawa and J. Alan Yeakley

Every year, fifth and sixth graders across the Portland metropolitan region climb into school buses and head for three nights to a week on the wet Oregon coast or in the high desert east of the Cascades. Sleeping with their classmates in cabins of various sizes, shapes, and levels of comfort at night, they spend the days crawling through lava tubes and tasting ants, stepping over banana slugs, and peering into tide pools. Children of staunch urbanites; of new immigrants from eastern Europe, Southeast Asia, or Latin America; and of rugged outdoor enthusiasts alike, all dirty their designer shoes and Kmart cargo pants as they encounter the best nature the state has to offer.

Outdoor School has been a routine part of the elementary school experience for more than 300,000 students in the Portland region since 1966 (Friends of the Outdoor School 2003). More than 47,000 high school students have served as camp counselors. While ostensibly part of the "science" curriculum, these students are also learning what might be called "environmental appreciation." The Outdoor School mirrors, and reinforces, the strong support that the environment has consistently scored among voters.

The State of Oregon is a national leader in environmental legislation. It was one of the first states to pass a bottle bill (1971) and a toxics use reduction act (1989). Voters in the Portland metropolitan region not only consistently list the protection of natural resources, parks, and open spaces as among their highest priorities they also back this sentiment up with their pocketbooks. For example, in 1995 they elected to tax themselves to the tune of $135 million through a bond measure for the purchase of open space. Anecdotally, while school children nationwide have been heard questioning the tobacco smoking habits of their elders, Portland area children have been known to insist that their parents use native vegetation to landscape their yards.

Plant selection for one's home or seeing the value of natural resources along the coast or within parks, however, may be quite a separate matter from limiting subdivision and construction on city lots that abut streams. Within city boundaries, land is perceived as scarce, and infrastructure for development is readily available, creating a compelling rationale for the sacrifice of natural areas to urbanized uses. In the backyard, alternative uses and aesthetic tastes compete for the homeowner's allegiance and investment. But natural resources within the urban area are increasingly recognized as critical elements of our broader ecosystems (Platt et al. 1994). Moreover, as urban sprawl spills over into the hinterlands, a failure to attend to natural resources within urban areas means an absolute loss across the broader landscape with serious consequences for the ecological system.

In the Portland metropolitan region, as in every locale in the United States, environmental protection occurs within a matrix of federal, state, and local policies. While federal policies provide a common context across the nation, the State of Oregon has distinguished itself from the other 49 states because of its 1973 state land use law. (Hawaii passed a state land use law the same year and other states have since passed growth management legislation. However, Oregon's action was early and uniquely ambitious in breadth.) At the same time, in Oregon as elsewhere, local jurisdictions maintain considerable discretion through their authority over land use decisions (i.e., what gets built where and how).

Given this potential for variation, do management approaches and policies in the Portland region differ widely? To what extent are local policies a response to state and federal directives? Or, to what extent are actions of nongovernmental actors critical? Finally, is there evidence that these management strategies create measurable on-the-ground differences? This chapter addresses such questions by examining the protection provided for a specific resource, riparian corridors. Although restoration efforts are becoming an increasingly significant factor in vegetation coverage, this chapter focuses on the prevention of loss. A close examination of the efforts directed toward protection of this resource may shed light on the interactions between the policies and responses of multiple levels of government and citizen groups that share responsibility for environmental protection. We find that environmental management in the Portland metropolitan region is best understood as an evolving process that involves many players, each of which contributes authority, inspiration, resources, and expertise. We posit that a similar dynamic may occur to varying degrees in other localities across the country.

This chapter begins by summarizing the ecological functions served by riparian buffers and factors in urban land patterns that present special challenges to stream corridor protection. We then present an overview of relevant federal and state policies and move on quickly to a narrative of the management histories of three cities in the Portland region up to 2002. This section ends with a preliminary assessment of on-the-ground conditions using two measures, the number of building permits issued within 30 meters of the stream for three cities between 1990 and 2002, and the loss in vegetation cover within the same "bandwidth" for two of these cities between 1990 and 1997. The stories of these three cities illustrate the flexibility and opportunities that federal and state policies represent to municipalities, the important role of citizen advocates, and the need for leadership in the management of environmental resources that cross jurisdictional boundaries.

## Riparian Areas and Challenges of Urban Environmental Management

Riparian corridors are a fundamental element of natural ecosystems, and yet urban environmental management has only recently targeted them. Typically vegetated in their undisturbed state, riparian corridors serve as the primary transfer area between terrestrial and aquatic components on a landscape. Vegetation along streams protects water quality by filtering heavy metals and sediment, assisting in the uptake of nutrients (primarily nitrogen and phosphorus), and cooling water temperatures by canopy shading and runoff absorption from impervious surfaces. The vegetation also increases the storage capacity of the stream and alleviates flood crests by diverting storm runoff. Finally, riparian corridors provide connectivity and migratory pathways for wildlife, and the proximity to fresh water provides a supportive habitat to various wildlife species, contributing to biodiversity in the region.

In cities, riparian corridors often represent relict green spaces that have been avoided by developers to some extent because of steep slopes or the threat of flooding (Spirn 2000). Alternatively, creek side locations may command high value from property owners who are drawn by the picturesque water feature. Often homeowners are tempted to clear vegetation in order to create an unobstructed view of the water and generally do so without public oversight. Consequently, while riparian corridors serve a unique ecosystem function, urban resource managers often neglect the contribution of such features to collective goals such as water quality, flood prevention, habitat preservation, and species diversity.

In fact, the management of riparian corridors in urban areas presents a number of special challenges. In contrast to rural, agricultural, or forest lands, urban lands are more fragmented in ownership and command higher economic rents. Equity conflicts arise, such as the fairness of restricting new development rather than requiring modification of existing practices, and the weighing of off-site impacts on water quality, such as runoff from impervious surfaces compared to the direct effects of cutting down trees.

Finally, as in many areas of environmental management, uncertain science and dismal science burden the protection of natural resources in urban areas. In general, riparian functions are still not well understood and are difficult to generalize among ecosystems that vary in geologic history, climate, soils, and the evolutionary history of fauna and flora. The major scientific studies on riparian functions have been conducted on forested and agricultural lands. Thus urban managers often must extrapolate from scientific work based on nonurbanized systems. It is also unclear what the benefits of lower stream protection and restoration are compared to upper stream protection. In addition, there is a serious lack of data about riparian conditions in urban areas and the relative cost of their protection. Consequently, urban environmental managers face severe obstacles to setting policies that adequately protect the riparian resource. Riparian corridor protection (and restoration) is an appropriate focus of examination precisely because of its political and technical complexity.

## The Policy Context

In his seminal work, "The Tragedy of the Commons," Garrett Hardin (1968) attested that common resources will be depleted in the absence of strong, central control because individual incentives to exploit a particular resource will outweigh the rational understanding of the need to restrain consumption to levels that will allow for natural replenishment of the resource. Traditional administrative theory proposes a hierarchical organization with strong leadership by a centralized authority. In the environmental field, the traditional model has prevailed with the federal government acting as a strong force for the past 40 years, pulling states along in the effort to clean up air and water quality, and with some success (Kraft and Vig 2000). However, the federal role has been periodically attacked by states rights advocates, and as funding and administrative support for monitoring and enforcement activities decline, "command-and-control" approaches in general appear increasingly less viable.

Urban land use and ownership patterns present an additional challenge to the hierarchical model, due to the place-bound and regional nature of many natural resource systems paired with the prerogative of local governments to dictate land use decisions within their jurisdictions. Urban environmental management requires not only coordination among municipalities but also the cooperation of individual landowners. The "new governance" models suggest a network of interdependent bodies, comprising both governmental and nongovernmental actors (Rosenau 2000, Salamon 2002). However, other scholars have pointed out the risks of dismantling the federal regulatory infrastructure (Gottlieb 1995, Rabe 2000). Our examination of riparian protection illustrates how these two approaches may coexist and complement one another.

The policy context in the management of stream corridors in the Portland metropolitan region involves federal, state, and regional bodies; local authorities; and citizen advocates. Figure 12.1 portrays elements of environmental management systems focusing on place-based resource issues. Development pressure, brought about by increasing populations and economic expansion, creates a demand for urbanization that can lead to degradation of ecosystems. Governments at various levels, as well as private and nongovernmental interests, have tried to mitigate this pressure by imposing regulatory controls and undertaking direct public actions. Many of these actions require substantial coordination. In the area of riparian buffer protection, for example, the federal Clean Water Act seeks to control effluents into water bodies and to protect wetlands. Implementation is achieved through the actions of state agencies empowered through agreement with federal agencies. Figure 12.1 portrays the overarching but indirect effect of federal law on local decisions.

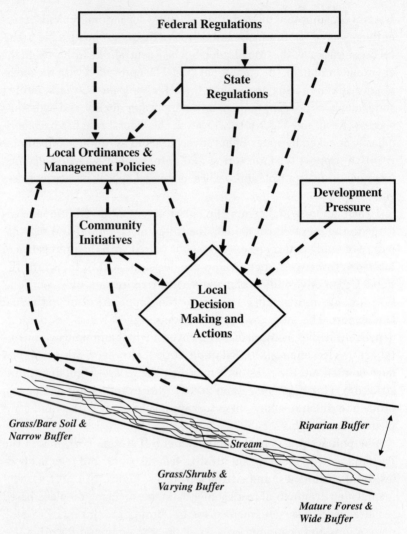

FIGURE 12.1. Forces and constraints on environmental degradation of riparian buffers. Source: Original.

In addition to the Clean Water Act, the federal influence has been exerted through the Flood Insurance Protection Act. Although both these pieces of legislation focus on water quality and the protection of human lives and property, they have provided the impetus and the funding for riparian protection, as will be discussed following here. More recently, National Oceanic and Atmospheric Administration (NOAA) Fisheries, then called the National Marine Fisheries Service, spurred action by listing endangered and threatened salmonids under the federal Endangered Species Act in certain west coast cities, including those in Portland, in 1998. This action similarly has spurred local governments to attend to factors that affect habitat conditions in salmon-bearing streams (Metro 2002a).

The Oregon state land use law set forth several goals for protection of riparian corridors, most specifically Goal 5 but also Goals 6, 7, and 15, as described in Table 12.1. These goals were set forth as a result of considerable public consultation about what Oregonians value (Oregon Department of Land Conservation and Development 2004). The state land use law requires every city, county, and regional authority with planning authority to prepare and submit a comprehensive plan to meet Goals 5, 6, 7, and 15 to the Department of Land Conservation and Development (DLCD) for approval. In the first round of comprehensive plan acknowledgments, DLCD pragmatically focused its review on a few, not all 19, of the goals. Development of more specific guidelines and expectations was an incremental and evolving process.

Consequently, it was not until the second round of comprehensive plan reviews, which began in the mid-1980s, that DLCD grew more attentive to Goal 5. Even then, however, the state agency was reluctant to impose punitive conditions on the cities that failed to make significant

### Table 12.1
*State goals affecting stream corridor protection in Oregon*

| Goal (year adopted) | Description |
| --- | --- |
| Goal 5: Open Spaces, Scenic and Historic Areas, and Natural Resources (1974) | To conserve open space and protect natural and scenic resources |
| Goal 6: Air, Water, and Land Resources Quality (1974) | To maintain and improve the quality of the air, water, and land resources of the state |
| Goal 7: Areas Subject to Natural Disasters and Hazards (1974) | To protect life and property from natural disasters and hazards |
| Goal 15: Willamette River Greenway (1975) | To protect, conserve, enhance, and maintain the natural, scenic, historical, agricultural, economic, and recreational quality of lands along the Willamette River as the Willamette River Greenway |

SOURCE: Original

progress toward resource protection (Brooks interview 2003). Instead, the state more typically would accept the progress made and prod the municipality to move forward in specific directions, such as by completing what might be a partial inventory of natural resources. In 1996, DLCD recommended new guidelines for Goal 5. These guidelines remained process oriented and did not mandate specific substantive outcome standards, except in the case of the "safe harbor" provision (Metro 2002b).[1]

In the Portland metropolitan region, the regional planning agency, Metro, has become a strong force in the management of resources of regional significance. (See Chap. 2, Seltzer.) By state administrative law, Metro has the authority to identify "regional resources" and to require cities and counties to comply with defined goals and objectives and measures to achieve them.

Adopted in 1998, Metro's Urban Growth Management Functional Plan comprises 11 titles, focusing on various aspects of growth management. Title 3 addresses water quality, flood management, and wildlife habitat. This section of the plan targets the protection of 775 miles, or 87%, of streams inside the urban growth boundary. At the time of adoption about 51 % of the 10,434 total acres of vegetated corridor areas were developed. Title 3 thus pertained to about 4,154 acres of undeveloped land and required minimum buffer widths that range from 15 to 200 feet, contingent on slope and flow characteristics (Metro 2003).

In addition, the agency's Metropolitan Greenspaces Master Plan inventoried and ranked the significance of natural resources in the area and set as a priority the acquisition of streamside open space. A 1995 bond measure provided $135.6 million for land purchase, of which all but $8 million had been expended by 2003. Anticipating future growth of the urban area, some of these spaces lie beyond the borders of the current urban growth boundary. In 2003, Metro had purchased approximately 63 miles of stream bank (Metro 2003).

Metro relies heavily on advisory committees in its plan-making efforts. These committees typically include representatives from environmental organizations, the local Audubon Society, the regional Coalition for a Livable Future, 1000 Friends of Oregon, local businesses, local, state, and federal agencies of relevance, and, as in the case of the Economic Advisory Committee, academic and private consulting economists. Hundreds of "friends" groups, or citizen-based voluntary organizations, as well as organizations favoring property rights participate by submitting testimony at public hearings (Ketcham interview 2003).

Although the Greenspaces Master Plan and the Water Quality and Flood Management Plans provide substantial protection to riparian corridors, the coverage is not complete (Metro 2002b). Therefore, Metro set out in 1998 to develop a fish and wildlife habitat plan for the region. The initial outreach, which involved meetings, surveys, and education campaigns regionwide with residents and representatives from local jurisdictions and state and federal agencies, demonstrated both substantial public support for more extensive natural resource protection and cautious resistance from local governments concerned about home rule (Metro 2000). Metro has moved forward with an economic, social, environmental, and energy (ESEE) assessment, and staff expect to bring a plan to the Metro Council in 2004.

## The Management Stories of Three Cities

We turn now to a narrative about the regulatory and management approaches of three cities in the Portland metropolitan region. The 23 cities and three countries under Metro's jurisdiction illustrate a variety of local responses, the influence of federal and state policy on local actions, and the roles and effect of nongovernmental actors. We chose three cities to demonstrate a range of these responses.

Portland was selected for obvious reasons, as the largest city in the state and the focal point of much of the region's activities. We chose the cities of Hillsboro and Oregon City because of their comparable, rapid growth rates in the 1990s, their physical locations at the western and southeastern edges of the region, as well as their reputations as communities respectively less and more progressive in their attitudes toward development and resource protection.

We end this section with analyses of building permit activity and vegetation loss to provide a sense of conditions on the ground. This report is limited to the cities of Hillsboro and Oregon City, as our efforts to analyze vegetation loss in Portland are still under way. Although this analysis is preliminary, it is suggestive, and presents a protocol for further research and future comparisons with other cities and regions.

### *The City of Portland*

As the largest city in Oregon, Portland essentially had an open field to shape the rules of Goal 5 compliance. In the mid-1980s, the City of Portland began to work in earnest toward a strategy for protecting natural resources within its boundaries. According to former Portland planner Duncan Brown, the planning team was urged forward by Audubon

Society of Portland advocate Mike Houck. Houck had been inspired by a meeting with David Goode, who in 2003 was the director of environment for the Greater London Authority, and by the initiatives of Bellevue, Washington, and Eugene, Oregon, and Pierce County, Washington. The Portland planners met with a biologist, Esther Lev, for direction and instruction about conducting qualitative assessments of the city's natural resource areas. Lev counseled the planners to consider the value of specific tracts with regard to plant diversity, canopy cover, and habitat quality, measured by availability of food, water, and cover. The planner team divided the city map into eight areas and headed out to cross check sites with aerial photographs and existing inventories. Based on the eight subsequent reports, with input from a technical advisory committee, through which Mike Houck remained active, the planners drew zoning maps delineating "preservation" and "conservation" zones (together known as environmental zones or E-zones). The zoning was approved by the city council in 1989.

Business interests were not oblivious to the planners' undertakings. An industrial landowner who feared that this zoning approach would infringe on his firm's business in the port district took the city to court in 1990. The lawsuit cited the lack of an ESEE analysis and ultimately forced the city to develop methods of quantifying the need for these environmental protection and conservation zones. The first of these documents was approved by the city council in December 1990 and the last in September 1994.

By 2003, more than 7,689 hectares (19,000 acres) had been designated in environmental zones. The E-zones provide an additional review step for new development, expansion of existing structures, land divisions, and topographical alterations. Permits for construction can be obtained either by demonstrating compliance with specific development standards or by a more customized review through which applicants must demonstrate that approval criteria are met through alternative means. In both cases, the application is subject to opportunities for public comment. Preservation zones (P-zones) essentially forbid any new development except pathways, roads, and the laying of pipes or cables. Conservation zones (C-zones) allow the construction of structures but set forth specific criteria for the percentage of disturbed area allowed, special construction conditions, and requirements for the replacement of vegetation, among other items.

The City began work to expand the environmental zones in 2001. The proposed changes would have affected an additional 13,000, or 10%, of the city's landowners. Some landowners in southwest Portland mobilized quickly to oppose the city's effort, arguing that the proposed changes would require compensation to landowners for lost value in their land under the state's then in-limbo property rights Measure 7. Measure 7 has since been found "invalid" by the state judicial system and the landowners leading the charge against the E-zone expansion, ironically, have moved out of the state. The city, however, has not resumed its efforts publicly as of autumn 2003.

The City of Portland has worked on other fronts toward improving the conditions near streams and other water features. One of its most visible efforts revolved around Johnson Creek, which flows from the foothills of the Cascade Mountains westward, crossing through east Portland and emptying into the Willamette River. Historically, annual flooding over the banks of Johnson Creek created fertile farmland. This constructive attribute became perceived as destructive as the city encroached on the farmland and houses crowded the edges of the stream. Decades of bickering among service districts, governmental agencies, and taxpayers delayed flood control efforts (Seltzer 1983). However, the 1987 amendments to the Clean Water Act, including attention to nonpoint sources of water pollution and the assignment of responsibility for water quality standards to cities with populations of 100,000 or more, prodded the City of Portland into action once again. Harnessing the energy, knowledge, and commitment of local residents who had been mobilized to ward off road construction in the canyons of the creek a few years earlier, the city's Bureau of Environmental Services successfully sponsored a facilitated management plan making process. After five years of information gathering and analysis, the plan was produced and adopted by the City of Portland in 1995.

One of the offshoots of the Plan was a "willing sellers" program to purchase properties in the flood-prone sections of the Johnson Creek floodplain from homeowners at market rate prices. Since 1997, 90 properties have been purchased. Most of these properties are within the Johnson Creek 100-year floodplain. The program has expended $10.7 million, with funds from Metro's greenspaces program, community development block grants, the Federal Emergency Management Act (FEMA), and the City of Portland.

The Johnson Creek Resource Management Plan experience led the group of citizen participants to a crossroad. They could become an official arm of the City of Portland, or they could apply for a state grant to launch an independent watershed council. The citizens chose the latter route. They have since maintained an active and vocal presence in watershed planning and restoration activities in the region and are recognized and included in land use development planning efforts (Adler and Ozawa 2002).

The City of Portland's Bureau of Environmental Services took the experience with Johnson Creek forward and expanded into a watershed stewardship program that includes six streams within city boundaries. The City works with local resident and business organizations to provide educational workshops, increase local awareness of current issues, and develop management plans and programs for maintaining and restoring watershed health.

Finally, the city's most recent and perhaps most ambitious initiative originated in response to the 1998 and 1999 listing of steelhead trout and chinook salmon as threatened under the federal Endangered Species Act. The City of Portland organized a staff of scientists and managers under the auspices of its new Endangered Species Act (ESA) Program, which recently produced a draft of the *Framework for Integrated Management of Watershed and River Health* (City of Portland, Bureau of Planning 2004). The *Framework* has several objectives including (a) creating a scientific information database that can inform city government decisions, (b) integrating the city's response to several federal regulatory statutes, and (c) guiding the development of watershed plans within the city.

The *Framework* is a comprehensive watershed-based plan that touches all land use or development within the city boundaries with any potential effect on aquatic or riparian habitat or conditions. Its goals encompass hydrology, physical habitat, water quality, and the biological community, and focus on the health of aquatic and riparian ecosystems. The *Framework* proposes an iterative watershed management process, and seeks to integrate the mandates of various city bureaus under one umbrella that focuses on improving watershed and river health. The *Framework* seeks to achieve this integration by (a) providing a set of common goals and actions for each watershed in the city, (b) guiding development of additional plans and documents needed to comply with federal and state laws, and (c) providing guidance for city plans and actions that do not specifically relate to watershed health to ensure that they are compatible with watershed health goals.

In addition to the Endangered Species Act, the *Framework* is driven by other regulatory requirements including the Clean Water Act (CWA), the Safe Drinking Water Act (SDWA), and the Comprehensive

Environmental Response, Compensation, and Liability Act (CERCLA), or Superfund. Locally, the *Framework* was also a response to the City of Portland's River Renaissance initiative, endorsed by the Portland City Council in March 2001, which seeks to ensure a clean and healthy river system for fish, wildlife, and people.

It is notable that in July 1998 the city council chose not only to respond to the federally mandated requirement to avoid or minimize *take* of threatened species, but also to commit the city to *recovery* of those species. The *Framework* is a thoughtfully presented, scientifically based document, reviewed by an independent science team (IST) of biologists, ecologists, and hydrologists from Oregon, Washington, and Idaho. The IST presented their findings before the Portland City Council in July 2003. While the members of the team had constructive criticisms on details of the *Framework*, the IST was largely supportive of the City's approach. The IST found that "The *Framework* is a well-written, scientifically defensible document. It provides a framework that will give sound ecological guidance to some of the decisions, actions and plans that will comprise Portland's watershed restoration program." The ESA program anticipates completing revisions to the Framework and seeking city council approval during 2004.

### The City of Hillsboro

While planners in Portland took an aggressive, proactive stance toward Goal 5 and the protection of riparian corridors, Hillsboro planners chose instead to "fly below the radar." Hillsboro was predominantly a farming community on the western edge of the metropolitan region until the 1990s, when it became the heart of the area's "Silicon Forest," with Intel and other transnational high tech firms located within its boundaries. (See Chap. 1, Mayer and Provo.) Population growth rates in Hillsboro during the 1990s were among the highest in the region, growing by 86% to 69,883 in 2000, making it the fourth most populous city in Oregon. The city planning department is led by a director, two supervisors (of current and long-range planning), nine staff line planners, and a planning database coordinator.

About 63.5 km of rivers and streams meander through Hillsboro, including the Tualatin River, which empties into the Willamette River several kilometers downstream from the city border. Despite the abundance of water features, the city planning department had not singled out riparian corridors for special protection until 2003. Until then, resource protection had been achieved through a jigsaw puzzle of significant resources identified through specific area plans, the review of "planned unit development" projects, or by referral to the Washington County water services provider, now called Clean Waters Services (CWS), which implements programs to meet federal water quality standards.

The City of Hillsboro responded to the objectives of Goal 5 in sporadic steps. A "regulated floodplain district" map was adopted in 1980, which essentially required erosion controls, and a partial inventory of "significant natural resource areas" was completed in 1991. These controls flagged a portion of riparian corridors for special design considerations but did not prohibit outright development or removal of vegetation. A potential avenue of protection was provided through the Planned Unit Development (PUD) Overlay District, which allows exceptions to setbacks and minimum lot size in order to avoid the destruction of sensitive resources without impeding development.

Throughout the 1990s, development permit applications were shuffled to the water service district organization for review, working from a set of maps that included the 1991 partial resource inventory, floodplain maps, and other similar documents. Regulations in place forbid structures or construction within 25 feet of stream banks, but exceptions would allow developers to encroach within 15 feet.

Since February 2000, the standards have remained essentially the same, but the review process has been refined. CWS routinely examines all applications that may include a Sensitive Area onsite or within 200 feet. (Sensitive Areas are defined as existing or created wetlands, rivers, streams, and springs with year round or intermittent flow, and natural lakes, ponds, and in-stream impoundments.) Sensitive Areas are identified by a CWS biologist through a field investigation conducted prior to permitting and again during construction. The required "no-build" buffer varies from 15 to 200 feet depending on slope, drainage area, and resource quality.

In spring 2003, the City of Hillsboro adopted a "significant natural resources program," which was intended to bring it into full compliance with state Goal 5 for the first time. The program consists of delineating a significant resources overlay district, which includes specified buffers around identified natural resource sites and impact areas. The ordinance recognizes the possibility of future revisions to comply with Metro's current Goal 5 work on fish and wildlife habitat. Hillsboro planners developed the ordinance with opportunities for public comment. However, there was no conspicuous presence of environmental groups.

Property owners did express opposition and the city lessened proposed restrictions on the impacted area (Rollins 2003).

## Oregon City

Set at the southeastern edge of the Portland metropolitan area, Oregon City is the oldest city in Oregon. The residents are proud of its historic role as well as its natural beauty. Located at the confluence of the Clackamas and Willamette Rivers, it has roughly one-third the population of Hillsboro, but also experienced rapid population growth in the 1990s, increasing nearly 74% from 14,698 to 25,533 over the last census period.

Oregon City has pursued resource protection through the creation of a number of special overlay districts, as displayed in Table 12.2. Development permit applicants must check the zoning maps to ascertain whether their property falls within any of these special overlay districts. If so, the applicant must demonstrate the extent to which the specified resources will be impacted and how such impacts will be mitigated. The overlay districts do not forbid incursions into vegetated stream corridors but they do flag situations when they are likely to arise and encourage avoidance or mitigation of adverse impacts.

The planning staff at Oregon City has turned over quite frequently in recent years; the public works director, who has been with the city since 1996, has been serving longer than any current planning staff member (Kraushaar interview 2003). Perhaps more significantly, the planning staff may or may not have the expertise to assess potential impacts; they typically rely on the technical reports of consultants hired by permit applicants.

In the early 1990s, Oregon City conducted a partial inventory of natural resources to comply with Goal 5. A major step forward occurred in 1999 when the city revised its overlay districts to conform to Metro's 1998 Title 3 water quality and flood management maps. Riparian areas are now protected primarily through the Water Quality Resource Area Overlay District, which stipulates vegetated buffers from 15 to 200 feet, depending on slope.

While the city council is apparently quite supportive of protective measures, the city's resources are stretched. The staff welcomes Metro's leadership and is comfortable relying on Metro's data and policy guidance. Citizen organizations are not actively involved in resource management in Oregon City, except on highly specific issues, when particular individuals rally around issues that affect areas of their special concern. The city council has recently approved $10,000 to fund a watershed group for Abernathy Creek. Clackamas Community College, located in

## Table 12.2
### Oregon City overlay districts

| Title of Overlay District | Year Adopted | Description |
| --- | --- | --- |
| Park Acquisition | 1980 | Reserves for the city the right of first option to purchase on all riverfront properties. |
| Flood Management | 1980 | Imposes special development standards in compliance with federal flood insurance standards. Revised (1999) in accordance with Metro 1998 Title 3 maps, 1996 flood data, and storm water runoff and topography data. Earlier maps were based on FEMA maps. |
| Unstable Slopes and Hillside Constraints | 1984 | Imposes special development standards to avoid and minimize disturbance to land and to protect vegetation. Based on Oregon State Department of Geology and Mineral Industries and Portland State University Environmental Assessment of Newell Creek. |
| Willamette River Greenway | 1984 | Created to comply with Goal 15 of the state land use plan. Directs development away from the river to the greatest extent possible and seeks to minimize erosion, promote bank stability, and maintain and enhance water quality and wildlife habitat. |
| Water Resources (later renamed Water Quality Resources) | 1993 | Stipulates "no build" zones based on slope. The Water Quality Resources Overlay District (1999) boundaries are based on Metro's Title 3 maps, modified in accordance with field data and a 200-foot extension to the water feature boundary. |

SOURCE: Original

Oregon City, has housed since 2000 an environmental learning center that hosts educational programs and outreach activities. As of fall 2003, however, the center had lost state funding and was actively seeking a community partner in order to remain open (Clackamas Community College 2004).

## Building Permits and Vegetation Loss in the 1990s

Ultimately, the test of public policy and private initiatives is the extent to which vegetation in urban riparian corridors is lost or gained in comparison with the corresponding gains or losses of other social benefits. Although from an ecosystem perspective, any loss is a cost that should be avoided, the current planning system in the United States views the loss of natural resources as a value to be balanced against other socially desirable gains or undesirable losses. Therefore, the effectiveness of any natural resource protection policy cannot fully be gauged by the amount of resource protected or maintained. Some loss may be socially acceptable, given other potential social costs.

Nonetheless, a rough evaluation of policies to protect targeted resources would measure the extent of resource loss, pollution, or incursions into protected areas. We have examined two metrics: new construction permits issued and net change in vegetation within 30 meters from streams. The number of building permits issued within stream corridors suggests the extent to which municipalities are limiting construction that may reduce vegetation and degrade the riparian corridor; an analysis of actual loss in vegetation cover more accurately indicates the extent to which the resource is protected.

Figure 12.2 shows the total number of permits issued for new construction in the three cities based on Regional Land Information System (RLIS) data obtained from Metro. The figure shows a relatively steady increase in permits issued over time, suggesting at least constant demand for new construction.

Figure 12.3 shows the number of permits issued by each city for new construction within 30 meters of a stream. The data are "normalized" for each city to account for differences in the amount of stream frontage to total land area. The City of Portland shows a clear decline in the number of new construction permits issued within 30 meters over this time period. The record for Hillsboro and Oregon City during this time is less clear.

Figure 12.4 shows the on-the-ground losses of two vegetation classes, unmanaged and tree vegetation, located near streams in Oregon City

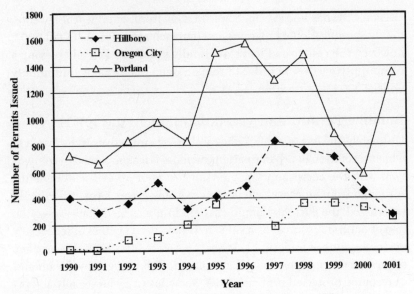

FIGURE 12.2. New construction activity, 1990–2001. Source: Metro RLIS Lite.

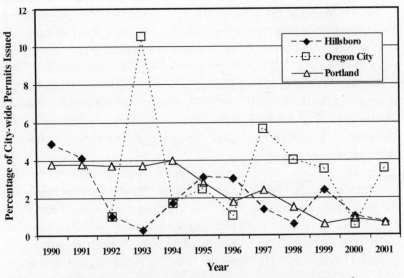

FIGURE 12.3. New Construction within 30 meters as a percentage of total permits. The data are normalized for ratios of stream frontage to land area. Source: Original

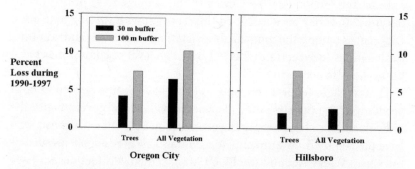

FIGURE 12.4. Percent vegetation loss within riparian buffers from 1990 to 1997. Two buffer widths are shown, 30 meters and 100 meters, both for tree vegetation areas and for all unmanaged vegetation areas. Source: Original.

and Hillsboro. (The data for Portland were unavailable at the time of publication.) We calculated these figures after orthorectifying and digitizing aerial photos taken in 1990 and 1997. Stream location data were obtained from Metro and site checked when a discrepancy appeared in the matching of our two data sources. The annual loss of vegetation within the 30 meter buffer is substantial in both cities, with a combined loss equivalent to about one high school football field (or 0.54 ha) every 16 weeks. Given that Hillsboro has nearly twice the length of stream frontage, the rate of loss in Oregon City is substantially higher for the 30 meter buffer width in Oregon City than in Hillsboro, as indicated in Figure 12.4. Interestingly, for the 100 meter buffer, the percentage loss of both tree and all unmanaged vegetation is similar, suggesting that the closer-in riparian areas are indeed under greater pressure in Oregon City than in Hillsboro.

## Analysis and Conclusions

Local governments in the Portland metropolitan region have recognized the vital importance of vegetated stream corridors to the overall health of the urban ecosystem. The City of Portland appears to have in place the strongest protection of riparian vegetation coverage. Hillsboro and Oregon City show less promise, although Hillsboro's loss relative to the volume of its streamside resources is less than Oregon City's.

The examples of these three cities illustrate that efforts to protect riparian buffers have varied over time and across jurisdictions. Despite the common framework of federal and state policies, local governments have retained considerable leeway in the management of this urban resource, and they have exercised this freedom with varying outcomes. Differences among the municipalities' staffing, resources, and administrative procedures certainly reflect both the level of commitment and the capacity to act on it.

Nonetheless, federal and state policies have been essential in both prodding and supporting the independent will of local governments, the individuals who stand behind the counters, and the citizen activists who have pushed their governments to new limits. Whereas policies such as the Clean Water Act and the Flood Management Protection Act have provided both the legal foundations and, as in the case of Portland's willing seller program, even monetary funds to protect stream corridors, the federal Endangered Species Act and the listing of salmon in the late 1990s and beyond have boosted efforts to create and maintain contiguous wildlife habitat. The experience of the Portland region suggests that federal policy and programs make an indelible imprint on the resource management landscape.

Observers often blithely attribute much of the Portland region's current conditions to the state land use law. However, although the protection of natural resources is among the state's 19 goals, the state has in fact commanded rather little and controlled even less. Despite the level of awareness and concern about the importance of riparian buffers, loss continued well past the passage of the law.

Fortunately, the state's acknowledgment of the importance of natural resources is more than symbolic, largely because of the authority the state has awarded to Metro, which has taken a proactive stance on the protection of resources of regional significance. Metro has organized and gathered critical information, has committed resources and expertise, and, most importantly, has helped level the field and has written the rules for fair play in riparian protection in the metropolitan region. While Metro's actions are relatively recent and their impact unproven, the public discussion that Metro generates provides local jurisdictions in the metropolitan area little choice but to either lead or be led. We expect on-the-ground changes to be far more uniform over time, and riparian vegetation loss to be tempered, provided the present processes that involve an informed citizenry in local decision making are allowed to continue.

Finally, the story of resource protection in the Portland metropolitan region challenges Hardin's "tragedy of the commons" notion by underscoring the complex interactive dynamic among different levels of government and the strength of informal and formal networks of relationships among the planners, citizen organizations, and activists. Individual advocates such as Mike Houck, naturalist at the Audubon Society of Portland; Esther Lev, biologist at the Wetland Conservancy; and members of watershed organizations and friends groups, who believe protection of nature is a given, have pushed Portland to the forefront of local protection strategies. (See Chap. 5, Johnson.) Such organizations and individuals are similarly vital to Metro's work. Alternatively, the dynamic in the Portland region might be viewed as a process dominated by policy elites. However, public acceptance of governmental regulatory efforts is a reflection of the cultural context in which it occurs. Efforts to cultivate a sense of environmental appreciation in this or in any other region should not be ignored. The legacy of the Outdoor School may be the imprint not only on children's minds but also on our landscape. Further analysis of change in riparian buffers over time should demonstrate the strength of our policies and popular support.

Our research to assess the on-the-ground changes under different management schemes is ongoing and not yet complete. It nonetheless provides a template for planners, scientists, and citizens in other parts of the country to similarly examine how well or poorly their own localities are faring with respect to protecting riparian buffers and maintaining the functions of a healthy urban ecosystem. With such efforts, we will better understand the relative importance of the various federal, state, and local bodies and actors, and how to best coordinate policies, resources, and actions to protect natural resources. Meanwhile, riparian protection in the Portland metropolitan region also reveals that the interplay of formal institutions and laws and local governments with the varying capacities to respond and initiate collective actions is only part of the story. Citizen advocates may bring an unregulated and serendipitous ingredient to the mix.

ACKNOWLEDGMENTS

We would like to thank graduate research assistants Shannon Axtell, Richard Friday, Aaron Hook, Jennifer Hughes, and Melanie Sharp for their help in various phases of this project; our anonymous colleagues at Portland State University who supported our applications for research grants; Portland State University for essential funding; Metro for sharing data; and the numerous local agency staff who shared their insights and expertise.

NOTES

1. The safe harbor provision allows local governments to opt out of certain requirements of the standard Goal 5 process by following specific criteria for particular features. For example, rather than inventorying riparian corridors within its jurisdictional boundaries, a municipality may employ a standard setback from all fish-bearing lakes and streams in accordance with particular physical conditions listed by DLCD, such as stream flow.

REFERENCES

Adler, Sy, and Connie Ozawa. 2002. *Pleasant Valley Concept Plan: Project Evaluation*. Portland: Metro.

City of Portland, Bureau of Planning. 2004. *Endangered Species Program*. http://www.fish.ci.portland.or.us (accessed 15 January 2004) or http://www.river.ci.portland.or.us (accessed 15 March 2004).

Clackamas Community College, Environmental Learning Center. 2004. http://depts.clackamas.edu/elc/index.asp (accessed 10 January 2004).

Friends of the Outdoor School. 2003. *About the Outdoor School*. http://www.passonthememory.org (accessed 30 August 2003).

Gottlieb, Robert. 1995. *Reducing Toxics: A New Approach to Policy and Industrial Decisionmaking*. Washington, DC: Island Press.

Hardin, Garrett. 1968. The tragedy of the commons. *Science* 162: 1243–1248.

Kraft, Michael E. and Norman J. Vig. 2000. Environmental policy from the 1970s to 2000: An overview. In *Environmental Policy*, 4th ed., edited by Norman J. Vig and Michael E. Kraft. Washington, DC: CQ Press.

Metro. 2000. *Fish and Wildlife Habitat Protection Plan: Public Involvement and Comments Report*. Portland: Metro.

Metro. 2002a. *Metro's Technical Report for Goal 5: Revised Draft*. Portland: Metro.

Metro. 2002b. *Draft Local Plan Analysis: A Review of Goal 5 Protection in the Metro Region*. Portland: Metro.

Metro. 2003. *Perfomance Measures Report Complete Results: An Evaluation of 2040 Growth Management Policies and Implementation*. Portland: Metro.

Oregon Department of Land Conservation and Development. 2004. http://www.lcd.state.or.us. 30 Years of Statewide Land Use Planning: Vision, Mission & Goals (Accessed 10 February 2004.).

Platt, Rutherford H., Rowan A. Rowntree, and Pamela C. Muick, eds. 1994. *The Ecological City: Preserving and Restoring Urban Biodiversity*. Amherst: University of Massachusetts Press.

Rabe, Barry. 2000. Power to the states: The power and pitfalls of decentralization. In *Environmental Policy*, 4th ed., edited by Norman J. Vig and Michael E. Kraft. Washington, DC: CQ Press.

Rollins, Ian. 2003. Citizens satisfied with new resource protection codes. *Hillsboro Argus News*, 15 May. http://www.oregonlive.com/ (accessed 20 May 2003).

Rosenau, Pauline Vaillancourt, ed. 2000. *Public-Private Policy Partnerships*. Cambridge, MA: MIT Press.

Salamon, Lester M. 2002. The new governance and the tools of public action: An introduction. In *The Tools of Government: A Guide to the New Governance*, edited by Lester M. Salamon. New York: Oxford University Press.

Seltzer, Ethan P. 1983. Citizen Participation in Environmental Planning: Context and Consequences. Unpublished dissertation. University of Pennsylvania.

Spirn, Ann. 2000. Restoring natural resources and rebuilding urban communities. In *Planning for a New Century: The Regional Agenda* edited by Jonathan Barnett. Washington, DC: Island Press.


INTERVIEWS

Brown, Duncan. 2003. Interview with author. 24 June. Former planner, City of Portland.

Brooks, Wink. 2003. Interview with author. 16 July. Director of Planning, City of Hillsboro.

Counts, Valerie. 2003. Interview with author. 16 July. Planning Supervisor, Long-Range Planning Division, City of Hillsboro.

Kraushaar, Nancy. 2003. Interview with author. 11 August. Public Works Director, City of Oregon City.

Ketcham, Paul. 2003. Interview with author. 6 August. Metro planner.

Rayber, Debbie. 2003. Interview with author. 5 August. Planning supervisor, Current Planning Division, City of Hillsboro.

Seltzer, Ethan. 2003. Interview with author. 26 July. PSU, former Metro planner.

# 13 | Portland's Response to Homeless Issues and the "Broken Windows" Theory

Tracy J. Prince

All across America cities are adopting the "broken windows" theory in their dealings with homeless people. City councils, mayors, and business improvement districts eagerly embrace the promises of a whitewashed downtown, sometimes without realizing the profound shift in tax dollars this approach requires or analyzing whether or not this is an efficacious or even humane community investment. While the rhetoric sounds wonderful—who doesn't want better "quality of life?"—the results of this policy bring many cities to the dark ages of social justice and simply sweep poverty, hunger, and homelessness away from public sight. The not so hidden cost of broken windows–inspired policies shifts tax dollars from addressing the causes and effects of homelessness toward the criminal justice system, since many of the daily activities of the homeless are criminalized. How does Portland fit into this changing national climate? What are the current and historical responses to homelessness in Portland? How do Portland's policies compare to those of its west coast neighbors—particularly Seattle and San Francisco whose cities have somewhat similar demographics, weather, and political leanings? At a time when cities are rushing blindly to embrace a policy that—whether they realize it or not—is social Darwinism, declaring, "if you can't fend for yourself, if you don't have a place to urinate or sleep, you must be removed," is Portland, which prides itself on its tolerance, any different?

# The Broken Windows Theory

In 1969 Stanford psychologist Philip Zimbardo conducted an experiment testing what would happen to two cars left abandoned in two different neighborhoods—both 1959 Oldsmobiles. "The license plates of both cars were removed and the hoods opened to provide the necessary releaser signals" (Zimbardo 1969). In one affluent and one nonaffluent neighborhood, the results were the same, although the vandalism took a little longer in the affluent neighborhood. In the Bronx, the car was completely vandalized in three days, with 23 separate incidents of vandalism. In Palo Alto, California (the wealthy neighborhood where Stanford University is located), the car was not touched for one week, but once Prof. Zimbardo and his graduate students helped things along by bashing the car a bit, people in the neighborhood quickly helped finish off the destruction.

In a 1982 *Atlantic Monthly* article titled "Broken Windows: The Police and Neighborhood Safety" political scientist James Q. Wilson and criminologist George L. Kelling (and Kelling and Catherine Coles's 1996 book on the same subject *(Fixing Broken Windows)*) expanded upon Zimbardo's study drawing the conclusion that broken windows on abandoned cars and in the cityscape seemed to signal that "no one cares." They drew a further correlation that social ills left publicly broken lead to more social ills. Some say this is an illogical assumption since they used one experiment with abandoned cars as the basis of an argument essentially claiming, among other things, that evidence of broken people in public spaces creates crime. Saying that the best way to fight "quality-of-life" crimes is to fight the disorder that precedes it, they called for more community policing and proactive efforts to prevent crime before it happens. While community policing and crime prevention sound quite reasonable, they also suggested that police pay more attention to the type of crimes often overlooked—public drunkenness, panhandling, public urination, graffiti, uncollected trash, and unrepaired buildings—in order to create a blight-free public space, which would then, conceivably, lower crime rates. "Therefore, the objective for preventing street crimes is to prevent the first window from getting broken, or prevent the first graffiti marks, or prevent the first drunkard from a public display. This has led to Neighborhood Watch programs and increased police foot patrols. These measures have not had a significant impact on crime, but they have succeeded in making neighborhood residents feel safer" (Williams 1998).

Wilson and Kelling's theory received an enormous boost when New York City mayor Rudolph Giuliani adopted the broken windows theory with a community-policing strategy focused on what he called "quality of life" and maintaining order—and crime rates dropped. Like George W. Bush's "compassionate conservatism" rhetoric, Mayor Giuliani spoke of his compassion when discussing his homeless policies. Giuliani's campaign was led in large part by powerful Business Improvement Districts such as the Times Square Business Improvement District, the Fifth Avenue Association, the Alliance for Downtown New York, the Madison Avenue B.I.D., the Grand Central Partnership, and the 34th Street Partnership. The rhetoric of this campaign referred to a "war on crime" aiming, in part, to "reduce sidewalk congestion" with "zero tolerance" on such issues as unlicensed vendors, loiterers, panhandling, and outdoor camping. "Community courts" and "quality of life" debates were often thinly disguised xenophobia against unhoused people, with an obvious focus on removing them completely from sight. Times Square was cleaned beyond recognition, graffiti was regularly washed from subway cars, subway turnstile-jumpers were arrested, trash was picked up, homeless people were arrested and moved along, and many of the effects of homelessness were removed from public sight. Giuliani's police commissioner, Howard Safir, encouraged the arrest of homeless people should they refuse shelter or police assistance. In *Sidewalk*, (1999) an excellent ethnography of the impact of Giuliani's policies on homeless people, Mitchell Duneier reveals the dirty underbelly of such policies. Although usually considered in the domain of human services, homeless people and issues in New York City are now frequently dealt with by the criminal justice system, as yet another "broken window." Furthermore, it has been argued by many that these campaigns simply moved the homeless to other boroughs and to New Jersey.

Nevertheless, focusing on these minor crimes seemed to work since crime rates dropped and in 2002 Manhattan experienced the lowest murder rate in 100 years (Salon.com 2002). Since New York City had such apparent success with these strategies, cities the world over began emulating their tactics. Many cities make it clear that they have fully accepted the view of homeless people as broken windows who need to be removed from public sight. However, other cities use the buzzwords "broken windows" with no apparent understanding of the term or the true social costs of implementing NYC-inspired policies. Santa Monica restricted homeless feeding programs in 2002 to discourage homeless people from coming to or staying in Santa Monica. Los Angeles police chief William Bratton brought his New York City training with him and implemented quality of life broken windows policies. He has said that he would like to corral all the homeless people into skid row so that they can be more easily controlled. The Hollywood Entertainment District business improvement group fully supports his ideas (Winton and Sauerwein 2003). Even historically tolerant San Francisco has embraced a hard-line approach to homeless policies and made enormous changes cleaning up the human broken windows in their city. Billboard campaigns to support drastically reducing homeless benefits with 2002's Proposition N (sponsored by the Hotel Council of San Francisco and other business groups) declared: "I want to be able to walk down the street without being asked for money," and "I don't want to have to hold my breath every time I pass an alley." Yet rates of violent crime have been dropping since the 1980s in American cities, well before Giuliani's tactics became popular. The Center on Juvenile and Criminal Justice (2002) debunked the commonly accepted idea that the implementation of the broken windows theory resulted in reduced crime rates. They found that since 1995 San Francisco, for example, reported a 33% reduction in violent crime rates even though during most of this time their policy was not to pursue aggressive arrests, prosecutions, and prison terms for homeless people. In comparison, during this time, New York City's experienced a 26% decrease in violent crime rates.

## Criminalizing the Homeless: Expensive, Ineffective, and Inhumane

Homeless advocates argue that criminalizing homelessness is exorbitantly costly, doesn't reduce homelessness, doesn't lower crime, and forces people into nightmarishly never-ending cycles of homelessness. For example, the taxpayer's expense for a night spent in jail is far higher than for a night in a shelter, which in turn is more costly than tax dollars spent on low-income housing. A prison bed averages $20,000 per year; typical rent subsidies average $4,500 to $6,000 per year; and the average annual cost for emergency shelter is $15,000 for singles and $25,000 to $30,000 for families (Culhane et al. 2002). The National Coalition for the Homeless argues that "the cost of arresting, processing and jailing homeless people is higher than the cost of creating housing . . . [and] criminalization of homelessness leads to increased barriers to accessing shelter and housing due to a criminal record and unpaid fines" (National Coalition for the Homeless 2002). In a "Policy Guide on Homelessness," the American Planning Association (2003) observes that the true costs of homelessness are masked in the budgets of law enforcement, corrections, health care, welfare, education, and other systems. In Portland, homeless advocate Rob Justice (2003), executive director of JOIN, makes the case that criminal records and fines for quality of life tickets would create a huge barrier to ending the cycle of homelessness. JOIN is an outreach group specializing in housing assistance for people who either do not utilize or are turned away from shelters and camp or sleep outdoors.

## Oregon's History of Poverty and Homelessness

In considering Portland's homeless community, it is important to have a snapshot of poverty in Oregon and contingent issues that lead to homelessness. The effects of Oregon's struggling economy are clear in the strain on social services and the increase in homeless people turned away from shelters. In 2002–2003 the state ranked number one in the nation in unemployment (Oregon Employment Department). Furthermore, even fully employed people find themselves struggling to make ends meet in today's economy. Oregon Housing and Community Services estimated in 2001 that a living wage needed for basic expenses ranged from $10.07 per hour for a single adult to $16.36 for an adult with two children. Yet 40% of the jobs advertised in Oregon pay less than the bottom end of this living wage scale. Consequently, the Oregon Food Bank reports that in 2002 Oregon was ranked as the hungriest state in the nation and continues to hover near the top of the list. The Oregon Center for Public Policy shows that poverty rates among Oregon's working families with children have doubled since the late 1970s, and the gap between the rich and the poor in Oregon grew four times faster than the country as a whole (Leachman 2001).

Although Oregon has been quite progressive in providing medical care for the uninsured (over 1 million uninsured Oregonians have received medical, dental, mental health, and chemical dependency services coverage under the Oregon Health Plan), this coverage has been seriously eroded in the enormous budget cuts of the past few years. The effects of these cutbacks are felt profoundly among the homeless and near homeless, especially those served by mental health and chemical dependency assistance. Of course, the difficult economic climate can be seen in dramatic increases in people seeking help from homeless service providers. Since 1993, the estimated number of single women turned away because of lack of space has increased 203% since shelter space has not kept pace with demand. Multnomah County reports a 38%

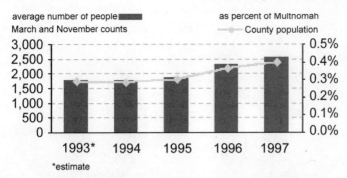

FIGURE 13.1. People seeking shelter nightly in Multnomah County. Source: Multnomah County Department of Community and Family Services, (November 1997).

increase in homeless families since 1993 and a 90% increase in those turned away from shelters (Graham 2003). Figure 13.1 reflects Multnomah County's research tracking a marked increase in people seeking shelter from the early to late 1990s.

In counting the numbers of homeless people, the city and county rely on two systems. One count is derived from Multnomah County's "one night shelter count," which counts only people seeking shelter assistance from public and private facilities in the county. The March 2003 count recorded 1,340 households and 2,220 individuals seeking emergency shelter, housing vouchers, rental assistance, or transitional housing assistance. One hundred and eighty households and 337 individuals were turned away because the shelters had reached capacity (Multnomah County Office of School and Community Partnerships 2003). The second count is conducted annually by JOIN, which only counts people sleeping outdoors or camping in Portland. In spring 2003 JOIN counted 1,571 homeless people.

Sisters of the Road Cafe, a homeless advocacy and outreach nonprofit, believes this number to be low. "Over 100 more homeless persons, 1,672 to be exact, were counted by JOIN in 2002; and from the increased demand upon social services there is little reason to assume that fewer homeless people are here now. Also, because JOIN was low on funding this year, it was unable to allocate a sufficient number of outreach people to conduct a thorough count" (2003a). They also point out the difficulty of counting homeless adults and families who are sleeping in cheap motels, rooming houses, or on a friend's couch or who opt to remain hidden deep within parks, in vehicles, or in abandoned buildings.

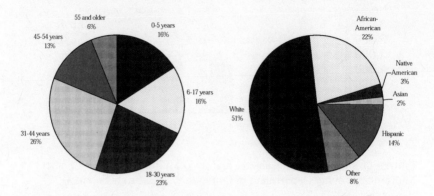

FIGURE 13.2. Age and race of people seeking shelter. Source:Multnomah County Department of Community and Family Services, (November 1997).

Likewise Multnomah County argues that 100% accuracy is impossible when counting the homeless because of undercounting (not all homeless people can be found) and double-counting (those who make multiple attempts to find shelter on the same night are counted with each contact made). Regarding the racial demographics of homeless people, the Portland–Multnomah Progress Board (1999), referring to the above chart, found that although more whites seek shelter than any other racial group, they also make up about 86% of Multnomah County's population (see Fig. 13.2). They point out that this means that the percentages of African Americans, Native Americans, and Hispanics seeking shelter are disproportionately overrepresented.

## Portland's History of Homeless Politics

Carl Abbott writes in *Greater Portland: Urban Life and Landscape in the Pacific Northwest* (2001) about the strong history in Portland of creating policies through consensus practices. Yet he points out the flip side of Portland-style consensus politics that rewards less confrontational activists—bringing "into the conversation 'well-behaved' advocacy groups that have gained attention. Once at the table, such groups can trade acquiescence with long term land redevelopment goals for substantial public commitments to low-income housing and social services." Abbott gives an example of how this consensus process has unfolded with debates about homelessness and low-income housing:

> In the 1980s, agencies serving the homeless population of Portland's skid road agreed to a cap on shelter beds in the Burnside/Old Town

district in return for a go-slow approach to redevelopment and an active program for relocating shelters and social services. A charismatic advocate for the homeless who declined to sign on found that contributions quickly dried up while newspapers headlined his own flaws of character and abusive behavior. In contrast, the Northwest Pilot Project monitors the loss of low cost downtown housing and repeatedly chides the city for neglecting the poor in its plans for a bright new downtown, but it also works within the framework of Portland progressivism to build coalitions among government, foundations, businesses, and social service agencies. In 1995, the Portland Organizing Project (POP) forced consideration of low income housing as a component of the River District north of downtown. Once the development leadership recognized the power of POP's populist appeal, however, they moved rapidly to enfold low income housing and its more consensus-minded advocates into the planning process (leaving POP on the outside and favoring the somewhat poor over the very poor). (151–152)

## Mayor Bud Clark

In important homeless-related policies of recent history, Mayor Bud Clark introduced community policing in the late 1980s, and his 1987 12-point homeless plan drew national attention, although it eventually achieved only half of its goals (Schrag 1984). It used city money to build much-needed shelters. Previously, shelters were run almost exclusively by faith-based programs. After a few years, though, it became clear that those shelters ended up cycling through, not moving out, the homeless. Thus, a new approach was needed.

## Commissioner Gretchen Kafoury

In her terms as both county and city commissioner, Gretchen Kafoury had enormous impact on Portland's homeless and low-income and affordable housing policies. In 1993 she appointed a task force on Strategies for Fair Housing (to respond to the Fair Housing Amendment Act of 1988), which was charged with making recommendations to the city council concerning homelessness and housing. A primary emphasis for the task force was to situate low-income housing throughout the city instead of ghettoizing it. In December 1993, the city council adopted their recommendations including changes to the zoning code, certification standards for homeless shelters, and a location policy regarding geographic concentrations of poverty. These three recommendations were designed to address community concerns while also making it, in some cases, easier to locate special needs housing. This was a crucial achievement by Kafoury's task force since locating special needs housing is always a difficult negotiation with the neighbors. As the APA points out, despite evidence in 20 years of numerous studies that such projects contribute to rather than detract from neighborhoods, NIMBY arguments often prevent supportive housing from being accepted in neighborhoods. A 1999 Urban Land Institute report, for example, indicates that supportive housing does not decrease property values or increase criminal activity (quoted in APA 2003).

The city chose to achieve the goals suggested by the task force by controlling funding for low-income housing in "impact areas." The funding sources include Housing and Urban Development's (HUD's) HOME funds (the largest federal block grant to state and local governments to create housing for low-income households), HUD's Community Development Block Grant (CDBG) funds providing funding for housing and community development projects, HUD's Housing Opportunities for Persons With AIDS (HOPWA) funds, and other low-interest loan programs. "Impact areas" are defined as areas with high concentrations of poverty, where more than 50% of the households in a census tract block group earn less than 50% of median income or 20% or more of the housing units are pubic and assisted (PDC 2003). But Commissioner Kafoury is perhaps best known for her "shelter reconfiguration plan," which the city has operated under for the past decade. This plan created separate shelters for men, women, families, youth, mentally ill, and domestic violence victims and included a component to provide permanent housing (although this housing, the Ritzdorf Court Apartments, wasn't completed until 2002). These shelters are now at full occupancy year-round with long waiting lists in the winter.

### Commissioner Erik Sten

Kafoury protégé, City Commissioner Erik Sten, oversees housing issues and is making his mark with collaborative community discussions toward a 10-year plan to end homelessness, following the lead of others nationwide including the National Alliance to End Homelessness. A major component of this plan focuses on a "housing first" strategy. The idea is to first assist people with stable housing, then address other issues such as mental health or addictions. This is the polar opposite of most current shelter programs in which sobriety and stability must be achieved first before people are allowed to transition into more permanent housing. Although now being discussed more nationally, the housing first model has existed since 1992 with JOIN's highly successful program. Of the 770 people placed into housing with JOIN's rental assistance program in 2001, 92% remained in housing a year later. This surprising success rate was achieved even though 70% of the participants had physical, mental, substance abuse, or criminal justice problems that their caseworkers thought might impair their ability to consistently pay for housing.

Though JOIN began its life in 1992 in a very confrontational mode with the city and the police, it has since developed collaborative ties with the city. The police in particular became an active part in helping find solutions for homeless people. Police Chief Charles Moose was supportive of police officers working closely with JOIN case managers when dealing with a homeless person. As a result of this collaboration the police found they needed fewer officers to respond to incidents (Anderson 2003). This collaboration has diminished somewhat since Chief Moose left in 1999.

Sten's "housing first" focus puts the city's concern with creating more low-income and affordable housing options on the front burner. However, the question is: Where will the funding come from? Homeless people and activists like those at Sisters of the Road Cafe are concerned that funding will be pulled from shelters and meal providers and are working with Commissioner Sten to make sure these concerns are addressed. Sisters of the Road, for example, was invited by Sten to participate in developing the City's official plan, so they are holding grassroots meetings to collect ideas from Portland's homeless community.

## Homeless Programs and Policies

### Collaborations on Homeless Youth Services

Multnomah County currently provides services for 1,000 homeless youth per year in Portland. In 1998 the Citizen's Crime Commission and the Association for Portland Progress questioned Portland's system of services for homeless youth, claiming that it was fragmented, lacked accountability, and was grossly underfunded. Under the influence of the HUD Continuum of Care model (which has required cities to act together to create collaborative and innovative responses to homelessness, analyze community needs, prevent gaps and possible overlaps of services provided, and make decisions about funding priorities at a local rather than national level) and the influence of Portland's historically collaborative climate, a Downtown Homeless Youth Continuum was formed.

(The Continuum of Care components are prevention, outreach and assessment, emergency shelter, transitional housing, permanent supportive housing, permanent affordable housing, and supportive services.) Community stakeholders, human service providers, business leaders, government agencies, homeless youth, and researchers provided input on ways to restructure the system and transition homeless youth off the streets. As a result of their efforts, between 1999 and 2001 the City of Portland and Multnomah County funding devoted to homeless youth services increased from $820,000 to $2,584,000. This additional funding allowed such improvements as more case management, more shelter and transitional housing space, a 24-hour access center, and other services (Multnomah County Auditor's Office 2001).

### Low-Income and Affordable Housing Policies

Since the affordability of housing is a clear factor in the ability to be permanently housed, low-income and affordable housing policies are an important part of addressing homelessness (see Chap. 9, Howe). Refuting the commonly held belief that addictions and the deinstitutionalization of the mentally ill have contributed to the rising rates of homelessness, Wright and Lam (1987) draw a direct link between the reduction in low-income housing opportunities in America and the rise of homelessness. Citing the lack of low-income and affordable housing as a major impediment for a community to end homelessness, the APA argues that planners can play a role in reducing homelessness by "determining local housing needs through their comprehensive plans, removing regulatory and legal barriers to the development of affordable and supportive housing, and fostering community support for permanent housing for the homeless" (2003). The APA's suggested tools to achieve more low-income and affordable housing are: promoting infill incentives, property tax abatement, density allowances, land assembly, and fast track permitting.

The APA also reminds us that the American Institute of Certified Planners (AICP) Code of Ethics requires that a planner "must strive to expand choice and opportunity for all persons, recognizing a special responsibility to plan for the needs of disadvantaged groups." In Portland, this message sometimes seems to ring true, with some focus on preserving low-income and affordable housing and alternatives to the ghettoization of poverty, and with some city council members, the Portland Development Commission (PDC), Multnomah County, and numerous homeless service providers moving to a "housing first" focus.

However, this has not always been the case (see Chap. 3, Gibson). The Northwest Pilot project estimates that since 1974 downtown Portland has lost 863 units of low-income housing to gentrification. Clients may wait three years for the subsidized housing that remains (Transition Projects, Inc. 2001). Reportedly, there is a shortage of 10,500 units of housing for low-income households in Multnomah County (Silverman 1999).

Opponents of the gentrification that is blamed for reducing stocks of low-income and affordable housing point to neighborhoods such as Albina, a historically African American neighborhood with interesting older homes in desirable proximity to downtown. In this neighborhood, average housing values doubled between 1990 and 1996 while, at the same time, the white population increased 12% or six times as fast as the African American population (Oregon Environmental Council 2003). These statistics point to displaced African American residents and gentrification rapidly changing a neighborhood. However, the Fannie Mae Foundation (2000) evaluates a different aspect of gentrification, expanding the tax base:

> The risk of displacement is often raised by critics of gentrification who view the return of middle-income suburbanites to cities as a zero-sum game. While the risk of displacement is real, we think it is outweighed by the even greater risk of losing a chance to secure a larger tax base. Taxing new middle-income residents and spending the money on programs for a general urban population is a benefit that at least partially offsets the pain caused by displacement.

In response to arguments against gentrification and displacement, in 2001 Portland's City Council adopted a "no net loss" policy on housing affordable to low- and moderate-income persons and households in the central city, to retain at least the current number of low-income and affordable housing units (at or below 60% area median income.) A specific goal to achieve the City's Comprehensive Housing Policy, Central City No Net Loss Policy, Consolidated Plan was set at 10,000 units by 2011. An additional goal was made to preserve or replace 1,200 units within the central city by 2006. The Housing Authority of Portland has also committed to no net loss of public housing within the city, and in 2001, Metro adopted a Regional Affordable Housing Strategy. Although in the 1990s the PDC was criticized as not having a comprehensive social agenda for its urban renewal programs (Wollner et al. 2001), in 2003 PDC added 3,550 units to the former 10,000-unit goal. This will be achieved with preserved or new rental units and an increase in first-time homebuyers and will be financed through traditional sources (CDBG, HOME, tax increment financing) as well as partnerships with the city and other organizations for resources through lines of credit, the City Lights Revenue Bond program, the Enterprise Foundation Smart Growth Fund, the Oregon Residential Loan, and the HOME 24 program (PDC Quarterly 2003).

### Ordinances Affecting the Homeless in Portland

In 1981 Portland passed the first of its Public Order laws (Portland Municipal Code 14A.50.020), an ordinance prohibiting temporary campsites on public property or public rights of way. Penalties include fines up to $100 and 30 days in jail. Although initially set up to discourage damage to public properties, Sisters of the Road Cafe argues that this code and others impacting the homeless are used to harass and criminalize the homeless. "Time and again law enforcement and city officials tell us that these laws will direct people experiencing homelessness through the community court system and to social services that will get them off the streets," says Rachel Langford, a volunteer with Sisters of the Road's program Crossroads. "At the same time they admit that these social services are overburdened, underfunded, and unable to meet the needs of many homeless citizens" (Newth 2003).

Portland Municipal Code 14A.50.010 prohibits drinking and open containers of alcohol on public property. This type of ordinance is a common civic strategy to reduce homeless loiterers. Portland police usually use this as an opportunity to question homeless people and ask them to move on if they are being disruptive.

Portland's de facto sit/lie law, Ordinance 14A.50.030 restricts people from blocking a doorway or the flow of pedestrian traffic or vehicular traffic. The Portland Police Bureau's enforcement guidelines state that panhandling alone does not violate this code. In 2001 an effort was led by the Portland Business Alliance (a business development group increasingly supportive of criminalization of the homeless) to create a tougher sit/lie law. They looked at Seattle's law as a model—it has restrictions against sleeping, blankets, chairs, etc. This effort failed when homeless advocates lobbied Mayor Vera Katz who announced that the existing laws were sufficient. Reportedly, only four arrests were made in 2002 enforcing this law (Jaquiss 2003).

Portland Municipal Code 14A.50.050 prohibits erecting permanent or temporary structures on public property or public rights of way. The police guidelines on enforcing this code require a 24-hour notice, require that police contact an outreach worker from JOIN, and allow for arrest and confiscation of property (to be held for 30 days) to be used as "evidence" of the crime. Recently added language encourages officers to give JOIN more than 24 hours' notice so that they have time to make contact with the campers (Portland Police Bureau 2003).

Portland Municipal Code 20.12.265 is a Parks and Recreation "trespass." This is usually enforced as a 30-day exclusion from a park. Fines may be assessed up to $600, though this method of enforcement is not the norm.

Like many cities Portland uses "drug free zones" to manage homeless people. Most of downtown is designated a "drug free zone." People may be excluded from a zone based upon arrest for probable cause (Portland Municipal Code 14B.20.030). In recent years Portland police have also discussed creating a "transient free zone" where arrests could be made, but homeless advocates and Commissioner Erik Sten have prevented this from proceeding further.

## Recent Flashpoints in Portland's Homeless Issues

Several events keep homeless issues in the public light in Portland. St. Francis Park in the SE Portland Buckman neighborhood has business leaders, police, neighborhood leaders, and the church at odds about homeless people who hang out in the park adjacent to the St. Francis Church. Like all Catholic organizations dedicated to the ideals embodied by St. Francis, it has a historical outreach to the hungry and homeless. In September 2003 the police declared the park a "chronic nuisance" and demanded that the church come up with a solution to help address day camping, loitering, and crimes occurring in or near the park. This situation is reminiscent of a similar neighborhood/human services provider conflict that occurred in 2001 at the Sunnyside Centenary United Methodist Church—another meal provider in Southeast Portland. That dispute drew attention from national advocacy groups when the city council put a limit on how many people would be allowed to worship there (Homeless People's Network 2000, *World Faith News* 2000, *Jewish World Review* 2000). St. Francis is still negotiating with neighborhood leaders to come up with an acceptable plan to reduce the impact on the neighborhood (Hannum 2002).

Dignity Village, a cooperative homeless campsite, was created in 2000 after Portland's 19-year-old camping ban was overturned. An editorial by Jack Tafari in *street roots,* a paper written by members of

Portland's homeless community, called for people to organize and form a tent city. The idea captured the imagination of homeless people, churches, donors, homeless service providers, the Oregon Law Center, and Mark Lakeman of the collective City Repair who helped create a master plan for the village (City of Portland Office of Neighborhood Involvement 2003). Some of the motivations cited for its creation were to accommodate many of those turned away from overcrowded shelters, to provide alternatives to shelters that require attendance at religious services, to provide a place for homeless people who own pets, and to band together to prevent police harassment and street crimes. The city has moved the village several times because of NIMBY (not in my back yard) issues and public versus private property issues. A highly organized group, Dignity Village has had the benefit of excellent pro bono legal and community design work. They have also created savvy publicity opportunities such as marching as a "Homeless Front" shopping cart brigade while moving to a new site, thereby drawing the attention of every news channel in town. After strong initial resistance, the city began working with the community to help locate an acceptable site. As of 2004, the camp is located near the Portland airport on part of a leaf-composting facility, leased from the city at $2,000 per month. This fee is to offset the city's loss of income from the lost space and thus lost leaf-composting revenue. The village has council meetings, rules of behavior, showers, educational opportunities, gardens, and hosts numerous visitors such as Portland Public School children who want to learn about their philosophy. Their stated aim is to be a self-governing, green, sustainable urban village. They continue to look for a permanent location.

Lastly, in 2003 an Oregon and Washington pizza chain decided to be creative about homeless handouts. It paid homeless people with pizza, soda, and a few dollars for holding a sign for about 40 minutes reading "Pizza Schmizza paid me to hold this sign instead of asking for money." Pizza Schmizza founder Andre Jehan said: "I got tired of not being able to make eye contact with these people. I thought, 'What skills could they have?' Holding a sign was an obvious one." Although an advertising watchdog group founded by Ralph Nader thought it was exploitation, Peter Schoeff, a 20-year-old homeless man who took them up on their offer said, "I think it's a fair trade. We're career panhandlers, that's the only way we can get money" (CNN.com 2003, Salon.com 2003, *Seattle Times* 2003).

# The Magnet Theory

The magnet theory is the idea that good homeless services in a city act as a magnet to draw homeless people from around the country. The Coalition on Homelessness in San Francisco (1999) points out the many cities that like to use this argument by posting names of places where civic leaders allege that their services draw more homeless people, including Akron, Ohio; New York City; Philadelphia; Portland, Pennsylvania; and Alexandria, Louisiana to name a few. The Sisters of the Road Cafe talks about this problem of perception and points to the reality that most users of homeless services are long-term residents:

> There is a misconception in City Hall, the Portland Police Bureau, and the Portland Business Alliance that homeless people and other "vagrants" flock to Portland because the supportive services are so plentiful. Yes, there is a strong matrix of support services in Portland, but there are many other cities with a similar support infrastructure. Where the misconception lies is that people don't come to Portland simply for its "vaunted" services. Many low-budget travelers pass through Portland because it is a scenic city with a vibrant underground culture and arts scene. Those folks typically are on the move to other places, even though they may frequently return to visit. Many people come because they are attracted to the bohemian lifestyle promised by districts such as Belmont, Hawthorne, Northeast 28th, and Northeast Alberta. Yet, for all those who come and stay, just as many leave for better opportunities elsewhere. Few will deny that decent-paying jobs are difficult to come by here. Finally, there is a significant number of homeless people here who don't take advantage of the services system at all. Perhaps the best answer is that the great majority of homeless people in Portland have been here for years. Although they may lack housing, they are full-time long-term residents. (2003b)

## Seattle and San Francisco in Comparison

In the Seattle–Bellevue–Everett Primary Metropolitan Statistical Area (PMSA) the population is 2.4 million; 82% are white. The Seattle/King County Coalition for the Homeless (2003) estimates that there are 7,980 people who are homeless in King County, Washington. Each year they conduct a one-night count, including a street count and counts at shelters and transitional housing programs. In 1993 and 1994 Seattle implemented several Civility Laws to help control the homeless people downtown. Under these laws, for example, a repeat offender who urinates in public can be fined up to $1,000 and jailed up to 90 days and a first time offender for aggressive panhandling can receive the same punishment (City and County of San Francisco Board of Supervisors 2002). Seattle's sit/lie ordinance restricts people from sitting or lying on sidewalks in certain business districts between 7 a.m. and 9 p.m., including sitting on a blanket or stool (Seattle SMC 15.48.040). If police notify individuals that they are breaking the law and they refuse to move they may be fined up to $50. If the ticket isn't paid or the offender doesn't appear in court the penalty reverts to up to 90 days in jail and up to $1,000. The sit/lie ordinance has been challenged in court several times but has not been struck down. Leaving no doubt about the influences driving these recent changes in Seattle, the Seattle Police Department Web site actually provides a brief lesson on the broken windows theory (Seattle Police Department 2003).

In the San Francisco PMSA the population is 1.7 million; 62% are white. In 2002 the San Francisco Mayor's Office on Homelessness counted 8,640 homeless people. This total has been highly debated, with activists claiming the homeless count is double this amount. The *San Francisco Chronicle* estimates that between 8,500 and 15,000 homeless people live in San Francisco but acknowledges that no one really knows the total. Proposition N (also known as the "Care not Cash" initiative), which passed with almost 60 percent of the vote in 2002, dramatically changed the city's response to homelessness. It authorized the city to reduce monthly checks to the almost 3,000 able-bodied homeless adults who don't qualify for state or federal aid, from about $395 to $59 (Lelchuk 2003). They are being told that they will receive shelter and food instead. The problem is that the resources are limited, shelters are overcrowded, and service providers are stretched to their limits. Thus it is impossible for the city to fulfill its promise. In another brutal effort to rid themselves of the homeless, the Matrix, also known as the "Quality of Life Enforcement Program," is the name for police operations to remove the homeless from downtown San Francisco via criminalization tactics. Laws prohibit public urination and drinking, camping, aggressive panhandling, and "intending to lodge." The police are moving along or arresting homeless people and often dump their belongings in the garbage. San Francisco's Coalition on Homelessness (1999) studied 80 cities and their efforts to criminalize homelessness under the guise of quality of life crimes or the broken windows theory. One hundred percent of the communities studied lacked enough shelter beds to meet demand, yet 90% are implementing antipanhandling laws.

# Portland at the Crossroads

It seems that Portland has not yet fully joined its neighbors, Seattle and San Francisco, to throw enormous criminal justice resources at running the homeless out of town or out of sight. While its downtown business district seems to be attempting to follow in the steps of New York City's Business Improvement Districts, the Portland Business Alliance has not yet succeeded in having the broken windows theory dictate policy or in criminalizing homelessness to the extent reached in many other cities. Portland's homeless advocates point to many egregious problems (lack of low-income housing, insufficient service provider funding, and gentrification leading to displacement are at the top of the list), but Portland has a history of long-range and progressive thinking about homelessness that may yet lead to a model to end homelessness—provided a "transient-free zone" isn't set up first!

Yes, the conditions are ripe for heading toward more criminalization of the homeless, and flashpoints such as the St. Francis/Buckman neighborhood debate demonstrate how conflict-ridden the climate remains. But this is also the same climate in which police are required to work with outreach workers from JOIN to help campers find permanent housing, where funding more than doubled for homeless youth after a community consensus was reached on restructuring homeless youth services, where the city council, the Housing Authority, Metro, and the Portland Development Commission have a no net loss policy for low-income and affordable housing, where after initial conflict the City of Portland and Dignity Village have created productive practices and dialogue, and where for over a decade the city has maintained policies to prevent geographic concentrations of poverty. It will be interesting to check back in a few years to see which way the winds have blown and how much Portland planners have involved themselves in these issues. Portland has established a national reputation for planning an egalitarian and sustainable community. Will it be able to foster a model for addressing homeless issues that rejects the politics of fear created by the broken windows theory? It seems quite reasonable to not want to smell urine on public streets and be endlessly panhandled in the urban center. But can Portland find an answer that addresses society's human tragedies rather than simply sweeping them out of sight? It seems clear that it is not an effective use of tax dollars to funnel people and thus funds through the criminal justice system. Perhaps the 10-year plan to end homelessness can find answers to both the business community's interest in a cleaned-up urban core and the social service community's interest in humane responses to homelessness, especially during these harsh economic times.

REFERENCES

Abbott, Carl. 2001. *Greater Portland: Urban Life and Landscape in the Pacific Northwest*. Philadelphia: University of Pennsylvania Press.

American Planning Association. 2003. *Policy Guide on Homelessness*. http://www.planning.org/policyguides/homelessness.htm?project (accessed 11 November 2003).

Anderson, Jennifer. 2003. Life turnabout hinges on basic premise: Housing. *Portland Tribune*, 22 April. http://www.msnbc.com/local/vcolptld/ M289418.asp (accessed 11 November 2003).

Center on Juvenile and Criminal Justice. 2002. *Shattering "Broken Windows": An Analysis of San Francisco's Alternative Crime Policy*. http://www.cjcj.org/pubs/ windows/windows.html (accessed 1 July 2003).

City and County of San Francisco Board of Supervisors. 2002. *San Francisco's "Quality of Life" Laws and Seattle's "Civility" Laws—11 Jan 2002. Legislative Analyst Report* (File No. 011704). http://www.sfgov.org/site/bdsupvrs_page. asp?id=5100 (accessed 23 February 2003).

City of Portland Office of Neighborhood Involvement. June 2003. *Planning at the Roots: Low-Income and Communities of Color in Portland, Oregon*. Portland: Office of Neighborhood Involvement.

CNN.com. 2003. *Pizza Company Hires Homeless to Hold Ads*. 17 June. http://www.cnn.com/2003/US/West/06/17/offbeat.pizza.ap/ (accessed 11 November 2003).

The Coalition on Homelessness in San Francisco. 1999. *Looking at America through "Broken Windows."* http://www.sf-homeless-coalition.org/ 799brokenwindows.html (accessed 1 July 2003).

Culhane, Dennis P., Stephen M. Metraux, and Trevor R. Hadley. 2002. Public service reductions associated with placement of homeless persons with severe mental illness in supportive housing. *Housing Policy Debate* 13 (1): 107–163.

Duneier, Mitchell. 1999. *Sidewalk*. New York: Farrar, Straus and Giroux.

Fannie Mae Foundation. 2000. Target marketing can help attract city residents. *Housing Facts and Findings* Spring 2 (1). http://www.fanniemaefoundation.org /programs/hff/v2i1-marketing.shtml (accessed 11 November 2003).

Graham, Rachel. 2003. Homeless for the Holidays. *Willamette Week*, 14 Mar. http://www.wweek.com/html/urbanpulse122899.html#family (accessed 1 November 2003).

Hannum, Kristen. 2002. St. Francis plan for park problems rejected. *Catholic Sentinel*, 31 October. http://www.sentinel.org/articles/2002-44/10660.html (accessed 11 Nov 2003).

Homeless People's Network. 2000. *Portland Church at Center of Gathering Storm*. 11 Feb. http://projects.is.asu.edu/pipermail/hpn/2000-February/ 000109.html (accessed 1 November 2003).

Jaquiss, Nigel. 2003. Bulldog. *Willamette Week,* 12 Feb. http://www.wweek.com/ flatfiles/allstories.lasso?xxin=3620 (accessed 1 July 2003).

Jewish World Review. 2000. *Zoning Out Religious Freedoms.* 24 Feb. http:// www.jewishworldreview.com/michelle/malkin022400.asp (accessed 1 November 2003).

Justice, Rob. 2003. Interview with author. 20 April. Executive director of JOIN.

Kelling, George, and Catherine Coles. 1996. *Fixing Broken Windows: Restoring Orderand Reducing Crime in Our Communities.* NY: The Free Press.

Leachman, Michael. 2001. *Hunger in Oregon.* Silverton: Oregon Center for Public Policy.

Lelchuk, Ilene. 2003. Ammiano zeros in on 1,350 homeless. *San Francisco Chronicle,* 10 April. http://sfgate.com/cgi-bin/article.cgi?file=/chronicle/ archive/2003/04/10/BA90033.DTL (accessed 1 July 2003).

Multnomah County Auditor's Office. 2001. *Homeless Youth Services Continuum: Review of System Outcomes.* Portland: Multnomah County Auditor's Office.

Multnomah County Office of School and Community Partnerships. 2003. *One Night Shelter Count March 26, 2003.* Portland: Multnomah County Office of School and Community Partnerships.

National Coalition for the Homeless. 2002. *People Need Their Civil Rights Protected.* http://www.nationalhomeless.org/facts/civilrights.pdf (accessed 11 November 2003).

Newth, Dan. 25 Feb 2003. *Dispatch from Portland.* Originally printed in *street roots.* http://www.alternet.org/sns/story.html?StoryID=15243 (accessed 1 July 2003).

The Oregon Environmental Council. 2003. *Healthy Albina.* http://www.orcouncil. org/reports/Albina/chapters/chapter3.htm (accessed 11 November 2003).

*PDC Quarterly.* 2003. PDC increases housing goals. *PDC Quarterly* 5 (2): 4. http://www.businessinportland.org/pdf/pubs_general/gen_quarterly_spring_ 2003.pdf (accessed 1 November 2003).

Portland Development Commission. 2003. *Housing: Location Policy and Impact Area Map.* http://www.pdc.us/housing_serv/general/iam.asp (accessed 1 November 2003).

Portland–Multnomah Progress Board. 1999. *Decrease Homelessness.* http://www.p-m-benchmarks.org/health_fam/31.html (accessed 11 November 2003).

Portland Municipal Code 14A.50.020. *Camping Prohibited on Public Property and Public Rights of Way.* http://www.portlandonline.com/auditor/index.cfm?c= 28513&#cid_15427 (accessed 11 November 2003).

Portland Municipal Code 14A.50.030. *Obstructions as Nuisances.* http://www. portlandonline.com/auditor/index.cfm?c=28513&#cid_15427 (accessed 11 November 2003).

Portland Municipal Code 14A.50.050. *Erecting Permanent or Temporary Structures on Public Property or Public Rights of Way.* http://www. portlandonline.com/auditor/index.cfm?&a=15431&c=28513 (accessed 11 November 2003).

Portland Municipal Code 14B.20.030. *Civil Exclusion.* http://www.portlandonline. com/auditor/index.cfm?c=28513&#cid_15427 (accessed 11 November 2003).

Portland Municipal Code 14A.50.010. *Alcohol on Public Property and Public Rights of Way.* http://www.portlandonline.com/auditor/index.cfm?c=28513& #cid 15427 (accessed 11 November 2003).

Portland Municipal Code 20.12.265. *Trespass.* http://www.portlandonline. com/auditor/index.cfm?&a=17286&c=28627 (accessed 11 November 2003).

Portland Police Bureau. 2003. *Manual of Policy and Procedure.* http://www. portlandpolicebureau.com/directives.html (accessed 11 November 2003).

Salon.com. 2002. *Manhattan Murder Rates Hit 100 Year Lows.* 31 December. http://www.salon.com/news/wire/2002/12/31/manhattan_murder/index.html (accessed 1 July 2003).

Salon.com. 2003. *Company Pays Homeless Workers with Pizza.* 16 June. http://www.salon.com/news/wire/2003/06/16/pizza_paycheck/index.html (accessed 1 July 2003).

San Francisco Mayor's Office on Homelessness. 2002. *Homeless Count Report: 25 November 2002.* http://www.sfgov.org/site/homeless_page.asp?id=3930 (accessed 1 July 2003).

Schrag, John. 1984. This Bud's for you. *Willamette Week* http://www. wweek.com/html/25-1984.html (accessed 11 November 2003).

The Seattle/King County Coalition for the Homeless. 2003. *The One Night Count.* http://www.homelessinfo.org/onc.html (accessed 11 November 2003).

Seattle Municipal Code SMC 15.48.040. *Sitting or Lying Down on Public Sidewalks in Downtown and Neighborhood Commercial Zones.* http:// clerk.ci.seattle.wa.us/~scripts/nph-brs.exe?s1=&s2=sit+lie&S3=&Sect4=AND &1=20&Sect1=IMAGE&Sect3=PLURON&Sect5=CODE1&d=CODE&p=1&u= /~public/code1.htm&r=2&Sect6=HITOFF&f=G (accessed 1 July 2003).

Seattle Police Department. 2003. *The "Broken Window" Theory.* http://www. cityofseattle.net/police/prevention/Tips/broken_window.htm (accessed 1 November 2003).

*The Seattle Times.* 2003. Homeless Serving as Billboards. 15 June. http://seattle-times.nwsource.com/html/localnews/134998925_pizza15.html (accessed 1 November 2003).

Silverman, Rachael. 1999. *Description and Assessment of Portland's Response to Homelessness of Adults.* Portland: Portland Bureau of Housing and Community Development.

Sisters of the Road Cafe. 2003a. *Portland's Anti-homeless Ordinances.* http://www.sistersoftheroadcafe.org/crossroads/Anticamp.htm (accessed 11 November 2003).

Sisters of the Road Cafe. 2003b. *Frequently Asked Questions.* http://www. sistersoftheroadcafe.org/crossroads/FAQ.htm (accessed 11 November 2003).

Transition Projects, Inc. 2001. *Women's Reality: Single Homeless Women in the City of Portland.* Portland: Transition Projects, Inc.

Urban Land Institute Report. 1999. *The Impact of Supportive Housing on Neighborhoods and Neighbors.* Washington, DC: Urban Land Institute.

Williams, Rebecca. 1998. *Philip Zimbardo: A Psychologist's Experience with Deviance.* http://www.criminology.fsu.edu/crimtheory/zimbardo.htm (accessed 1 May 2003).

Wilson, J. Q., and G. L. Kelling. 1982. Broken windows: The police and neighborhood safety. *Atlantic Monthly,* March. http://www3.theatlantic.com/election/connection/crime/windows.htm (accessed 1 May 2003).

Winton, Richard, and Kristina Sauerwein. 2003. LAPD tests new policing strategy. *Los Angeles Times,* 6 February. http://www.latimes.com/templates/mi...evive2feb02&section=%2Fnews%2Flocal (accessed 1 July 2003).

Wollner, Craig, John Provo, and Julie Schablitsky. 2001. *A Brief History of Urban Renewal in Portland, Oregon.* Portland: Institute for Portland Metropolitan Studies.

*World Faith News.* 2000. Portland City Council throws out attendance limit for church. 3 March. http://www.wfn.org/2000/03/msg00052.html (accessed 1 November 2003).

Wright, J. D., and J. A. Lam. 1987. Homelessness and the low-income housing supply. *Social Policy,* Spring: 48–53.

Zimbardo, P. G. 1969. The human choice: Individuation, reason, and order versus deindividuation, impulse, and chaos. *Nebraska Symposium on Motivation* 17: 237–307.

# Conclusion

In 1993, James Kunstler, an observer of American cities, wrote in his book, *The Geography of Nowhere*, that Portland, Oregon, "embodies the most hopeful and progressive trends in American city life and especially in urban planning" (Kunstler 1993, 189). Kunstler went on to describe Portland's lively day-and-night downtown, mixed-use permissive zoning codes, pedestrian-friendly building design standards, a then unusual public investment in light rail, parking caps on downtown spaces, and the generous sprinkling of parks and greenery throughout the downtown. Kunstler attributed much of the city's vitality to the innovative urban growth boundary established in response to the 1973 state land use law that acted to constrain urban sprawl and that frustrated conventional real estate developers who were seeking thousand-acre subdivisions.

He ends his passage on Portland saying that, "It remains to be seen how well the Urban Growth Boundary will work. . . " (Kunstler 1993, 206). How has Portland done? A little more than a decade later, the light rail system has been extended out to the western edge of the urban growth boundary, east to the airport, and north to the edge of the Columbia River, just across from southeastern Washington state's Clark County. The Pearl District, connected by a streetcar to the neighborhood of Northwest 23rd Avenue and the Portland State University campus, hosts trendy shops and restaurants, some of the city's highest-priced condominiums, and Jamison Square, whose fountain

302

draws children and their parents from across the region on warm, sunny days.

Although the population of the region has increased, spatial expansion of the urban area has been minimal. The region is growing in a pattern more tightly knit than other North American cities. Although traffic congestion is a problem in the region, residents have alternatives to the automobile and use them. Housing is expensive and prices climbed steeply over the past decade, but these increases are a reflection of demand and improvements in housing stock, rather than a consequence of rising land prices from supply constraints due to growth management tools, specifically the urban growth boundary.

The light rail system, the Pearl District, and the extensive park and open space system did not arise as a consequence of "voluntary" forces (Beito et al. 2002). As the chapters in this volume detail, the fate of the Portland metropolitan region was not left to chance or private entrepreneurship. The planners and elected officials have relied on the state land use system and Metro in particular to provide a fairly steady hand in guiding growth.

The chapters in this volume also illustrate the important roles that federal policies and programs play. Transportation planners directed federal highway and urban renewal grants into the light rail system. Portland planners relied on federal emergency management act (FEMA) program monies to purchase flood-prone properties to create a watershed system that mimics nature. Portland social services used federal Housing and Urban Development (HUD) funds to support homeless youth. Even KBOO, the volunteer-run, community radio station, obtained a federal grant to purchase essential technology during its early development.

But it is people that bring programs, plans, and laws to life and movement to institutions. The combination of people and institutions works to create (or not) a sense of community. In the Portland metropolitan region, these chapters have argued that extraordinary leaders and publicly spirited citizens together with public institutions have labored diligently to create and sustain a sense of belonging and responsibility to this remarkable landscape. The range and scope of membership and activity in civic organizations in the region are considerable. These organizations provide outlets for the expression of offbeat culture, alternative news about the community, and a venue for social interaction directed toward a collective good, whether that good be a healthy watershed or a local sense of the social ownership of airwaves.

Thus far, the region's public institutions have been reasonably responsive to active citizens. Metro has constructed an elaborate apparatus to bring the jurisdictions and public interest advocates into its decision-making processes. Various city bureaus have a more mixed record of public involvement, though allowing citizens no voice has clearly not been accepted in this part of the country up to now.

Yet the chapters also illustrate the difficulty of keeping institutions vibrant and open and ensuring that our notion of community is inclusive of all the people who live in a place. Housing affordability and homelessness are issues that Portland and every urban area must address. As the Portland metropolitan region and all urban areas today experience not only growth but growing diversity among its citizens, it will become increasingly challenging to ensure that individuals feel a sense of agency in their lives, a sense of responsibility to others, and a sense of belonging in a place.

The purpose of this volume was not simply to tell "the Portland story." We had hoped that by doing so, however, we would add to larger discussions about how to recover, sustain, and create strong communities. We offer no recipes for "How to create community." Nonetheless, it is clear that the level of livability in the Portland region is no accident. Through the experience of this place, we believe we have identified a few key ingredients of a strong community and welcome others, in other communities, to join us in dialogue.

REFERENCES

Beito, David T., Peter Gordon, and Alexander Tabarrok, eds. 2002. *The Voluntary City: Choice, Community, and Civil Society.* Ann Arbor: University of Michigan Press.

Kunstler, James Howard. 1993. *The Geography of Nowhere: The Rise and Decline of America's Man-Made Landscape.* New York: Simon & Schuster.

# About the Contributors

Carl Abbott (Ph.D., University of Chicago) is Professor of Urban Studies and Planning at Portland State University (PSU), where he has taught since 1978. He is the author of numerous books about urban and western history, including *The Metropolitan Frontier: Cities in the Modern American West* (1993), *Political Terrain: Washington, D.C. from Tidewater Town to Global Metropolis* (1999), and *Greater Portland: Urban Life and Landscape in the Pacific Northwest* (2001). He is currently working on a book about the ways in which American science fiction writers forward the narratives of western America.

Sy Adler (Ph.D., University of California, Berkeley) has been a faculty member in the School of Urban Studies and Planning at PSU since 1981. He teaches and does research in the areas of the history and theory of planning, urban transport politics and policy, urban politics, and community development. He is especially interested in the evolution of planning institutions, and the relationships between planning institutions and planning practices. He was a coeditor of the *Journal of the American Planning Association* (1998–2004).

Nancy Chapman (Ph.D., University of California, Berkeley) is Professor Emerita in the School of Urban Studies and Planning at PSU. She is an environmental and social psychologist whose publications include articles about housing and environments for the elderly, informal helping networks, and privacy. She collaborated with Deborah Howe to develop materials to educate planners about the challenges of an aging society and to explore the use of accessory apartments by older persons. Her interest in testing the social and behavioral claims of New Urbanism is reflected in the research of several of her students.

Jennifer Dill (Ph.D., University of California, Berkeley) teaches courses in urban planning, transportation policy and planning, and planning analysis in the School of Urban Studies and Planning at PSU. She conducts research on transportation and environmental planning, travel behavior, air quality, and transportation–land use interactions and has published articles on transit and land use, transportation demand management, regional air quality planning, bicycle commuting, and vehicle retirement programs. She is currently researching factors that influence decisions to walk and bicycle, including street connectivity and New Urbanist neighborhood designs.

J. R. Estes is pursuing her Ph.D. in Urban Studies at PSU. Her dissertation focuses on media and policy analysis, specifically media discourse and the political economy of environmental deregulation. With an English M.A., J. R. also teaches writing across the curriculum at PSU and is currently researching the relationship between writing and student learning.

Karen J. Gibson (Ph.D., University of California, Berkeley) is an assistant professor in the School of Urban Studies and Planning at PSU. Her research centers on racial economic inequality and antipoverty policy. Past topics include the Pittsburgh Urban League's Industrial Welfare Workers, 1918–1920; black and white poverty in Detroit and Pittsburgh; occupational segregation, and; the Housing Authority of Portland's Family Self-Sufficiency program. She is currently evaluating its revitalization of Columbia Villa, the largest public housing community in Oregon.

Leslie T. Good (Ph.D., Stanford University) is an associate professor in the Department of Communication at PSU, as well as a photographer. Her research focuses on visual communication and mass media, and she has edited a scholarly book series, *Critical Studies in Communication,* for Hampton Press. She is currently completing a history of photographic inquiry within media studies and is examining the role of visual documents in cultural memory and community identity.

Deborah Howe (Ph.D., University of Michigan) has been a professor of urban studies and planning at PSU since 1985. Her scholarly and professional interests include community planning for aging, the Oregon land use system, planning with Native American communities, and affordable housing alternatives. Dr. Howe coedited *Planning the Oregon Way: A Twenty-Year Evaluation* (Oregon State University Press, 1994) and served as coeditor of the *Journal of the American Planning Association* (1998–2004). She was honored with membership in the American Institute of Certified Planners College of Fellows, Class of 2000, in recognition of her contributions to planning education.

Steven Reed Johnson (Ph.D., Portland State University) is a native Oregonian, a community activist for 25 years and recipient of the City of Portland's Spirit of Portland award in 1992. In 2002 he was awarded the best dissertation of the year in urban politics from the American Political Science Association. He has a forthcoming book on the transformation of civic life in America since the 1950s, with Portland as a case study, and teaches courses on citizen participation and community studies.

Hollie Lund (Ph.D., Portland State University) is an assistant professor of urban and regional planning at California State Polytechnic University in Pomona, California. Her primary research area is at the intersection of transportation planning and policy, neighborhood design, and community development. Dr. Lund currently teaches land use planning and theory, planning applications of geographic information systems, and community planning studios and is now serving as director of the Center for Community Service–Learning at Cal Poly Pomona.

Heike Mayer (Ph.D., Portland State University) completed her dissertation on the evolution of Portland's high-technology industry, and joined the faculty at the Department of Urban Affairs and Planning at Virginia Polytechnic Institute and State University in August 2003. Her research interests focus on economic and community development and her work on high-technology and biotechnology regions has been published by the Brookings Institution.

Chet Orloff is an adjunct professor in the School of Urban Studies and Planning at PSU, Director Emeritus of the Oregon Historical Society, and founding president of the Museum of the City. He practices history with numerous public and private agencies and firms throughout Oregon and has served on the Portland Planning, Landmarks, and Arts & Culture commissions and the Portland Parks Board. He helped initiate the national and Oregon Lewis and Clark Bicentennial efforts.

Connie P. Ozawa (Ph.D., Massachusetts Institute of Technology) is a professor of urban studies and planning at PSU. She is author of *Recasting Science: Consensus-Based Procedures in Public Policy Making* (Westview, 1991). Her research interests include participatory democracy, environmental mediation, collaborative planning, and planning education. She currently serves on the editorial board of the *Journal of the American Planning Association* and is associate editor of the *Negotiation Journal*.

Tracy J. Prince (Ph.D., University of Nebraska) is an adjunct assistant Professor in Urban Studies and Planning. Her teaching and research interests include poverty, affordable housing, homelessness, race relations, cultural studies, gender studies, citizenship, and national identity. She has worked on community development projects such as teaching African American, Native American, and women's studies courses at a homeless shelter; working with Oklahoma and Nebraska city planners and city councils to help create "Continuum of Care" collaborations; and creating two transitional housing facilities for the homeless.

John Provo is a Ph.D. candidate in PSU's School of Urban Studies and Planning. As a part of the School's Institute of Portland Metropolitan Studies he has been a part of regional efforts to study industrial clusters and define a regional economic development strategy. He has taught housing and urban development and coauthored a history of urban renewal in the City of Portland. His dissertation "Placing Equity Issues on the Regional Agenda in Portland, Oregon" examines how the region's governance structure has addressed questions of equity in the areas of affordable housing and economic development.

Ethan Seltzer (Ph.D., University of Pennsylvania) is currently Director and Professor in the School of Urban Studies and Planning at PSU. He was the founding director of the Institute of Portland Metropolitan

Studies at PSU and worked for Metro, Portland City Commissioner Mike Lindberg, and the Southeast Uplift Neighborhood Program prior to joining the university.

Gerald Sussman (Ph.D., University of Hawaii) is a professor of urban studies and communications at PSU. He is the author of *Communication, Technology and Politics in the Information Age* (Sage, 1998), author or editor of three monographs on the political economy of telecommunications, and coeditor of *Global Productions: Labor in the Making of the "Information Society"* (Hampton, 1997) and *Transnational Communications: Wiring the Third World* (Sage, 1991). He is completing a book manuscript, *Globalizing Politics: Campaign Consultants, Communications, and Corporate Financing in the Neoliberal Order* (Rowman & Littlefield).

Matthew Witt, (Ph.D., Portland State University) was born and raised in the Portland metropolitan region. He is currently Assistant Professor of Public Administration at the University of La Verne, where he chairs the Bachelors Public Administration program. He has published research in *Administrative Theory & Praxis* (1999) and *The Hansell Symposium* (2000) (International City/County Management Association). His research interests include public administration theory and citizen involvement in local governance. Dr. Witt has also served as a consultant to the City of Los Angeles Human Relations Commission.

J. Alan Yeakley (Ph.D., University of Virginia) is an associate professor of environmental science at PSU. Dr. Yeakley's research activities span urban ecology, riparian ecology, and watershed hydrology. He has been a principal investigator (PI) or co-PI on several federal grants and has published articles in journals such as *BioScience, Ecology, Landscape Ecology, Water Air and Soil Pollution, Hydrology and Earth System Sciences*, and *Ecosystems*.

# INDEX